IMMIGRANTS
IN THE VALLEY

IMMIGRANTS IN THE VALLEY

Irish, Germans, and Americans in the Upper Mississippi Country, 1830-1860

Mark Wyman

Nelson-Hall nh Chicago

LIBRARY OF CONGRESS CATALOGING IN PUBLICATION DATA

Wyman, Mark.
  Immigrants in the Valley.

  Bibliography: p.
  Includes index.
  1. Mississippi River Valley—History—1803-1865.
2. Irish Americans—Mississippi River Valley—History
—19th century. 3. German Americans—Mississippi
River Valley—History—19th century. I. Title.
F353.W97 1984   977'.02   83-11459
ISBN 0-8304-1023-6

Copyright © 1984 by Mark Wyman

Manufactured in the United States of America

10 9 8 7 6 5 4 3 2 1

The paper in this book is pH neutral (acid-free).

For Eva
—twice an immigrant

Contents

Acknowledgments

This work was made possible through the assistance of a research grant from the National Endowment for the Humanities. The findings and conclusions presented here do not necessarily represent the views of the Endowment, of course. The other major source of assistance was Illinois State University, which provided a sabbatical leave, released time for research, and typing.

Special thanks go to the following persons who aided this project in the United States:

Prof. Arnold Schrier, University of Cincinnati; Roland A. White, Champaign, Illinois; Prof. Kerby Miller, University of Missouri, Columbia; Judith Anne Kaufhold, Historic Preservation Commission, Belleville, Illinois; Dr. Tom Spencer, University of Notre Dame; Father James Culleton and Richard A. Middleton, Bloomington, Illinois; and four who read drafts of the manuscript: Prof. Robert M. Sutton, University of Illinois; Dr. Roger Bridges, Illinois State Historical Society; Dr. Walter Havighurst, Oxford, Ohio; and Rev. Andrew M. Greeley, National Opinion Research Center, University of Chicago.

Abroad, assistance came from Prof. Joseph Lee, University College, Cork, Ireland; Ann Barry, Cork Archives Council; Rev. Kevin Condon, All Hallows Seminary, Drumcondra, Dublin, Ireland; Dr. Edith Goldschmidt, Bonn, West Germany; Dr. Emil Goldschmidt, Hamburg, West Germany; and Prof. Günter Moltmann, Universitat Hamburg, West Germany.

Many libraries and historical societies opened their collections to me, most notably the Illinois State Historical Library, the Illinois Historical Survey and the Main Library of the University of Illinois, and Milner Library at Illinois State University.

Assistance was also received from the following institutions:

Iowa State Historical Department; State Historical Society of Wisconsin (which provided notes from its History of Wisconsin Project); Newberry Library; Chicago Theological Seminary; Chicago Historical Society; Notre Dame University Archives; Area Research Center of the University of Wisconsin-River Falls; Area Research Center of the University of Wisconsin-La Crosse; Bancroft Library, University of California, Berkeley; Garrett-Evangelical Theological Seminary; Northwestern University Library; Central Illinois Conference of the United Methodist Church; First Congregational Church of La Salle, Illinois; Catholic University Library; National Library of Ireland; Public Record Office, Dublin, Ireland; Public Record Office of Northern Ireland, Belfast; Queens University Library, Belfast; British Library of Political and Economic Science of the London School of Economics; British Library Newspaper Library, Colindale, England; and the Commerz-Bibliothek, Hamburg, West Germany.

Prologue

The landscape of the Upper Mississippi Valley is strewn with reminders of distant homelands. These are the names on the land, in reality, clues to the past. Many that were once proclaimed boldly on signposts live today only in old platbooks, on yellowed scraps pressed in albums of a bygone era, or in memory.

The names were there once, though, and many continue in use today. Tumbling down to us from more than a century ago come Irishtown, Irish Ridge, Irish Settlement, Irish Grove, Little Ireland, Erin, and even Irish Diggings in the Wisconsin lead region or the Kerry Patch section of St. Louis. And German Hill, Germantown, Germania, Rhinelander, Holstein, Hamburg, Hanover, Berlin, and a string of names derived most often from the Americans' misuse of *dutch* for *deutsch:* Dutch Hollow, Dutch Hill, Dutch Flats, Dutch Creek. Add to these such community names as Scotch Grove, Swedesburg, Vienna, Bern, Brussels, Holland, Helvetia.

These are place names of the Upper Mississippi country, the states of Illinois, Wisconsin, Iowa, Minnesota, and Missouri. More than merely revealing origins of early settlers, these designations, traced to the rush of settlement from 1830 to 1860, show that newcomers often sought to re-create certain aspects of their former lives. If their religion and folkways could cross the ocean, why not also the appellation of the city of their birth? And so they hopefully added "New" to the townsite over and over again: New Erin appears, New Dublin, and New Ireland, along with New Baden, New Berlin, New Holstein, New Munster, New Trier, New Westphalia, New Ulm. From other points came New Glarus, New Sweden, New Denmark, New Vienna, New Amsterdam, New Windsor. Norwegians there were, and Swedes, English, and Scots, but the overwhelming majority of European immigrants in the 1830–1860 period came from Ireland and Germany. (*Immigrant* is used in this book to mean a person who leaves his or her home to travel to another country for permanent settlement.) Many of these people chose place names that linked their new community with their native land. Their past was not to be forgotten, not to be rejected completely.

So the maps of the region read today like a crazy quilt of international nomenclature, and to browse through these documents is to confront a visual cacophony of distant birthplaces. But if the records show a New Erin and a New Baden, there is also a New Boston—several, in fact—as well as multiple New Havens and New Londons, plus a Yankee Settlement, Vermont Settlement, Bunker Hill, Yankee Hill, Plymouth, New Bedford, New Rutland, New Virginia, New Pennsylvania. One Illinois county today contains both a Virginia and a Philadelphia; another manages to harbor an Irishtown and a Germantown.

Place-names, of course, serve travelers as guides to their whereabouts. These names can also provide clues to our whereabouts in history, telling us where we have been as a people. The colonial era saw the founding of New England, New France, and New Spain, and those names remind us today of aspects of that European settlement process. The *New* in the early colonial period, as later in the nineteenth century, was also tied to dreams and hopes: it represented a beginning as well as a desire to hark back to a former dwelling place that served as a point of reference.

Collect these names scattered across the Upper Mississippi Valley, and the result is a heterogeneous list, linked by experiences and memories to Europe, New England, the East, and the South. And the list hints at more: bring the peoples of these communities together, suddenly, and the result may be struggle, accommodation, or sometimes violence. The manner of spending the Sabbath, Bible reading in the schools, drinking, the retention of European languages—these and similar issues raised hackles and provoked controversy in many communities, rural and urban. Illinois received the most immigrants and, with its large blocs of southerners and New Englanders, became a crucible of forces during that stormy era. Major emphasis in these pages will be placed on events in that state. But this drama of settlement was played out as well in Wisconsin, Iowa, Missouri, and Minnesota, and those states will be given attention also.

One final caution: this story is written mainly for those who wish to know how their ancestors settled in this new land long ago and for those desiring to understand the immigrants' changing impact upon American culture. If readers are surprised at the discord described in these pages, that surprise may in itself be a measure of modern America's acceptance of diversity. And this acceptance may be the major legacy of the antebellum era when the frontier lay open across the Upper Mississippi Valley and people from diverse homelands arrived to create their New Erin and New Baden, their New Virginia and Yankee Settlement.

1. The Prairie as a Land of Hope

In the beginning was the prairie. It was talked of, written about, pointed toward in sweeping gestures by wondering people hundreds and thousands of miles distant. Reports came first from the Indians, who told of a sea of grass, but such tales were scarcely believable to those who had not seen it. Early white explorers of the Upper Mississippi Valley tried to explain the existence of the prairies in ways that seemed logical to those confident of the inseparability of soil and trees. One of the earliest of these, the French explorer Louis Jolliet, reported that he had imagined "it was a country ravaged by fire where the soil was so poor that it could produce nothing." Others coming after him sought similar explanations when they learned of the vastness of this prairie. For example, James Monroe reported in 1786 that the land around the Mississippi and Illinois rivers "consists of extensive plains which have not had from appearances and will not have a single bush on them, for ages."

But to finally walk through it, to plunge fingers deep into the moist black humus, unloosed other feelings and explanations. The variety of grasses, flowers, birds, animals was overwhelming; the soil so fecund that it pushed the bluestem grass as high as the head of a mounted horseman by late summer. The impact was especially great on the men who had struggled through thick forests from the Atlantic Coast; to them the sudden prairie was "like a lake of verdure most cheering to our eyes just emerging from the dark woods of Indiana," as an English traveler put it in 1817. A German echoed him two years later, finding that after growing weary of forests the westbound traveler "believes himself transferred to another region of the world as soon as he crosses the Wabash."

1

There was nothing in the experience of Americans or Europeans that could explain it—nothing that would help them describe for relatives and friends in stony, stump-filled, or forested lands just what the endless, luxuriant prairies were like. Many came up finally with a common experience that perhaps those at home could grasp. "I could compare it to nothing but the sea," wrote a traveler to his brother in Scotland. A British writer described the Delavan prairie in central Illinois as "outstretched and undulating, [it] lay around us a vast ocean of meadowland; in some parts bounded and stretched in upon, or dotted with coasts, capes, or islands of forest-wood." Persons crossing these prairies shaped their course from point to point of timber, as a ship's pilot follows islands. Near the middle of the nineteenth century, a Boston newspaper reporter also fell back on sea images: "For miles and miles we saw nothing but a vast expanse of what I can compare to nothing else but the ocean itself. The tall grass, interspersed occasionally with fields of corn, looked like the deep sea; it seemed as if we were out of sight of land, for no horse, no barn, no tree was visible, and the horizon presented the rolling of the waves in the far-off distance.... We saw at intervals, groves of trees, which looked like islands in the ocean."

Like the foaming brine of the Atlantic, this sea of grass held dangers, the newcomers soon learned. A newly arrived Irish abbot saw "one vast weaving sheet of green" in the Iowa prairie near Dubuque, but later he learned that it was growing "only to be devoured by fire in the fall," the flames "rolling and roaring for miles." Winter would bring blizzards, the winds sweeping over the faded stalks of bluestem, snow piling high in spots where a creek or grove existed at variance with the roll of the land. At times the prairies could be lonely, and humans who challenged them could feel isolated and vulnerable.

But for much of the year the prairies were not regarded as dangerous. Summer breezes crossing this sea of grass came laden, not with salt air, but with perfumes of the abundant prairie rose and other flowers, for this vastness was "profusely sprinkled with pale yellow and flame-colored, or blue and pink flowers," wrote one traveler. A touring Irish priest was impressed by the blossoming prairie as he went by stagecoach into the lands bordering the Mississippi in the Dubuque-Galena area. "Saw in Illinois-Iowa wild gooseberry current and cherry apple plum trees everywhere and prairie covered wild strawberry blossoms and several nice flowers,'' he penned in his diary.

The islandlike groves held mainly hardwoods—walnut, ash, maple, oak, beech, and hickory—many reaching mammoth proportions. Thickets were prized for wild plums, crab apples, sassafras, gooseberries, blackberries, and wild cherries. Wildlife was abundant. The buffalo was almost gone by the early nineteenth century, remembered mainly by the occasional bones found in the earth or in their wide thoroughfares remaining through the grass, but there were black bear, deer, wolves, prairie chickens, turkey, squirrels, and the sky-darkening flocks of passenger pigeons, with lesser numbers of quail, ducks, cranes, plovers, and green birds the newcomers called ''paroquets.''

The tall prairie grasses, their roots anchored in rich black loam, grew like a protective blanket on much of the Upper Mississippi's prairie—the upper two-thirds of Illinois, almost all of Iowa, and portions of northern Missouri, southern Wisconsin, and southern Minnesota. An 1838 traveler in Iowa estimated that ''probably three-fourths of the territory is without trees,'' and this appears to have been generally true of the prairie region. But the grasslands were speckled with numerous ''slews,'' or swamps, as well as frequent groves, and by timber along the streams and rivers. This was especially true near the larger waterways: the Wabash, Ohio, Illinois, Kaskaskia, Rock, Iowa, Des Moines, and of course the Mississippi. Many of the hills along the rivers were large and steep, especially in the Shawnee Hills region of southern Illinois. Steamboat passengers thrilled to the sight of ''bold beautiful cliffs, or green cone-like hills,'' along the east side of the Mississippi, while three hundred-foot bluffs were marvels to Rock River travelers. The lead-bearing region where Wisconsin, Illinois, and Iowa come together was compared to mountain districts, and the Galena-to-Dubuque topography was described ''as if an ant should cross the teeth of a mill saw longitudinally—a fearful alternation of hill and hollow.''

To the northward, the traveler encountered other riches. Much of southern Wisconsin and Minnesota abounded in ''oak openings'' where hardwood forests curled over soft hills, while far to the north in both states stretched one of the world's great forests, a massive stand of white pine and other evergreens that would eventually provide housing for much of the growing nation. But the timber era would wait until later in the century.

Most visitors hailed the vast prairielands enthusiastically—but not all. Charles Dickens crossed them in 1842 and described the "Looking-Glass Prairie" near Belleville, Illinois, as "oppressive in its barren monotony." Others would echo this, but such men were not farmers; their lives had not been shaped by the need to grub out stumps or haul rocks. To farmers who had spent their lives battling a hostile nature, the prairies were like a prayer finally answered. Thus, an Englishman proudly described his newly purchased prairie acreage as "without stones or stumps to interfere with the plough." (And when it was found that traditional plows would not scour clean in the prairie soil, men like John Deere soon developed new ones that did.) From Iowa, an Irish immigrant wrote home that "there is no grubbing through roots, or hopping round stumps when ploughing here." Similarly, a Scottish immigrant proudly reported from Logan County, Illinois, that "there is no stones in the ground. I have often ploughed a week at a time and never turned over a stone the size of an egg."

These men were more representative of the world's population than Dickens, and on the prairie they found many of their former problems existing no more. The battles had been won, not against nature but *by* nature. Manure was found to be unnecessary, for centuries of the prairie grass cycle had left a thick loam soil several feet deep. It was, wrote a Scottish immigrant in 1841, "the best land in the world." Many agreed, despite Dickens.

Such a land easily elicited superlatives, and the more visitors who toured the Upper Mississippi prairies, the more boastful became the reports. No rich, black soils like this in the eastern states, none in Europe ("I do not fancy there exists in the old world such a sight as we beheld," wrote a Scottish scientist during his tour). The prairies' use in agriculture was predicted to become a boon for the world's population.

What had come about to suddenly throw open this Eden to the world's farmers? Part of the answer lay in a conjunction of the continuing westward push of settlement with technological innovations and refinements that together brought the steamboat charging up western waters, wagons rolling through traces and roads, and ultimately the railroad winding into the Old Northwest. Indian trails were steadily evolving into wagon roads, and on the prairies the Conestoga wagons of the Pennsylvanians and southerners mingled with the New Englanders' narrow-tread, low-boxed wagons drawn by horses instead of oxen.

The major route into southern Illinois from Kentucky, Tennessee, and the Carolinas crossed the Ohio at Ford's Ferry and then passed through Equality, Mount Vernon, and Carlyle. Government roads began to carry heavy traffic also. The Cumberland Road reached Wheeling by 1818; its western extension was completed as the National Road to Columbus by 1833 and to Indianapolis by 1850. Wagons, humanity, and livestock were soon flowing west over them. The whole nation seemed in motion. "The National Road has the whole season been blocked up with movers' wagons," *Niles' Register* reported in 1839, claiming there were enough people then heading west to form another state. Northern travelers often took their wagons over the Great Sauk Trail, an Indian route from Detroit to the southern end of Lake Michigan. It had become a government post road by 1825. Fall traveling was favored by these pioneers due to the dryness of the roads—they were mud holes after a rain—and seven to nine weeks were required to travel from the eastern states into the prairies. Waiting for fall to leave home also meant that crops could be harvested, cattle fattened, and rivers forded more easily.

Part of the national craze for "internal improvements" were the canals spreading inland from the East, connecting river systems and roads. The most prominent was the Erie Canal, which opened in 1825, although there were others such as the Union, Pennsylvania, and Wabash and Erie that eased the way westward for emigrants traveling with bulky goods. Completion of the Erie meant that a water route from New York City and other Hudson River towns was open all the way to Buffalo, a city that thereby became the great embarkation point for what was then universally known as "The West."

The rapid development of the steamboat speeded up the settlement process while throwing open another major route to mid-continent: upstream from New Orleans on the Mississippi, with its numerous navigable tributaries. Families floating on flatboats down the Ohio now watched steamboats pass by, the decks crowded with westbound settlers. This form of travel grew rapidly. In 1833 only eleven steamboats were traveling regularly from Buffalo westward across Lake Erie to Detroit; they carried 43,000 persons during the season, although sailboats transported many others. Two summers later, an estimated 1,200 persons left Buffalo each day for the West, and in 1839 a steamer line with eight boats established regular traffic between Buffalo and Detroit, with light boats making a connecting run to Chicago. Many of the Chicago passengers then headed north to Wisconsin or pushed westward to Iowa. By 1839 the eastern shore of the Mississippi across from Burlington, Iowa, reminded onlookers of a permanently encamped army, so ineffectual were the ferry's efforts to reduce the numbers wishing to cross.

The fare for the Buffalo-Chicago trip was $20 in 1840, and this fell to $10 a decade later. Steerage was half this. Continued improvements in ship technology and knowledge of the lakes enabled the steamboat *Milwaukie* to cut the Buffalo-Chicago trip by water to under nine days by 1841; by combining steamboat and railroad, it was possible to go from New York to Chicago in five days by 1847.

To the south, emigrant traffic on boats from Cincinnati increased drastically also. By traveling down the Ohio and up the Mississippi, or by coming into the Gulf of Mexico (from New York or from Europe) and then up the Mississippi, a person could avoid overland travel until the final phases of emigration. Passage from New Orleans to St. Louis was $30 in the 1830s, but deck passage was $8, and to continue on to Galena was another $3. Steamboats were soon running up the smaller western rivers as well.

Stagecoach service also expanded, although little comfort for passengers could be expected. As early as 1831 stages traveled between St. Louis and major Illinois settlements, and newcomers into the region in the mid-forties found lines operating daily out of both St. Louis and Chicago to all sections of the Upper Mississippi Valley. The telegraph soon followed. Its electric wires reached Chicago, Springfield, and St. Louis by 1848 and stretched to Wisconsin and Iowa soon thereafter. By the time railroad construction was booming in the region in the 1850s, eastern rail lines were so extensively developed that a traveler in New York could choose from three railroads for a thirty-six-hour trip to Chicago. Thus

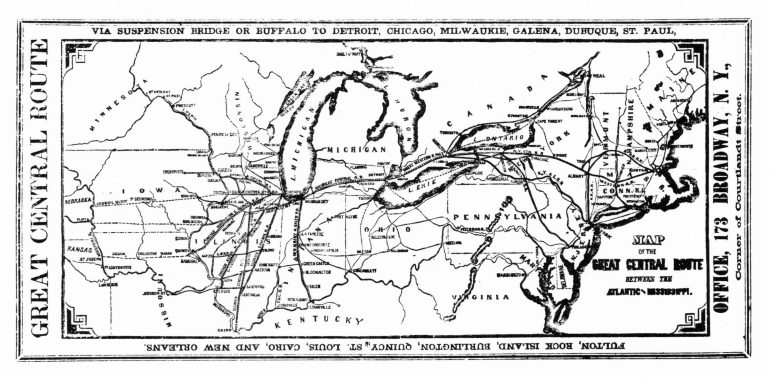

By 1855, the East Coast traveler or immigrant had direct rail transportation to the Upper Mississippi country, and within the region a variety of lines were completed or planned.

did technology and the moving line of settlement throw open the Upper Mississippi Valley to the world.

To the Indians—principally the Sac and Fox, Kickapoo, Illinois, Winnebago,
Iowa, Sioux, and Potawatomi—the prairies and forests had been good homes, and
they yielded to this invasion grudgingly, struggling against smallpox and the
white soldiers and settlers in sporadic encounters that they usually lost. The Black
Hawk War of 1831–32, involving a band of the Sac and Fox, was one of the
Indians' final attempts to maintain a presence in the region until the 1862–63
Sioux Uprising in Minnesota finally brought down the curtain on the Indians' independence there. Chicago was filled with Potawatomis for the tribe's final treaty
session the summer after Black Hawk's defeat. The tribe staged a final fierce
parade—really a recessional—through the city in August 1835, shouting, dancing,
and waving tomahawks as they moved down Lake Street and out of the city en
route to Iowa and then the Great Plains. Whites moving into Iowa were enabled to
settle on the "New Purchase" west of the Black Hawk country after treaties of
1843, 1846, 1848, and 1851 removed the Sac and Fox. However, most of the
Winnebago, Chippewa, and Menominee won in their attempts to remain in
Wisconsin, generally agreeing to settle on timberland in deference to the influx of
whites onto the prized prairies and oak openings. The federal government yielded
to the Indians' requests after unsuccessful attempts to move them to Minnesota.
The Minnesota tribes remained a threat to settlers until Indian treaties were
signed after the Civil War.

The role of governmental agencies, so apparent in Indian removal and land
sales, underwent several changes as the Upper Mississippi's population increases
brought the end of territory status. Illinois gained statehood in 1818, Missouri in
1821. In 1838, Iowa Territory was split off from Wisconsin; the two eventually
became the nation's twenty-ninth and thirtieth states, Iowa in 1846, Wisconsin in
1848. Minnesota's inaccessibility in these years delayed its statehood until 1858.

The passing of the Indian, the onrush of settlement, the creation of new states in
the wilderness seemed evidence to many of divine intervention. Alexis de Tocqueville, after visiting in 1831, pronounced the Mississippi Valley to be "the most

magnificent habitation ever prepared by God for man." Clergymen carried de Tocqueville's concept further, seeing special purposes involved in God's selection. A missionary recalled riding across the Illinois prairies in the early 1830s and passing near a mound with a bark-covered enclosure at the top. Inside, he discovered the body of an Indian chief in full regalia, "the arms hanging by the side, and its hands crossed upon its lap, and its legs fully extended...with his bow, quiver and tomahawk lying by his side." The missionary learned that the chief had requested that his body be left in this way, so that "when the 'pale faces' came, he would awake to life, and be in readiness to lead the tribe on to the conflict." However, by midcentury a school building stood on top of the mound, the unbroken prairie below had been largely replaced by grain fields and fenced farms, and clergymen carried the word of God. It was part of a divine plan, the missionary concluded: "In viewing the change I am often constrained to exclaim, 'What hath God wrought!'"

The white population, whose entry the late Indian chief opposed fruitlessly from his mound-top sepulcher, had grown in fits and starts through the colonial era. French explorers who ventured down the region's rivers in the seventeenth and eighteenth centuries established forts and trading posts; their marks on the land can be encountered today. Land holdings were held in narrow strips running back from the waterfront, perpendicular to the rivers, forming a system still evident in platbooks of such former French posts as Prairie du Chien, Wisconsin, and Prairie du Rocher, Illinois.

Then came the Americans. St. Louis, which began as a French center in the 1760s, was transformed as Americans, primarily southerners, traveled north after the War of 1812. The upper South's proximity to southern Illinois and the reach of such southern tributaries of the Ohio River as the Cumberland and the Tennessee helped draw many settlers (including blacks, both free and fugitive) northwestward into Illinois. Several southern traces, including the Wilderness Trail and the Nashville-Saline Trail, had also evolved into major thoroughfares into Illinois by the early nineteenth century. The 1850 census showed that 70 percent of the settlers in the Shawnee Hills of southern Illinois were of southern origin, predominantly from the upper South. These groups carried their mountain pioneer culture with them, hunting in the forests of hilly southern Illinois rather than venturing as farmers onto the prairies. Formal education remained rare in the area—soon known as "Egypt"—and a visiting Presbyterian missionary later complained that "not half of the adult population can write their own names, and not one in fifty can repeat the Ten Commandments."

Many of these southerners continued up the Great Valley to the lead-mining region of southwestern Wisconsin and the adjacent areas of Illinois and Iowa. The lead country became a distinctive area, marked by the large numbers of people who had originated in the South or in such southern extensions as southern Illinois and the Missouri lead region below St. Louis. Iowa also received a major southern settlement along its Missouri border region and in the Des Moines River Valley. Some even brought their slaves into Iowa, believing they were in Missouri.

Migrations before 1830 included few foreigners. Except for the Missouri and southwestern Wisconsin lead regions and isolated fur-trading posts, settlement during the opening decades of the nineteenth century was principally in two bands: along the Wabash on the eastern side of southern Illinois (Shawneetown was the principal city) and along the Mississippi on the west, around Kaskaskia on the American Bottom and St. Louis on the western shore. But some foreigners were present, of course. Irish veterans of the American Revolution came in the 1790s to O'Hara Settlement in Randolph County, south of St. Louis on the Illinois side of the river. Congress in 1818 authorized townships to be set aside in Illinois for emigrants fleeing Ireland's turmoil, with land sales at two dollars per acre. Hundreds of Irish emigrants arrived in New York City in the spring of 1819, and many were soon bound inland to the prairies of Illinois. The lead mines in the Dubuque and Galena area soon had Irish employees, while Kane County, Illinois, recorded an "Irish Settlement" by the late 1830s. By this time another group of Irish families had started farming in the Merna area of McLean County, Illinois.

Some Germans arrived early too, although confusion exists because many of the early German-speakers in the Shawnee Hills were apparently Pennsylvania Dutch rather than emigrants coming directly from Germany. German philanthropist Ferdinand Ernst traveled through southern Illinois in 1819 and encountered a fellow countryman farming near Edwardsville, but the larger movement of Germans would wait one more decade. By 1830 the German population was increasing rapidly west of St. Louis, in St. Clair County, Illinois, and in nearby Fayette County. Darmstadt, Illinois, was started in 1832 by a group of German farmers and tradesmen. This was the decade of German beginnings in St. Louis and Milwaukee, soon to become major German centers, while numerous river towns—Galena, Quincy, Warsaw—also became known for substantial German populations.

A colony of English farmers was launched on the English Prairie near the west bank of the Wabash in 1817; they founded the towns of Albion and Wanborough. Soon after that, English, Welsh, and Scottish miners were laboring in southern Illinois coalfields and in the new lead region. Soon the Scandinavians began to arrive, settling mainly in southern Wisconsin and northern Illinois, especially around Chicago, until their numbers increased sharply later in the century and they moved in a swelling tide into Minnesota and Iowa. Norwegians came to the Fox and Rock River Valleys and Wisconsin's Lake Koshkonong area in the 1830s and 1840s, while Swedes settled in Rockford, Galesburg, Bishop Hill (a religious communitarian settlement), and several smaller communities. The Irish and Germans were most numerous by far among the foreign-born, however.

But Americans, rather than Europeans, predominated in the rush to settle the Upper Mississippi country, particularly after the "Military Tract" west of the Illinois River was opened in 1817 to soldiers who had served in the War of 1812, and with the rush to the lead region after 1824. Prominent in many communities were New Englanders, who began to appear in southeastern Wisconsin and northern Illinois by the 1830s. New England folk formed Princeton, Illinois, in 1831 as a colony of Northampton, Massachusetts; Metamora was launched in 1835 by settlers from Hanover, New Hampshire; Geneseo in 1836 by a group of New Yorkers; and Wheatland by Vermonters at the end of the decade. The New Englanders and New Yorkers were joined by an increasingly heavy settlement from Middle Atlantic states such as Pennsylvania and from adjacent Indiana and nearby Ohio.

Diversity became the pattern for all states of the region through this immigration, although only Illinois's population developed in layers: southern Illinois was overwhelmingly made up of folk from the upper South; northern Illinois was heavily New England and Middle Atlantic in origin; and the state's central region had a heavy influx of Americans from other parts of the Old Northwest. (Architecture today reveals this settlement pattern, for "dogtrot" cabins of the southern style predominate in southern Illinois, while the upright wing of the New England cottage can still be found in some communities at the northern end of the state. Church architecture sometimes betrays settlement patterns as well.)

Few towns retained their initial composition for long, of course; and with the exception of southern Illinois, most areas of the Upper Mississippi Valley developed as heterogeneous conglomerations of peoples. Not here a New England unity, proud of its pure strain of English dissenters; no heavily German state like Pennsylvania, no Scotch-Irish domination as in the Appalachians. On the contrary, the states that formed the target of this onrush of immigration fast became a rainbow of national, regional, and religious types. Milwaukee developed a Yankee Hill section but also a Tory Hill, a German Town, the Irish "Bloody Third," and the "wooden-shoe district" or Hollandsche-Berg. A missionary noted this diversity in his field of labor in Wisconsin: "On the south is a settlement of Scotch emigrants. Next succeeds a neighborhood of settlers from the island of Guernsey, some of whom cannot speak English. Among their number is a Methodist clergyman, who sometimes preaches to his countrymen in their own language. A society of Free-will Baptists comes next; and immediately contiguous is a colony from Wales composed of Baptists and Whitfield Methodists....Interspersed with the above described population are members of our church."

To the south, across the Illinois border in Freeport, another minister encountered people from New England, the Middle Atlantic states, "occasionally a Marylander, Virginian, and Carolinian, with a foreign mixture of Norwegians, Prussians, Germans, French, Irish, Scotch, and English," all belonging to twenty-one church denominations. Even those meeting together as Presbyterians were members of Congregational, Associate Reformed, German Reformed, Irish Presbyterian, and New School and Old School Presbyterians. The "Campbellites," or Disciples of Christ, were active as well in most areas. Atheists and rationalists were found also, particularly as refugees from the German revolutions began to arrive in numbers. Spiritualists established groups, as did followers of local messiahs. Mormons briefly found havens in the Upper Mississippi—in

"Farm on Missouri Coast, about 1842."

Gustavus Pfau, a German artist, toured the Upper Mississippi country and left a valuable record of paintings of pioneer life. The "Virginia fence," the importance of corn, and the location of the river nearby were all common to farming across the Upper Mississippi region before the coming of the railroad. Soon, barbed wire would provide fencing, wheat and other cash crops would compete with corn, and farming would develop in the interior opened by the Iron Horse.

Courtesy of the Illinois State Historical Library.

Jackson County, Missouri, then in Nauvoo, Illinois—before opposition drove them to continue their quest for a new homeland farther west.

This shifting diversity soon became part of the fabric of a region that lived on hope—hope for rich harvests from the black prairie soil; hope for the new towns already mushrooming and for those existing only in speculators' minds; hope for the prosperity promised by roads, canals, and railroads; hope for "The West," which was increasingly hailed as the nation's future center of political and economic power.

With this mood in ascendance, Cairo, at the southern tip of Illinois, became known as the state's "great city of prophecy." A look at the map showed its obvious destiny. Not only did it lie where the Ohio met the Mississippi, it was also the point where planned railroad lines would unload freight and passengers from the entire Old Northwest and East for transshipment to the South. Noting the approach of railroad lines, a visitor asked the obvious: "With all these advantages can Cairo fail to become a vast city?"

If Cairo eventually became an example of a dream deferred, Chicago was the opposite, always exceeding its boosters' predictions. Incoming vessels were forced to anchor far off the shore during the village's early years until funds were appropriated in 1833 for development of the harbor. By 1835 the hundred-ton schooner *Illinois* was able to move into the Chicago River through the deepened cut. City fathers were so enthusiastic over these improvements that they advertised wharf-leasing privileges for 999-year terms, until the state legislature forced a reduction to a more modest maximum of 5 years. Soon Chicago was the region's leading port, and it continued to build on its importance for transportation. Once a network of Indian trails had met at the tip of Lake Michigan, but increasingly lake shipping and rail, wagon, and canal lines reached or connected with Chicago. The city's trade and transport area reached as far south as St. Louis by the late thirties and took in much of Wisconsin as well.

Chicago became a bustling community, always on the move. Visitors were frequently astonished to meet in its busy streets a "house that is out for a walk"— even buildings three stories tall were rolled to new locations as the city by the lake built out onto the prairie. A village of fewer than 100 in 1830, Chicago in 1835–36 had 456 recorded boat arrivals, and in July 1837 officially reported 4,179 persons within its city limits. Connections by wagon with the Illinois River had been established by then, and in 1839 a stage line ran between Chicago and the Mississippi River at Galena.

William Cullen Bryant was astonished by the changes when he returned to Chicago in 1846 after a five-year absence. The population had jumped from 5,000 to 15,000 in the interim. The city featured long rows of warehouses and shops, a busy waterfront, and even suburbs "of the cottages of German and Irish laborers, stretching northward along the lake, and westward into the prairies, and widening every day." It had become the center for farmers within a radius of several hundred miles for shipping wheat, beef, pork, and other goods. This was the new, bustling metropolis of the lakes and prairies. And elsewhere up and down the region's waterways, in old St. Louis as well as rising Milwaukee, Racine, Muscatine, Burlington, Alton, Quincy, and smaller towns, dreams were forming of a future filled with prosperity. The 1840 census pointed the way. Illinois already had a population of 476,183, highest in the region; Missouri was next with 383,702 (16,469 in St. Louis), followed by Iowa with 43,112, and "Wiskonsin" with 30,945 (Milwaukee reported 1,712).

But if the prairies and oak openings were becoming magnets to the farmers of the Old World and the older states of the nation, and if the rising western cities welcomed capitalists into a burgeoning frontier economy, this land was regarded with concern and even anxiety by many religious leaders. Wealth meant worldliness, and behind this drive for riches in the West the men of God discerned some distinctly un-Christian traits.

The act of emigrating frequently involved breaking with tradition, cutting ties to institutions and customs. Partly because of this fact frontiersmen had long been suspect in the East as a people morally adrift. This concern was magnified as the nation suddenly began pushing westward rapidly—Texas, California, the Oregon country—and each migration called forth prayers, funds, and missionaries to help the westering people.

In the Upper Mississippi country especially, missionaries saw hard labor ahead. "Intemperance, Sabbath-breaking, and profanity grow rank all around us, from the very outset of settlement," complained a preacher at one of the Minnesota river towns. Competition whetted the missionary appetite. "If the gospel of Christ be not there," the Presbyterians and Congregationalists were told, "Romanism will be there, or Mormonism, or Millerism, or Mesmerism, or Spiritual Knockings, or some other equally stupid and debasing form of faith or infidelity." Catholics felt competitive pressures also, and the Irish immigrant leader Thomas D'Arcy McGee sent a warning to Catholic leaders back in Ireland that "there is now going on here a hand-to-hand battle for the Faith, unprecedented, I verily believe, since the 'Reformation,' in any quarter of the world."

This competition was further heated by the fact that many of the Protestant missionaries who poured into the West in the decades leading up to 1860 came out of an environment caught up in the spirit of reform. These campaigns for moral suasion were based on a belief that the immediate perfectability of individuals and society was possible and, therefore, necessary. This was the "hot air period," when movements proliferated, from temperance to care of the insane, from free land to public education. Most of these became linked with religion and were carried on by specialized voluntary organizations. Antislavery was but one among many reform movements until events of the 1850s elevated it above the others in the public consciousness.

Clashes were perhaps inevitable in such a divided, heated environment. Just as Indians resented and then fought the encroachment of whites onto soil they regarded as theirs, so white Americans challenged other white Americans, and many of these disputed the arrivals of Europeans, especially of Catholic Europeans. There were many who agreed with the Reverend Lyman Beecher when he argued that "a homogeneous people" had launched the American experiment in self-government, but immigration was threatening those foundations. He called for the government to regulate both the influx of foreigners and their naturalization to prevent the overthrow of national moral and intellectual culture.

The main confrontations took place not in national councils or church seminaries, but on the prairies and in the hills, within the new settlements, in shops and land offices, on steamboat decks and in railroad cars, at camp meetings and political rallies all across the Upper Mississippi country. In such settings differences in speech or dress or custom could, under the right conditions, trigger disputes that leaped rapidly from picayune matters to philosophical debates on the natural order of things.

Suspicion as well as hope grew on the prairies. When English settler Morris Birkbeck entered southern Illinois in 1817, he learned that settlers regarded visitors as "invaders of their privileges," and newcomers were called "land-hunters" with "some expressions of contempt." Fifteen years later, when New Englanders entered the Black Hawk Purchase in Iowa and located in the town of Denmark, a North Carolina native said he was "sorry when he heard that the Yankees were coming." Other southerners nearby referred to the new town as "Yankee Heaven." Similarly, a newcomer to central Illinois wrote to his eastern in-laws that "they sneer in this country at every thing of a Yankee origin."

Europeans seemed especially noxious to religious Americans. The elders of a Presbyterian church in Madison County, Illinois, included in their plea for eastern financial help and prayers the lament that they were "surrounded by a population...more than half German, and these strangers manifest no interest in vital religion, or sound morality."

As the 1820s gave way to the 1830s, the stage was being set for this region to become a confrontation ground—an enormous debating arena—and to assume a new role in national political and economic life. This process would be played out in community after community, in each New Erin, each New Baden, New Virginia, Yankee Settlement, as the arguments over religion and reform mingled with the day-to-day tasks of clearing land, buying and selling goods, and establishing homes, churches, and communities. The beliefs and aspirations of these westering peoples had already been molded within sharply differing environments. God's will, the right path, holy destiny—these were seen quite differently by each arriving group. Perhaps that fact was not apparent along the Rhine or Hudson or Firth of Clyde, in the Schwarzwald, Appalachians, or County Kerry. But it was certainly present within the minds and fibres of the travelers who packed their chests and made the mental break with tradition that was always the first requirement for the move west. Their differing backgrounds would become increasingly evident as these peoples jostled, competed, and cooperated in the newly opening lands of the Upper Mississippi.

2. From the Irish Island

Beyond the seas, under the same sun and moon as the prairies of North America but linked to a crueler past, the soft, green hills of Ireland and the steep slopes of the Rhineland were nurturing men with new dreams. Caught in a maze of political traditions and economic dislocations, they saw the distant lands of America as a vision of hope. The burdens of the past were different in each land, but events of the 1830s and 1840s in Ireland and in Germany magnified them until life seemed intolerable and escape became the goal. The Old World was in turmoil; it seemed a deteriorating environment. In late 1845 an agent of the British Commissioner of Woods took the space and time in his official report on Irish crown estates to comment on the manner in which children prepared potatoes for dinner: "They first peel off the skin," he wrote, "then they scoop out the black or diseased spots on all sides, as the disease enters into the potato at different depths. It has rather a curious appearance when cleared of all the black spots," he added, "and even it looks much worse boiled than raw."

These were the times when workhouse directors at Dundalk, north of Dublin, were surprised to see before them one day Andrew English, a "first rate farmer" applying to be admitted as a pauper:

> MR. M'CULLOCH: Why; is it possible that you are come to this?
> ENGLISH: Yes indeed, sir, I kept away as long as I could: but it was no use.
> MR. M'CULLOCH: I remember that man a very respectable farmer in this county, not very long ago.
> MR. CONROY: Yes, indeed, he held thirty-three acres of land, and was a right good farmer.

The guardians, agreeing on his integrity and honesty and dismayed at his condition, granted English's application to enter the workhouse. He thanked them and withdrew, but not before one of the directors observed that they would have "one hundred fifty cases of the same description" within two years. The prediction was accurate, even understated. From such conditions, multiplied a thousandfold, came a massive exodus of Irish men and women and children to the New World.

There was more to it than the Irish famine of the 1840s, of course; more, still, than opposition to British control of the island, although many would link the two. One of the most famous Irish nationalists would begin his account by stating unequivocally, "The famine is to be thus accounted for: The act of union, in 1800, deprived Ireland of a native legislature," and so on. But by mid-century, British control of Ireland as a colony had become a festering sore that imbued the Irish people with a sense of frustration and a determination to accept no further persecution. These experiences in Ireland became guides for Irish behavior later in America.

The British connection was an overbearing fact of life to the Irish. The English, rulers over most of the island since the twelfth century, treated nineteenth century Ireland as a colony, seeking to snuff out local opposition and to mold the people to English ways. "In those days we were forbidden to *speak our native language in school*," an immigrant recalled of his childhood near Ballygar after 1810. "Our teacher would put a stone in our coats as a telltale to report if we spoke Irish." More than merely discouraging use of the native language—a campaign that some Irish groups supported because they regarded use of the Irish (Gaelic) as representing backwardness—the United Kingdom continued to enforce portions of the Penal Laws, anti-Catholic statutes dating back to 1695. These laws sought to reduce Catholicism to "helpless impotence" by prohibiting Catholics from holding important positions in law, commerce, or the military. In the eighteenth century the laws were the vehicle for breaking up Catholic estates, and widespread ruin accompanied their use. But the major long-term result was the degradation of the Irish peasantry.

Certain aspects of the Penal Laws had been softened or ignored over the years, however; and by the time the Act of Union between Great Britain and Ireland took effect in 1801, Catholics could vote in parliamentary elections, although they still could not be elected to office. Such restrictions stimulated efforts to unite Ireland's Catholics, and their first mass political movement was the Catholic Association, begun in 1820. A local bishop accurately hailed it as "an Irish revolution." The tenant farmers and others who provided the mass of votes were sometimes led to the voting stands by priests instead of by their landlords as before. They marched to the balloting in groups as large as five hundred for the 1828 Ennis election campaign, when Daniel O'Connell, leader of the movement, was victorious, 2,057 to 982 over his Protestant opponent. As a Catholic he still could not take his seat, but in the resulting clamor the British Parliament gave in, and the Catholic Emancipation Act was passed the following year. Irish Catholics could now sit in the parliament that claimed to speak for them.

But other aspects of British control continued to gall the Irish. The Protestant Anglican church remained the official church, receiving tax funds and other advantages. From 1798 on, religion became part of politics, as Catholics were forced to seek changes in British law to follow their religion. Priests increasingly led local groups opposing British restrictions. Through such developments Catholics lined up as enemies of the established government. They regarded non-Catholics as enemies of the people. It was the accomplishment of Daniel O'Connell to bring together various opposition groups and focus these through the growing spirit of Irish nationality. Mass meetings for repeal of the union between Ireland and Britain brought crowds numbering into the hundreds of thousands during the 1840s. After O'Connell's death in 1847, the ardent agitators left in the fray—mainly the "Young Ireland" movement—launched a futile revolt in 1848 and split the movement through their quarrels. But they enunciated ideas that would remain important in Irish politics throughout the century as political consciousness continued to develop among the Irish people.

What they came back to, over and over, was the land question. British control had placed British landlords on most Irish land in preceding centuries, and Protestant Irish controlled much of the rest. By the early nineteenth century, the masses of Irishmen worked either as small farmers known as cotters, renting tiny plots of less than five acres, or as farm laborers. (Years later and a world away in Wisconsin an Irish immigrant farmer complained of crop prices in a letter home, then added the telling comment, "But we own the land." It was the crucial difference.)

These were a preindustrial people whose lives flowed with the rhythm of the seasons—of potato planting and harvesting, of digging turf (peat)—rather than the demands of a timekeeper. To many prefamine visitors, the Irish seemed indolent and lazy, although hospitable and much given to music and dance. A lady told of seeing County Kerry men who would walk ten miles into town for a pennyworth of tobacco or twopence worth of fish and thought their day was well spent. Light in their one-room hovels came from peeled rushes dipped in grease, and furniture was rare. An 1837 survey in Tullahobagly, County Donegal, found only 10 beds, 93 chairs, and 243 stools for a population of 9,000. Two touring Welsh clergymen reported that Irish girls "sit on their heels on the ground....Seldom does one see either a chair or stool in the whole land." Pigs had the run of the house. Cotters were forced to work without pay for their landlords, planting and digging potatoes, reaping, haymaking, digging turf. No wonder Kerry folk "become prematurely old," the lady visitor remarked; "they lead a dreary life of hard work and privations, yet cheered by the blessed consciousness of fulfilling their duty."

Fully two-thirds of the Irish people were dependent on agriculture for a livelihood as late as 1841, in a system which promoted tinier and tinier subdivisions. First there was the rental of large tracts of land on long leases to individuals, who then sublet and split farms into smaller holdings to obtain more rent. Since the demand for farmland was high, the landlord could always count on renting even the tiniest plot. Additionally, in the west of Ireland a joint tenancy system known as *rundale* had developed, with land held in common and then divided so that each tenant received a portion of different qualities of land. Rundale, together with subdivision and inheritance divisions, could carry land division to extremes. A Donegal man finally gave up when his land was cut into forty-two different pieces. At Liscananawn in County Mayo, 110 inhabitants had three portions each of the 330 parcels into which 167 acres were divided. If they could have improved this— fenced, fertilized, drained—with any promise of longevity, the system might have been better; but, as John Stuart Mill lamented, "In Ireland alone, the bulk of a population wholly dependent on the land cannot look forward to a single-year's occupation of it.''

Those statistics of the 1841 census hinted at but could not reveal the underlying hatreds and distrust built up over preceding generations: of landlords who charged what tenants felt were exceedingly high rents, confident that they could always find someone to farm their land; of British officials and their apologists who enforced the system; of Anglican clergy who drew sustenance from the land through taxes, while Catholics were often forced to hold mass in the open air for lack of a building in which to meet.

Overdependence on the potato must be placed high among the factors creating the famine. In the eighteenth century, when Ireland shifted from pastoral to tillage farming and land division increased, the population adopted the potato as its basic food. It was nourishing, it was economical. An acre and a half would supply a six-member family's wants for most of the year. And it freed land for cash crops such as wheat, which required four to six times as much land as the potato for equal production of food.

Portions of the island had encountered some of the dangers of a one-crop system during the regional famines that had ravaged the land on four occasions in the thirty years prior to 1845. Then came premonitions of disaster from westward across the Atlantic. In 1842 the potato crop along the eastern seaboard of the United States and Canada had been hit by disease, but the availability of other food at the time almost erased that occurrence from the records of American agriculture. In 1844 a blight swept through potatoes in the northeastern section of the United States. Then, in the summer of 1845, notices began to appear in British government reports and in the press of potato crops dying from a similar blight, and it was affecting the Continent as well. By September it had reached Ireland, touching Waterford and Wexford first, but soon covering half the island. Since local failures of the potato crop were not new, this problem excited little extra comment.

Hopes were high for the potato crop of 1846. When a priest traveled from Cork to Dublin at the end of July, he saw potatoes blooming ''in all the luxurance of an abundant harvest.'' But when he returned a week later, he wrote, ''I beheld with sorrow one wide waste of putrefying vegetation.'' Others told similar stories of the entire green countryside suddenly turning scorched, as if a fire had passed over. Leaves withered, tubers decomposed. A people who had never known such all-encompassing disaster before searched desperately for expedients. They covered parts of the fields with cloth, they cut up the blighted potatoes and soaked them in water, they dried them in ovens, and they persisted in trying to eat them. One report from Clare told of people dining on food from which ''so putrid and offensive an effluvia issued that in consuming it they were obliged to leave the doors and windows of their cabins open.''

In this condition, where starvation already seemed possible, Ireland entered the winter of 1846–47. It was the worst in many years: gales swept fiercely over the island, snow lay deep everywhere, and typhus, dysentery (the ''bloody flux''), and ''famine dropsy'' or hunger edema were widespread. Ireland's travail did not subside until 1851, despite a better crop in 1847.

People begged along the roadways and in the towns, searching for food—any food—and stealing when they could. Cork reported five thousand beggars in its streets, and a visitor said ''every corner of the streets is filled with pale, careworn creatures, the weak leading and supporting the weaker,'' while women ''assail you at every turn with famished babes, imploring alms.''

In early 1847, the streets of Westport in County Mayo were filled with ''gaunt wanderers,'' while at Bundorragha across the harbor the population ''were like walking skeletons, the men stamped with the livid mark of hunger, the children crying with pain, the women, in some of the cabins, too weak to stand.'' All animals were gone from the farms except one pig, a visitor noted.

Many people in Kerry ''live rather more like animals than people,'' two travelers reported in 1852. They told of a family ''living in a hole at the side of a large bank by a river,'' and they encountered an old woman at the side of the road ''creeping out of a sort of hut similar to a dog-kennel.'' As publicized as these conditions were, members of a Protestant visiting society who ventured out among church members in Skull near Bantry Bay were surprised at what they encountered. Their rector reported that the group saw ''many families of from five to eight members, all obliged to sleep on one wallet of straw, with only one sheet

down on them, and no other covering except the rags which they wear by day!...
By the successive blight of their crops for the last four years they have barely
existed.''

Stealing food became commonplace, and records of the 1849 summer assizes
for Limerick Gaol show numerous cases of theft of sheep, goats, cows, geese, hay,
and potatoes, as well as "milking cows by night" and "milking a cow and stealing
the milk value 1/2 property of Thomas Abjohn." That summer's record for
Limerick showed that forty-six cases—39 percent of the total—involved stealing
food for humans or animals. When eight young girls were arrested in Kilkenny for
"an organised plunder of potatoes," having opened "seventeen drills in one
night," one of the girls told the barrister, "I would work if I could get it. I was
hungry."

Death was the portal out of this land of famine for many. In Dunmanway,
County Cork, one parish lost a fourth of its population to "disease and
starvation" in a twelve-month period in 1847 and 1848. This story was replayed in
most areas of Ireland in the years following 1845, until by 1851 the population of
the island had fallen from 8.5 million to 6.5 million. Only half of the 2 million absent by 1851 had escaped bodily over the water; the rest died from hunger and
disease.

It was increasingly evident that there were too many persons on the land. The
bulge in Irish population in the early nineteenth century contributed to the severi-
ty of the famine, both in the starvation which followed when blight killed the
potato crop and in stimulating countermeasures by landowners to save their
estates. When Parliament in June 1847 put the responsibility for Irish relief on
landlords, taxes quickly rose as workhouse populations mushroomed. The law
divided Ireland into 130 "unions," averaging 62,884 each in population. Each
union was to have a workhouse under control of some elected guardians and some
ex officio guardians subject to Dublin. The 1847 amendments created outdoor
relief—principally road repairs—while blocking any relief for those owning more
than a quarter of an acre.

Landlords who saw their taxes climbing to support the workhouses were already
aware that improvements in agriculture and income meant reducing the

Harper's Weekly, Feb. 14, 1880. Courtesy of the State Historical Society of Wisconsin.

**The distress in Ireland—
exterior of a cabin.**

The famine of the 1840s was devastating in its impact upon the people of Ireland, driving thousands to emigrate as an alternative to death by starvation.

Harper's Weekly, Feb. 14, 1880. Courtesy of the State Historical Society of Wisconsin.

**The distress in Ireland—
interior of a cabin.**

population on the land and increasing the size of individual farm units. "From my general knowledge of the present state of the West and South West of Ireland," reported a government official visiting the royal estate of Kingwilliamstown in 1849, "I am decidedly of opinion that no permanent improvement can be effected until the surplus population of the estate be removed." It was a well-worn statement by then.

Soon most Irish landlords had two desires in common: to reduce taxes by removing the destitute from their union district and to improve harvests by reducing the number of tenants. It was a difficult combination to deal with, and some 10 percent of Irish landlords went bankrupt during the famine years from the decline in rents. Crops dwindled, farm work was stifled, tenants fled without paying their debts. "Old Mrs. McCarthy is in great distress," a landowner near Limerick reported, "as one of her younger sons has run off, it is supposed, to America with £14 which she said was my rent." A Dublin official surveying records from Tipperary in 1849 found that "more than half the occupants" were gone from many estates, "some gone to America, some to the Poor House, and many had died." But in all cases, he added, the land was left with the proprietor, "generally with the entire loss of rent for three years." Irish records of the period show almost frenzied efforts by landlords to reduce their taxes and remove excess tenants.

Work relief immediately became popular among landlords. Some wanted the crown to require that landowners employ the poor on their own estates' road and draining projects and thereby reduce poorhouse charges. Most of the poor who were thus "relieved" ended up some distance from their old homes, however, and the work was crushing to many in their enfeebled state. Sir John Benn-Walsh, an English landowner, looked in on a workhouse in 1851 and "saw the paupers in a state of mutiny" at the establishment of a capstan mill (a mill with grinding wheels turned not by a river current but by men who pushed the spokes of a cylinder endlessly around). But eventually "they succumbed," he added. Work relief in Skull required the "unfortunate creatures" to arrive early in the morning for roll call and remain until evening, walking five or six miles to and from the work site "without having tasted food, and with their miserable clothes dripping wet on their wretched frames."

One critic of the work-relief program charged that "aged widows and others with scarcely a rag to cover them and nothing to screen them from the severities of the weather" were forced to work eight hours a day sweeping streets or "breaking stones on a bog road" in bad weather. This work, he added, "seemed more effective if designed (according to the opinion of some) speedily to rid the Union of what was considered an incumbrance rather than to afford relief to the perishing pauper."

Workhouses were quickly overcrowded with refugees from the famine and land clearances. A landowner visiting his estate in August 1848 admitted to being "utterly dismayed and appalled" after talking with the poor-law agent. There were 22,000 paupers on outdoor relief, out of a population of less than 78,000, and the union was £40,000 in debt because of it. Nearly an eighth of Tralee's population was in that union's workhouses in January 1851. Parliament had discovered the previous summer that some 336,000 persons were on some form of relief in Ireland. Many of these workhouse residents were helped to emigrate, and in Connaught it was reported that employed laborers subscribed sixpence each toward a fund which was then used to pay the lottery winner's passage to America.

With taxes for poor relief climbing, landowners sought ways to cut expenses. Emigration of tenants proved an efficient answer, removing the cotters, leveling their mud-walled cottages, buying them tickets for "Amerikay." Sir Benn-Walsh told of a Clare landowner who had emigrated fourteen hundred persons, and Benn-Walsh's own journal shows frequent use of this solution. At Forhane "the worst tenants have been got rid of at the expence of emigrating them." On his land at Derrimdaffe, "I have emigrated the families of three insolvent tenants.... They are, I should think, nearly twenty persons." And "some of the cottiers [at Tullamore] have been emigrated and their cabins leveled. Bat Madigan died, his family have been emigrated, and his lot thrown into the others." Summing up an 1851 tour of his property, Benn-Walsh wrote that "to induce the larger farmers to surrender their holdings when they became insolvent, I emigrated several, either with their whole families or in part." The latter decision was expensive, he wrote, "but it enabled me to consolidate and make comfortable sized farms of from £30 and £40 up to £140 per annum." This was the goal, increasingly, for Ireland's landowners.

Emigration of excess populations had been attempted earlier, but before the famine there had been much less interest among the cotters. Now they seized the opportunity to leave. At Ballykilcline in County Roscommon, an old crown estate, tenants had turned down their landlord's offer to help them emigrate in 1836, at a time when the 602-acre estate had 463 subdivisions and a population of 500 persons. In 1847 the tenants themselves petitioned to be emigrated.

In this way thousands upon thousands of Irish cotters and farm laborers were sent across the Atlantic, joining the masses emigrating without the landowner's assistance. Soon the absence of people on the land was apparent to all; some feared the island would shortly be depopulated. Thurles and some areas of Tipperary "appear to be almost totally deserted," a report claimed, while a Mayo magistrate and landowner expressed the fear that the county would be without "sufficient hands to till the ground." Connemara was hit by clearances so extensive "that it must, in a short time, become a complete desert," a visitor predicted. After several hundred tenants had been helped to emigrate from the crown-held estate at Ballykilcline, it was reported that **the estate** was "perfectly untenanted."

Agriculture was given a new thrust in Ireland as larger units could be farmed with reliable, proven tenants, and there were those who even claimed that "the destruction of the potato is a blessing to Ireland." But it had brought tragic human destruction as well.

It would be too much to expect any people to give up without a struggle the land they and their forefathers had lived on for generations. Violence became a common ingredient of Irish life. It was abetted by several factors coming together in addition to the famine, including the long tradition of secret societies (Oak Boys, White Boys, Ribbon Men) that had flouted the law, killed British agents, and carried out "people's justice" for generations, usually with the acquiescence of the local population. Their acts were often stimulated by the fact that many of the new landowners were "improvers," efficient and cost conscious, who hesitated little in removing what they considered surplus, inefficient, ignorant tenants. New laws aided the landowners in these efforts after 1849.

Forced removals of Irish people from land they considered their own, carried out by officials who were to them an occupying power, brought a wave of violence across Ireland that has been somewhat downplayed in history because of the enormity of the era's prominent feature, the famine. Newspapers of the period provide some evidence of the resistance: "Mr. Ralph Smith, of Tullamore, is so obnoxious to his Carlow tenantry, because he served ejectments for non payment of rent, that they will not suffer him to cut down and save his crops, which are rotting in the fields. The ears were cut off the horses of three persons who volunteered their assistance, and the horse of another was shot." These were the "midnight legislators," the "rockites," who fought ejectment and, when that failed, fought the new occupants. When a "respectable farmer" in 1850 took over land in Clare from which tenants had been removed for nonpayment, all houses on the property were burned down the night before he was to take possession, and he refused to remain. That example kept another would-be local tenant from taking possession of his land. Bailiffs attempting to evict tenants at Ballykilcline were attacked, but a local jury acquitted the attackers. The evictions were finally carried out, but only with the aid of sixty policemen, twenty-five cavalry, thirty infantry, and a magistrate. Twelve policemen remained behind as guards.

The travail of Robert Pike of King's County shows the degree to which anti-eviction violence was upheld—or at least acquiesced in—by the tenantry. Pike's job was evicting tenants from his employer's land, tenants who had not paid rent for up to two years. He was almost killed when shots were fired at him as he drank tea in his home. Because of such incidents he went armed with a brace of pistols and a cane sword. But when going to evict seven families in Killyon in August 1850, Pike was attacked as he walked with a local farmer. The assailants ordered the farmer to leave, then beat Pike with his own sword. Pike suffered gunshot wounds in the back, chest, and abdomen and a skull fracture. No one but his walking companion could be found to testify on the incident although it occurred "in broad day light, upon an open public road…numbers of the peasantry going to market—several inhabited houses within a short distance of the spot, and nearly fifty people working in the bog."

This was a time of warnings, of notices posted on doorways, of letters tied to rocks and thrown through windows. A Nenagh bailiff left his home one morning and encountered a paper tied to a stick in a heap of manure in his yard. It featured a drawing of a blunderbuss firing and this warning: "Dillon, if you do not give up the decrees mark the consequence—yo don damage enough to take this warning and do no more or you'll get you earning, Mr. Sheriff. Serve no more ejectments, nor throw no more houses." Two Clonmel men who became tenants after earlier occupants were evicted were warned to "give up the land ye took of late or if not ye will get the most horrid death any person ever got...by Christ we shall burn yearselfs and year houses to ashes." The notice ended with rockite poetry:

> Give up the Land
> Give up the Land
> Give up the Land
> By god there is a bird a live still.

The creation of tenant associations refined such threats into elaborate philosophies. These groups appeared in the south of Ireland in 1847 and 1848, were led by Catholic priests, and spread quickly. There were at least twenty such societies in existence by July 1850, when a national Tenant League Association was founded seeking the "three F's"—fair rent, fixity of tenure, and free sale. Members tended to be market-oriented grain growers rather than downtrodden cotters, however.

Arguments arose based on claims of legal right as well as traditional anti-landlord hostility, but landlords had to deal with both types. James Ryan fell back on legal claims when he was hailed into Insolvent Court in Clonmel on an eviction attempt by his proprietor. Ryan had not paid rent for nine years. The account of the hearing in a prolandlord newspaper is probably slanted but still provides a tenant's view:

> COURT: How came you to owe so much rent, and what brought you here?
> INSOLVENT: On account of the heavy rent I was paying. I was paying a heavy rent, indeed.

Mr. Lane (attorney for the receiver): Why, man, you paid nothing. How in the world can you complain of heavy rent, when you didn't pay a farthing these nine years.

Court: Will you give up the land?

Insolvent: Yes, my lord, if I am paid my "rights."

Mr. Lane: What rights?

Insolvent: What I'm *tould* I'm entitled to.

Court: Will you give up the land?

Insolvent: When I'm paid.

After being ordered to jail and told he would remain there until he yielded the land, Ryan gave up.

Crop liftings became another facet of the tenants' opposition. When Thomas Scully, accompanied by a group of bailiffs in Kilkenny, was driving off cattle after attempting to collect rent, his tenants attacked the group and fled with the livestock. A group of some two hundred tenants at Tullekesane cut down grain in the presence of the landowner, then faced down the lawmen who came to retrieve it so "that the Constabulary deemed it prudent to withdraw without effecting the object in view." In another attempt at recovery, constables were cowed by some thirty or forty men "armed with pitchforks, billhooks, hatchets and other offensive weapons." Tenants near Holycross, many owing two and a half years' rent, took all the corn, wheat, oats, and barley, then drove off horses, cows, and pigs, all the while blocking the landlord's agent from leaving his house. When the owner arrived on Monday morning "he could find nothing but recently threshed straw—no stock was to be seen—the houses all closed up—and those dishonest tenants were nowhere to be met with." The account noted that the lands were near Cashel, "where the tenant right meeting was held a week since."

Rage over the continued export from Ireland of wheat, barley, butter, and other foodstuffs stirred angry attacks in many ports as starvation spread. Barges leaving from Clonmel to Waterford had to travel along the River Suir, accompanied by fifty cavalry and eighty infantry for protection. At Youghal near Cork a crowd of country folk whom the police called "enraged" tried to block a vessel exporting oats. Laborers at Dungarvan refused to load boats with export crops after a riot there. Some of the hostility was also directed at harvesting crops for export, and troops were dispatched from Limerick to stop people from cutting traces of the horses used to haul the grain wagons away.

An 1848 commission investigating the wave of Irish murders termed the primary cause to be "circumstances connected with the possession of land." This was obviously the major cause in the incidents cited above. But it is also evident from a historical standpoint that several long-standing traditions merged with the famine distress to bring on or worsen violence in the late 1840s and early 1850s.

Struggles between various family or regional groups were long known to Ireland, and an 1834 visitor reported that the Tralee court docket was crowded with arrests in such feuds. The visitor wrote that he was present during "the memorable affray at Balybunian, when nearly two score persons were driven into the Shannon, and drowned, and knocked on the head like so many dogs." These "faction fights" were occasionally arranged beforehand, like medieval battles, and magistrates as well as onlookers were afraid to act against them. In addition, as they lost faith in legal methods, many Irish people turned again to secret societies and "Whiteboy codes" for salvation, instead of to the laws of Britain. This occurred while they were winning the support of their religious leaders for their basic goals.

Most of the other major traditions coming to play upon the famine era struggles involved religion—Catholic versus Protestant; Presbyterian versus Anglican versus Catholic; the pope versus the proselytizers; "faith" versus "fanaticism." Ireland was little affected by the Protestant Reformation, but English conquerors such as Oliver Cromwell attempted to fasten their brand of anti-Catholicism upon the Irish people, with only scattered success. It was people moving in from the east, such as the Lowland Scots brought to Ulster in the seventeenth century, who carried Protestantism with them. Thereafter, although Catholics formed more than three-fourths of the population, there were also Protestants in most areas. By the 1840s it was still true that most leadership positions were held by Protestants, however, and each town had its Protestant inn and its Catholic inn, Protestant stagecoaches and Catholic lines, and a host of other divisions along the Protestant-Catholic cleavage.

Presbyterians, who in the late eighteenth century seemed ready to join Catholics in battle against the Anglicans, increasingly backed off from joint activities. During the early nineteenth century the British government increased the Presbyterian endowment considerably, and the Catholic priests' growing power in antigovernment activities repelled many Presbyterians.

Protestant privilege was lessened by the struggle for Catholic emancipation, especially in its success in 1829. Compulsory taxes to support the Anglican church could not be collected in many areas, and the development of Catholic political consciousness and political skills during Daniel O'Connell's period of leadership threw further fears into Irish Protestants.

The famine, then, became a cauldron in which these religious animosities boiled. For example, Irish Catholics had traditionally held charity to be a duty for the donor. Poverty, they felt, carried not shame but even some merit. Emerging from a past where communal ownership was widespread, the Irish peasantry accepted begging as part of the yearly cycle; the community helped its less fortunate members without question. Prefamine estimates put the Irish farmers' annual donations of potatoes to the poor at a value approximating a million pounds. Long before the famine, priests had moved into leadership in organizing relief, and if unable to feed the beggar, the priest at least could locate sources for aid, even to the point of soliciting it. But this philosophy was rejected by many Protestants, in pulpit and press. Poverty held little merit for them, and they insisted that charity be handled so that it did not create a new class of beggars or endanger the economy. The fact that priests held important positions in dispensing local relief caused some Protestant agencies to refuse to donate famine help except through Protestants. Catholics, in turn, referred to those Catholics receiving help in Protestant soup kitchens as "soupers."

The priests' political role further polarized relations between Protestants and Catholics as the famine wore on, due to the identification of Protestants as members of the "law church." A priest told a tenants' rally in Scariff that he had read in a newspaper "that this agitation were merely a few priests at the head of it; that the landlords were the natural protectors of the people, and that the priests were exciting bad feeling, and creating differences between the tenants and the landlords, who were their natural protectors." He asked his audience to look around—"Who levelled those houses yonder?...These were monuments to show if the landlords were the natural protectors of the people."

To further deepen this chasm between Protestants and Catholics, an outbreak of No-Popery swept England in 1851, quickly crossing to Ireland, where Catholics responded by forming the Independent Irish party. The English No-Popery campaign developed as Parliament forbade Catholic clerics to accept church territorial titles, recently assigned to several bishops by the pope. The wearing of religious habits was also banned. As the dispute escalated, Irish Archbishop Paul Cullen lashed out at "the bigoted fanatical proselytizing Orange faction," and the grand chaplain to the Orange Order claimed that Catholics held top jobs, that the census was falsified to inflate the number of Catholics, and proclaimed that the mission of the United Kingdom was "to aim at Protestantizing the world." Organizations seeking to Protestantize Ireland multiplied, adding new fervor to what was already a religious war waged over a land and people ravaged by hunger.

Old ways of life were under attack. To Protestants, Catholicism meant superstition and idolatry, and they found much to condemn in the Irish peasantry's folk customs. This was a land where travelers encountered piles of stones along the roads marking spots where deaths had occurred; religious peasants would add a small stone to the heap as they passed by, so that eventually large mounds were formed. Holy wells dotted the landscape, each named for a saint. Pilgrims would ask the patron saint of the well to intercede for them to obtain relief from God, tying a piece of cloth on a limb or branch of a nearby tree. An immigrant recalled the religious references in everyday greeting customs:

John comes into Patrick's house, he says, "May God save all here."
"May God and the Virgin salute yourself."
"I wish you a hundred thousand welcomes."
"How are you, Bridget and the children?"
"They are all well, great thanks be to God."

One Protestant cleric complained that on the Sunday before July 8 each year, crowds of Catholics gathered at a tiny pond called Quinlan's Lake in Tuosist, "romanists of every grade, the respectable and decent along with trick-o' the loop men, prostitutes, fiddlers...and cripples with the diseased and disabled." They came because of "some popish lies of miraculous cures," and although the crude altar was no longer used for mass, pilgrims continued to come each year and pluck a hair to deposit at each turn as they crawled around the mound on their knees. The minister ridiculed such practices in a letter to the *Kerry Evening Post*, attacking "all these superstitious, idolatrous, profligate and savage abominations committed here in the outraged name of religion....As popery has no degrees," he asserted, "so she has no shame, but battens on such rankness as this bog-hole."

Proselytizing was not confined to the Protestants, although their missionaries were most obvious in the role which Catholics labeled as "stirabout gospelers," winning converts through relief kitchens. A letter to an anti-Catholic journal complained of beatings of Protestants and charged that priests in the Cong area were "scouring the country for miles round, entering every house, and forcing men, women, and children to confession," extracting a "solemn declaration that they will not again attend a Protestant school, Protestant sermons, or even speak to a Protestant, but when they meet one on the road they shall cross themselves."

Many of these conversion attempts were carried on in schools, where each side hoped to get to the children before their parents' religious choices became engrained. The Catholic curate of Kilcoe said he would continue to denounce a local school "while a single Catholic child attends it." The mistress was a Catholic, he admitted, but she was "a decoy-bird, the better to entrap innocent females." It was visited by the "bigoted fanatical evangelizing puritans of Ballidahob, whose touch is contagion" and whose breath was "rank poison to uneducated starving Catholic females, to their faith and morals." Noting Anglican assertions to have won a thousand converts in western Galway, the pro-Catholic *Limerick Reporter* claimed that a subsequent visit by two priests won almost all of them back: "with tears in their eyes, [they] threw themselves before the eloquent preachers, and promised to abandon their hypocritical course," asking to join the Catholic church again and resolving "to meet death rather than again fall into the tempter's power." When a Catholic visitor went through nearby

Outerard the next morning he reportedly looked in on a Protestant school where 110 "perverts" had been attending the previous week and found 9 left.

Violence was never far removed from such an environment. Two Welsh visitors discovered a Presbyterian church in Tralee in 1852 that could only hold services with two policemen present, otherwise the local "ignorant and superstitious people" would have thrown stones through the chapel windows, "making it very dangerous to worship." A popular local official in Listowel was pelted with stones one night by attackers who mistook him for one who worked with "the Protestant officials of the Union" against local priests. They apologized to their victim. At a Cork election in 1852, women armed with sticks, stones, and knives barred voting by a "Bible reader," one of them yelling, "By C——, Smith, if you attempt to vote I'll rip your bloody Protestant guts up."

In practice, violence was usually avoided. The kind of threatening situation that often resulted from such festering bitterness was demonstrated in an attack on a Protestant church at Templenoe in County Kerry one Sunday in the autumn of 1850. Stones showered on the church roof, and as the congregation later crossed the yard to the school the minister, who was also a local landlord, was kicked by someone in the crowd. This incident occurred, as noted in a Protestant account, "in the midst of his own tenantry, and in sight of the numerous improvements which have given employment to the people, and kept many of them from starvation and death." While church leaders examined pupils in the schoolhouse, the mob surrounded the building and pressed its verbal and stone-throwing attack. The rowdies repaired occasionally to a nearby public house, where the parish priest "harangued the mob in most exciting, though ostensively soothing terms, telling them to despise, as he did, the proselytizing soupers, for that he would soon put an end to them." The priest claimed that on the previous Sunday the two Protestant clergymen had lectured to Catholics walking out of mass, "telling them they were all going to hell and damnation, and trying to induce them to abandon that religion." Members of the mob then rode horses across the minister's yard, tearing up flowers and blowing horns, and committing "other depredations." These incidents closed a Protestant-Catholic confrontation in Templenoe.

Out of this stormy, often tragic environment came thousands of Irish to the New World. It was a heavily Catholic emigration, for which religion was of extreme importance. Sensitive to attempts to convert them to Protestantism, the Irish leaving their homeland in the 1840s and 1850s had learned to guard their churches, schools, and other institutions against interference by the state or by proselytizers seeking to change their traditions. The government they left behind was viewed with hostility, and *puritan*, a hallowed word in America, was a derogatory term with them.

News from across the ocean told of a different way of life. Emigrant letters sent back to Ireland were usually optimistic. People leaving their homes looked ahead, not back, as the ship crossed the Atlantic. And the tales that reached County Cork and elsewhere contrasted sharply with experiences of the famine-beset, landlord-ruled land at home.

"I think on the hole you would better your self mutch by coming to this country," Henry Hutchinson wrote from Detroit to his brother in Caran in 1845. "Here every man is Lord of the soil he owns, there is no rent yearly. It is his and hairs for ever." An Irish travel book written in the form of letters sent home from America emphasized this point also: "The American farmer, Patrick, never pays any *rent*. When he takes a farm he buys it for ever." William Porter, a Chicago carpenter in 1851, admitted in a letter to his parents in County Down that "my heart wanders back to my native soil," but he stated, "You have a chance of rising in the world here which you have not there and the fear of want is not always staring you in the face." Wealth was not obtained "for the lifting" in America, but "what I mean is that people enjoys the fruits of their labour here."

Advertisements and letters in Irish newspapers gave the impression of abundant jobs in the United States and Canada. A British government emigration agent at Quebec sent a printed notice in 1851: "1,000 labourers wanted immediately, on the line of the St. Lawrence and Atlantic Railway"; spinners, ropemakers, tailors, smiths, male and female servants, and farm laborers were also called for. Similar reports reached Ireland in family letters.

A railroad worker in Vermont wrote a scornful letter back to the Galway Collector of Excise in 1848, announcing that "instead of being chained with poverty in

Boughill I am crowned in glory." He wrote that he was "better pleased to come to this country than if you bestowed me five acres of land in Boughill."

Such stories were repeated often in the grapevine running between North America and Ireland. There was work, there was land, there was opportunity. Few negative reports made it back to Ireland, although as New York filled with immigrants some new arrivals sent word for their friends and relatives to head inland. "The seaports are filled to capacity with emigrants so that no chance can be had in them," one immigrant lamented in the prefamine era. By 1850, when the flood was great, an Irish girl similarly wrote home to Kingwilliamstown that "the emigrants has not money enough to take them to the interior of the country which obliges them to remain here in New York and the like places," bringing on a labor surplus and wage cuts. This was echoed by the Wisconsin emigration commissioner, who reported in 1853 that few Irish applied for information from his office, because most arrived "with but limited means," requiring them to "seize upon the first work offered them for subsistence."

Sometimes stronger warnings were sent home, including tales of signs proclaiming "No Irish Need Apply" and of the lengthy hours of labor in America. "If men and women worked at home as they work here they would have America in Ireland, but God help any one who has to work for his living in America," wrote one expatriate whose letter was printed in Irish newspapers. The writer urged Irishmen not to believe "half the favourable letters you see from America," for in reality people were fired from work one day to the next and had trouble locating another job.

More prestigious was the letter from Thomas D'Arcy McGee, the radical leader who had crossed to America in 1842, and as editor of the *Boston Pilot*, served as spokesman for his emigrating countrymen. In an open letter to Irish editors in 1850, McGee urged his compatriots to stay at home for the present because of a surplus of both educated job seekers and the unskilled. The big construction projects were finished, he contended. "There is, the coming year, no prospect of a large public work being organized," he warned, adding that New York was overstocked with 100,000 Irishmen "and how one-half of them live in honesty is a mystery to the other half." Another report in Irish newspapers at the same time said Irishmen were "begging in droves" in the streets of New York.

Newspapers in Ireland, the German states, and elsewhere in Europe were filled with advertisements by shipping companies for passage to the Americas. Early transport from Ireland to America required an initial trip to the English port of Liverpool, but as the emigration swelled, many ships began to leave directly from Ireland. The *Iowa*—bearing an American name as further inducement—took passengers to New Orleans, closest port for entering the Upper Mississippi country.

Waterford Mail, Oct. 18, 1851, p. 3. By permission of the British Library.

WATERFORD MAIL

Reduction in Teas.

JOSHUA BARTON,

TEA & COFFEE

DEALER,

16, Little George's-Street,

INVITES attention to the following Reduction in the Price of his TEAS :—

TEA, Superior to that heretofore
Sold at .... 4s., now 3s 8d
Do., do. .... 4s 4d, " 4s 0d
Do., the finest imported ...... 4s 8d, " 4s 4d

EMIGRATION
FROM
ROSS TO NEW ORLEANS.

The Splendid New and First-Class   Coppered Packet Ship

"I O W A,"

1650 *TONS BURTHEN*,

AND NEARLY 9 FEET BETWEEN DECKS,

IS INTENDED TO SAIL FROM

Ross for New Orleans,

WITH PASSENGERS.

About the 3d Day of NOVEMBER Next.

NEW ORLEANS is the highway to the far west of America—Steamers of great size and speed run daily from it, carrying Passengers at low fares thousands of miles up the Mississippi and Missouri rivers to the rich districts of Illinois and Missouri, and other Western States, in all of which Land is cheap and fertile, and wages universally high. The passage to New Orleans is far safer and easier than that to New York.

For freight or passage apply to

WM. GRAVES & SON,
New Ross ; or to
GEORGE WHITE,
Waterford.

TO ALL OWNERS, MASTERS AND CONSIGNEES OF VESSELS

Arriving at the Port of New York, the Commissioners of Emigration of the State of New York give the following

NOTICE.

THE Legislature of the State of New York, on the 11th of July, 1851, passed an act very materially amending and altering the former legislation relating to alien passengers arriving at the port of New York.

TO THE
INHABITA
OF
WATERFO
AND NEIGHBOU

Andrews &
OF DUBLIN

BEG to return their than Families who have p TEAS, through their Agent,

Mrs. Lunh

THEIR LEADING T

THE

Fine Strong C
at 4s per

AND THE

Rich Ripe Sou
at 4s 8d pe

ANDREWS A

Beg to direct particular at above TEAS, which will be tisfactory.

Nothing can exceed the SO 4s 8d per lb , for richness flavour.

Mrs. LUNHAM is constantl the above Teas in Packages also Canisters of 7lb. each, 10lb. each.

Mrs. Lunham.

Agent for ANDREW

Of 19, 20, 21, and 22,
DUBLIN.

Here is your R

HOLLOWAY'S O

A MOST MIRACULOUS CUR AFTER 43 YEARS' ST
Extract of a Letter from Mr. W Saint Mary's street, Weymout 1851

[handwritten marginal note: over saturated labor mkt / discrimination / low wages]

But McGee's prose barricade left one opening. "To such as can go direct from New York to Illinois or Ohio, this warning, though not needless, is yet inapplicable," he wrote. This became the goal for many: the new lands to the west. A magistrate for counties Clare and Galway told a parliamentary committee in 1849 that a former tenant of his had just returned from a visit to the United States: he "assured me that for 600 miles along the banks of the Mississippi (and he is a very respectable man) he had traversed the vast tracts of land, the worst acre of which was better than the best acre that I have in the world, and I have some of the very best in Ireland." The West lured others as well, such as William Williamson of County Armagh, who wrote to his brother that after arriving in New York "the rest of us put for the Good land of Illinois," where they eventually landed at Belvidere and promptly encountered an Irishman with "fifty acres of as good land as is in the state of Illinois. It is what is called here prairie, no trees or any [amount] of timber on it."

Such reports overwhelmed the thrust of negative comments. Dreams and hope fed on each other in never-ending circles, for an Irishman looked on America, a contemporary noted, "as the refuge of his race, the home of kindred, the heritage of his children and their children." Catholics saw no justice possible under the Union Jack. Although many emigrated initially to Canada, few remained there. Most headed south quickly. Because of these beliefs, a song penned by McGee probably enjoyed more circulation and had more impact than his 1850 warning:

> 'Tis ten long years since Eileen bawn
> Adventured with her Irish boy
> Across the seas and settled on
> A prairie farm in Illinois
>
> *Chorus:* The Irish homes of Illinois
> The happy homes of Illinois
> No landlord there
> Can cause despair
> Nor blight our fields in Illinois!

Continued improvements in ship technology and knowledge of the Atlantic cut traveling time drastically, while British parliamentary regulations improved conditions for passengers. By 1851, the *Souvenir* was bragging of an eighteen-day crossing and assuring passengers that "Tea, Sugar &c., as required by Act of Parliament" were provided.

Kerry Evening Post, June 21, 1851, p. 3. By permission of the British Library.

Sweet waves the sea of summer flowers
Around our wayside cot so coy
Where Eileen sings away the hours
That light my task in Illinois.

Lured by this vision of the West, thousands of Irish immigrants came by ship, canalboat, wagon, and foot to the Upper Mississippi Valley. Illinois had 27,786 of them by 1850 and 87,573 just a decade later. Missouri's Irish total rose from 14,734 in 1850 to 43,464 in 1860. Wisconsin went from 21,043 to 49,961 in the same ten-year span, while Iowa's Irish total was rising from 4,885 in 1850 (mainly in Dubuque County in the lead district) to 28,072 in 1860. This meant that the number of Irish in the region tripled during the decade before the Civil War, from 68,448 to 209,070.

The effect of this exodus on the homeland was traumatic in its enormity, for as more and more letters told of the wonders of life in America, the numbers of Irish people choosing to emigrate increased at an even higher rate. Many left only after attending an "America Wake" on their last night at home. This was an offshoot of the tradition of sitting up with a body the night before burial, the wake rooted in Irish antiquity. Because most emigrants of the 1840s and 1850s believed they would never see home again, the early "America Wakes" became sad, sigh-filled events, where talk centered on those who had emigrated, and requests were made to carry messages to relatives already in America. One participant recalled a wake as "not of a dead person, but of a living one, who next day would be sailing for the promised land." It was recollected that, in the time of the famine, "people made very little difference between going to America and going to the grave."

Mainly the better-off Irishmen left in the early years, but increasingly, poor peasants went as well. While "the better class of farmers in the county of Wexford" were reported in the exodus in the summer of 1850, an account from County Kerry the following summer also noted that "a very large proportion of those who are now leaving the county are poor persons." The reason: they "have had the means of emigration supplied to them by friends already in America." This observation impressed a Quaker leader testifying before a parliamentary committee on his relief work. A "very remarkable feature" of this exodus, he stated, was that relatives emigrating have "to an extent almost incredible, remitted money to their kindred at home."

It impressed Americans, too, when they saw poor Irish immigrants sending one pound a week home to help others in their families to cross over. Buried in the reports of individual American agents transferring $50,000 to Ireland over a twelve-month period were tales of individual heroism and sacrifice: the Irish immigrant woman toiling for two years to raise money to bring her six children to Chicago; the newcomer working to pay for his aged mother's trip. The process was eased when steamship lines began permitting Irish people in America to purchase fares for their families' journeys "from any port in Ireland, thro' to Milwaukee or Chicago."

Aided by earlier emigrating relatives or by landlords, or with their own meager savings, the Irish left in such numbers that roads to the Irish ports were often clogged. Some five hundred persons passed through Galway one week in 1853 to board one of the ships by then sailing directly to America from Ireland rather than from the English port of Liverpool, from which most Irish immigrants left for America. A man walking inland from Dublin met people "in gangs of from forty to sixty, in all directions, wending their way to the coast to emigrate for America."

All ships were assured of being filled to capacity. In Galway, it was reported, "as soon as a vessel is on the berth, she is at once filled with emigrants." When the summer emigration hit Cork late in August 1850, with two ships preparing to leave, the press of passengers was so great that men armed with heavy sticks were stationed along the decks to beat back the would-be travelers. Many "jumped recklessly on board at the risk of life" to catch the *Nimrod*. The military was sent for, and after the captain finally got his ship en route to Liverpool he still had to stop to remove some two hundred passengers, sending them back in smaller boats. The *Nimrod* eventually made it to Liverpool with seven hundred passengers riding on her open deck.

Scenes on the docks were emotional, and "to say they were crying at their parting would be too feeble a description," a Waterford reporter wrote. He witnessed "*men* actually bellowing and roaring like bulls" as the ship began to move. When the *Mars* slipped from her Waterford moorings one morning in October 1851, her 420 passengers, "who appeared rejoiced," gave "three hearty cheers, which were but feebly responded to by those they left behind." The crowds lingered on, watching the ship move out into the Irish Sea, and did not leave until it was out of sight.

But as the ships crossed the open Atlantic, the passengers' rejoicing ended abruptly. During the years following the famine, shipboard conditions deteriorated rapidly, and although by 1850 travel time had improved to under forty days to cross to Quebec and Montreal, this was still long enough to allow serious shipboard problems to develop. Passengers found that supplies promised by shipping agents were inadequate, although back in port they had sounded satisfactory enough. "Provisions at the rate of 2½ lbs. biscuit, 1 lb. flour, 5 lbs. oatmeal, 2 lbs. rice, 2 ozs. tea, 1 lb. sugar and molasses, and 21 quarts water, will be issued to each passenger weekly, with abundance of fuel and medicine," claimed a ship running from Cork to New York. A literate and articulate traveler in 1847 reported to Parliament that "the meat was of the worst quality" and, although enough water was taken on board, it was not distributed in adequate amounts, so that salt and rice had to be thrown overboard. He wrote that some passengers stayed for days "in their dark close berths, because they thus suffered less from hunger." But to this complaining passenger, disease and death did not form the only outcome of such a trip. A worse result, he said, was "the utter demoralisation of the passengers, both male and female, by the filth, debasement, and disease of two or three months so passed."

Other problems appeared as the vessels crossed the Atlantic. An Englishman traveling on a ship filled with Irish emigrants noted horrible conditions but blamed it on the Irish: "They where durty beyond all reason, did nothing but sleep all day, and prowl about at knight." Fighting placed someone in irons most days, he added, but he admitted that some of the trouble could be blamed on the ship's accommodations: "one stove for 300 passengers to cook by," resulting in many getting scalded, while "fighting for there crock of scilley called so by Irish." Anything laid down was lost if not guarded; "turn your head to one side it vanished to be found no more."

A new British passenger act in the spring of 1850 brought improvements, and complaints from immigrants began to decline. As a result, tales of shipboard life were varied among the 1.7 million Irish emigrating to "Amerikay" during the first decade after the famine began in 1845.

Many new arrivals in America searched to find other Irishmen, not a difficult task by mid-century. Daniel Guiny wrote from Buffalo that higher wages were possible if his group split up, "but we would sooner be all together." Soon after William Porter reached Chicago, he left his boardinghouse and "went to board with people from Ireland and I feel quite as well as if I was at home."

Many others also found their way inland quickly, directed both by advertisements and by reports of earlier travelers. An immigrant in Washington County, Iowa, told his friends in Ireland to "get a passage to Phildalfe then tak the rail roads fur Pitsburg...then over the Ohio river to the mouth ove the Mississippi river, thens to St. Luis, thens to Burlington in Iowa." Advertisements in Irish newspapers told of ships going directly to New Orleans, "the highway to the far west of America," where passengers could connect with steamboats up the Mississippi and Missouri rivers "to the rich districts of Illinois and Missouri and other western states." Soon reports told of vast numbers of immigrants on the Ohio and Mississippi riverboats, the greater number of them as deck passengers, where they were thrown in with the heterogeneous frontier population described by a traveling Irish priest: "Cards gentlemen and ladies all the way—such folks as met on Mississippi never met before—pick rascals of the United States."

To many, however, arrival in the New World brought no immediate relief from their suffering, but only prolonged it. When the ship *Waterford* landed at St. John's, Newfoundland in 1848, the British emigration officer there reported that he "observed some very miserable and emaciated persons"; all were able to walk to the reception buildings "although afflicted with fever and dysentery to a certain extent." He concluded he had rarely seen "a more dirty, reckless, and apparently lawless set of people" than the majority of those passengers. Long suffering, he added, "seems to have deprived them of all moral sense." Soon the arrivals of immigrants coming up the Mississippi to St. Louis brought such scenes to that city, and a special hospital was built near the docks for ailing or dying immigrants.

This portion of the emigration was ready prey for the hordes of sharpers in the ports. William Lalor admitted that his early troubles in America came mainly from his "total ignorance of the ways, manners, customs, prices...of the country by which I got fooled out of all my money within three weeks after landing." After that he became ill for some time. Many other immigrants lost out to the "runners" who soon surrounded them as they left the boat or inland stagecoach. "They thrust themselves upon [the immigrant]—they pull him this way and that—they stick their noses quite into his face—each claiming him as his own exclusive property." These runners fought for his trunk, demanding to take him to a hotel, which often was "a dirty, seven-by-nine barroom filled with loafers," in which he was forced to pay a dollar to escape. Some runners boarded trains, pretended to be railroad officials, and told immigrants their tickets were inaccurate but that properly made tickets could be bought from the runner. One report claimed that runners on trains coming westward to Chicago were changing thirty to forty tickets a day in this manner.

America was not turning out to be the paradise many had expected. One Irishman making his way west was greeted with help-wanted signs in Pennsylvania that read: "Niggers or Irish need not apply." A touring Irish priest was similarly dismayed by his irreverent traveling companions on a stagecoach crossing southern Wisconsin: "1 fellow ridiculed me hard and blasphemed at me three several times—others said nothing to him.... Today all rascals in stage—oh, oh!! obscenity oaths blasphemies.... Oh, what I suffered."

This was the New World: opportunity, but hard work; jobs, but insecurity of tenure; freedom of religion, but a surrounding population of critics, ridiculers, and proselytizers. The shock must have been great for many who had expected to find streets paved with gold. Irish immigrants landing at Boston's Deer Island reception station in 1850, accompanied by their priests, were taken first to a bathhouse, stripped of their clothes (which were burned), scrubbed with soap and water, given a haircut, and then required to attend Sabbath services. The priests' attempts to interfere with these arrangements were firmly rebuffed.

It would be no easy journey, this new life in America.

3. Auswanderers

The carpenter glanced up as the distinguished looking visitor entered his Freienseen workyard one day in the autumn of 1854. "Count Otto Solms appeared once more," he would later recall, "and asked me why I was going to America." He responded quickly, without excuse or embellishment: "I answered quite simply that I could provide better for my family."

It was a scene repeated over and over during the 1830–1860 years across the patchwork of duchies, principalities, and kingdoms that constituted linguistic Germany. For the thousands of *Auswanderers,* the decision to emigrate was seldom taken lightly, despite the brevity of the Freienseen carpenter's explanation to his landlord. In addition to the emotional sundering of kinship ties, leaving the German homeland usually required numerous trips to obtain permission and certificates from the local pastor, tax collector, school officials, and others, as well as the presentation of proof that the prospective traveler was free or forgiven of private debt. In many areas, the law decreed that the *Auswanderer* be officially advised he was being foolish.

There were other obstacles to emigration, barriers that were difficult to cross. The accumulated traditions, beliefs, and relics handed down from generation to generation within families constituted chains holding back the would-be emigrant. To leave them was to cut off family and homeland. But despite these restricting forces, the emigration from Germany after 1830 began to surpass all previous records. Over half a million crossed the ocean during a three-year spurt in the early 1850s, 1.5 percent of the total population of the German states. The Rhenish Palatinate lost 10 percent of its people between 1849 and 1856, and a devastating impact was felt in all of south and west Germany. Almost all went to America, where the German-born population rose from 573,225 in 1850 to 1,301,136 in 1860.

And most of these headed for the newly opening lands of the Mississippi Valley. The U.S. consul in Stuttgart, kingdom of Württemberg, sent a plea in 1850 to the governor of Illinois for maps, detailed materials on land sales, and similar information. He added that in his nine months as consul "a great many inquiries have been addressed to me with respect to the advantages Illinois affords for German settlers."

As they pushed toward midcontinent, Germans mingled with the human tide of Irish, New Englanders, "York staters," and others heading west, part of the giant movement that would not end until it reached the shores of the Pacific. For many, however, the journey halted on the rich prairies or lightly wooded sections of the Upper Mississippi country. A missionary in Macoupin County, Illinois, reported that when he arrived in 1851 "there was but one German family within four miles of Brighton." But by 1854 "there are probably more than one hundred, and still they come," he wrote. "Each new family in turn brings a circle of relatives and acquaintances who settle around them, and these again, by their glowing descriptions of the New World, attract others." It was a theme to be repeated over and over in those years, for, as a leading historian of immigration has emphasized, "America had never been more attractive" than at midcentury—and never more accessible.

If it had threads in common with the Irish emigration of the period, the German web of history also included strands of other sorts. Unlike the Irish, the Germans had not been dominated by a foreign power. When the French Revolution of 1789 reverberated eastward, German life was only disrupted, not transformed, and the counts and dukes and kings eventually came back into power. The same thing occurred after the revolts set off by the Paris outbreaks of 1830. But in the process, local German rulers in the thirties gave ground on many peasant restrictions, and in one crucial regard the past was forever swept away: the concept of a fixed position for each member of society—unchangeable, inescapable—was severely weakened, even destroyed. Self-improvement became a German byword of the early nineteenth century, and peasants who formerly would have accepted their plight now argued over injustices and inequalities as if these could be changed. When the counterattacks of the aristocracy succeeded in 1833, these did not restore the *status quo ante bellum* regarding human status.

As the German aristocracy in the early nineteenth century struggled to retain power, many of its members were also supporting a movement that eventually pointed in another direction—toward union. This movement began as a drive to transform Europe economically—to build rail lines, promote steamboat traffic, and modernize marketing methods. For many, these advances also meant a disruption of life-style. But these economic changes repeatedly came up against the toll barriers that greeted every European traveler. An 1819 petition complained that "to carry on business between Hamburg and Austria or between Berlin and Switzerland, one must traverse ten states, master ten customs and toll systems, and pay transit duties ten times."

It was Prussia that took the lead in creating a customs union (*Zollverein*) in its own territories in 1819. This union was gradually expanded with reciprocal agreements. The campaign culminated in 1834 with the establishment of the German Customs Union, which covered eighteen German states with a population exceeding 23 million. Just as German travel and transport were being united through the railroad and steamboat, economic union was being furthered by the *Zollverein*.

Bandwagons are seldom joined by all, however, and the great economic advances trumpeted by the modernizers were often regarded with less enthusiasm by lower echelons of German society. In such areas of south and west Germany as Rhenish Prussia (*Rheinprovinz*), the Rhenish Palatinate (*Rheinpfalz*), Baden, and Württemberg, high population density over the years had led to extreme fragmentation of landholdings. This was mainly due to the requirements that inheritances be divided among all living children. In some other areas, notably much of Prussia, Pomerania, and Mecklenburg, estate owners were discovering in the decades after 1815 that they could buy up peasant holdings and drive the residents off the land they had occupied for generations. They made the investment profitable by hiring labor only to plant and harvest. The peasants also suffered a growing wood shortage as the magnificent forests of earlier times fell to the axes and depredations of foraging armies during the eighteenth and early nineteenth centuries. There simply was no fuel for many; the area lacked the abundant peat that carried the Irish through the winter months.

Many of the peasants displaced by these varied pressures were able to rent land again, but only at high prices. In the process they often discovered that the creditors who advanced them loans required set amounts for repayment rather than a portion of the crop, as had been the case with landlords earlier. And these creditors lacked the sense of obligation toward the peasant that had characterized feudalism, leaving the tillers of the soil "victims of a new economic servitude with no traditions, no personal contacts, and no generous interpretation." These developments varied from place to place and year to year, but even where they did not appear, farmers were aware of their existence. And farmers constituted 72 percent of the German states' population in 1846.

One answer to this uncertainty, to being forced to exist on smaller and smaller plots of land, was to do what the Irish peasants had done slightly earlier—turn to the potato. The potato was the salvation of Germany and, as in Ireland, ultimately a cause of its tragedy. Once prejudice against the tuber had eased, it gained in popularity for the same reasons as in Ireland, for it fed large numbers of people nutritiously from small amounts of land. By 1841 the statement could be honestly made that "the potato is half the life of Germany, the foundation of peace and public welfare."

But as midcentury neared, economic dislocations combined with age-old antagonisms to raise tensions in German society. Despite the *Zollverein,* local jealousies and loyalties remained strong, arising from the "carnival jacket" of 314 German states and 1,475 estates into which the country was divided before 1800. Rapid industrialization in some areas added workers' class feelings to this changing world. Young radicals, fired up by the ideas emanating from France in 1789 and 1830, sought to promote uprisings. Religion proved to be a divisive force across this land where Protestantism had broken out in revolt three centuries earlier, where religious wars had been waged longer and had left deeper scars than elsewhere in Europe, and where Catholics and Protestants existed in roughly equal numbers overall despite heavy imbalances in the different states.

Then politics and religion confronted each other again, clashing in a series of struggles that would leave their marks on the minds of emigrants fleeing to other lands. Mennonites, Dunkards, and Schwenkfelders came early to America, and other sects followed. In the 1830s, across the realm of Frederick William III of Prussia, traditional groups sometimes known as *Alt Lutheraner* (Old Lutherans) rebelled at their sovereign's orders that the Lutheran and Reformed churches unite in a national church, as well as at growing "rationalism" within the Lutheran church. Dissident pastors resigned from the state church and led clandestine services at night. One immigrant to Dodge County, Wisconsin, recalled such incidents in Germany as secret gatherings in his family's house, the arrest of a pastor resulting in a fifty-year prison term, and efforts to hide clergymen under hay piles when police came to search the premises.

Rather than give in to government policies they considered ungodly, the *Alt Lutheraner* began casting about for new areas where they could practice their religion unfettered. In 1836 some six hundred Silesian Old Lutherans asked permission to emigrate to Australia, some sailing from Hamburg in 1837. Saxon Lutherans emigrated soon afterward, bound for New Orleans and eventually St. Louis. A Pomeranian group of *Alt Lutheraner* came to Wisconsin in 1839, the body of eight hundred providing a stimulus to Milwaukee's then-depressed economy. Other groups unhappy with Prussia's unified church campaign arrived in the 1840s, one group relating how their ship was boarded by police while in port in Hamburg and their pastor pulled off and arrested.

C.F.W. Walther emerged as leader of this Lutheran group in the Upper Mississippi, saving them from despair and confusion after their previous head, Martin Stephan, was expelled from the Missouri settlements for "defalcation and gross wickedness." Sentiment rose to return to Germany, until the struggling colonists were convinced by Walther that they represented the true church as long as they maintained the true faith, regardless of the discontinuity of human organization. Called to head the congregation in St. Louis, Walther launched *Der Lutheraner* and proceeded to stimulate, organize, and defend the "German Evangelical Lutheran Synod of Missouri, Ohio and other states," known as the Missouri Synod. It became one of the major branches of Lutheranism in America, a group conditioned by its European background to be concerned about interference from the state or other outsiders.

For Catholics of south and west Germany the era also carried threats to tradition and custom. After the Protestant Prussian government took control of the Rhine province, one of its disputes with the Catholic church brought the arrest of the archbishop of Cologne in 1837, setting off protests from Catholic leaders in other countries. Emigration became the escape for Catholics also, and Catholics from the Moselle began to show up in northern Illinois by 1837, carrying with them, as others had, suspicion of state interference and fear of losing faith through separation.

To many a young German of the 1830s and 1840s, churches constituted a large part of Germany's problem because of the obedience to tradition and feudal hierarchy that kept the people in thrall. Rationalism thrived among many of these challengers to the status quo, drawing charges in retaliation that they represented the antichrist. (Rationalism is the belief that reason, not supernaturalism or mysticism, can explain life. Its adherents argued against revealed truth and divine intervention.) A missionary in Illinois who encountered a group of German rationalists found that "the majority of them consider true religion as a hindrance for the liberty and welfare of the human race." When German rationalists and German Evangelical Lutherans confronted each other in Warsaw, Illinois, and in numerous other Upper Mississippi communities, sparks flew; the controversies of the Fatherland echoed again on the Mississippi's shores. The "infidel Germans" in Warsaw hated the Evangelical preacher and "often insult him in the street," an American clergyman reported.

Such disputes were a natural outgrowth of the religious contests prevailing in the German states; these arguments and dislocations in the 1840s had led to an exodus of the disenchanted, all determined to retain the practices increasingly denied them at home or perhaps to restore a life or position they had once held. The religious emigrants were therefore little different from the farmers, small merchants, and artisans who formed the bulk of the 1830 to 1845 emigration. These were people who, in Mack Walker's phrase, "had something to lose, and who were losing it, squeezed out by interacting social and economic forces."

These currents came together in Germany amid a burst of upheaval and revolution in 1848 and 1849, as all Europe seemed poised to throw off the rule of kings and princes. This was the time of barricades and marches, of hopes that age-old dreams would finally be realized. But behind the eruptions that led to the famous Frankfurt Parliament lay worsening agricultural and economic conditions. Hard times forced thousands to leave their homes and homeland. Crop failures, severe winter weather, food shortages, high prices, business depression, high unemployment, uprisings by peasants and industrial workers—these contributed to the revolts that flared up across the German landscape after Paris provided the spark.

The potato blight that robbed the Irish of their staple hit the German states in 1845 and 1846; as in Ireland, the stench of rotting tubers marked the disease's advance across Germany. Prussian officials tried to prevent the export of healthy potatoes, then abandoned all duties on imported grains to lower prices, and finally were reduced to encouraging the eating of horse meat and distributing recipes for making bread from ground grass roots.

But it was more than the potato; grain harvests also were reduced in 1845 and 1846, sending food prices upward and creating conditions for disaster. In the two years following July 1845, wheat prices went up 250 percent and barley 300 percent, while potato prices soared 425 percent. As in Ireland, crowds of beggars appeared on the roads, and such sights remained common for a decade. Typhus and cholera added to the death toll from starvation. The frequent uprisings were increasingly directed toward food problems, as when a gang of youths in the Rhenish Palatinate jumped a wagon train transporting potatoes out of their district. The teamsters were beaten, and their load of potatoes was distributed among the poor. Elsewhere, mobs burned the books that kept track of feudal obligations and payments of tithes. A traveler who returned to Chicago in 1849 from a business trip to Germany described affairs there as "wholly unsettled." In most of the Rhine provinces, he told a newspaper reporter, "law and order are completely at an end. The Revolutionists are constantly increasing in numbers, armed men are passing to and fro thro' the country." Not until 1854 would agricultural production return to normal over most of Germany and quiet come again to the areas where rioting had followed crop failure.

German cities were left reeling from the agricultural disasters and by the increased business competition that followed creation of the *Zollverein* and improved transportation. Charity was the major support for almost a third of the population in some of the cities of south Germany, while in Berlin it was reported that five-eighths of the workers' families were living at bare subsistence levels. Between 1840 and 1847, one-sixth of Württemberg's weavers went bankrupt, while other artisans were left with little work.

Although the German revolutions of 1848–49 were generally carried out by urban residents, the agricultural disasters were so broad in their coverage and dramatic in their impact that arguments over rural conditions came up frequently in the public debates of those years. A large rally in Offenburg produced a call for abolition of the sovereign's right to give land or lucrative offices to his offspring, a direct attack on the pressures felt by peasants forced off the land. (The rally also called for fusion of the army with a civil militia, a progressive income tax, and separation of the church from the school system—the latter a common plea of rationalists.) A peasant leaflet distributed during the revolution's heady days called for destruction of the nobility; elimination of all kings, dukes, and princes; execution of all officials; and banishment of all Jews. For the peasantry there were some gains from this agitation; frightened rulers finally ended the lingering feudal obligations. While it is true that for farmers these actions often merely opened the way to heavy dependence on local moneylenders, the accomplishment was no mean one and stands as one of the major ongoing results of the Revolution of 1848.

In the revolutionaries' Frankfurt Parliament little was done specifically on the agricultural problem, possibly because Germany's troubles were generally blamed on a lack of national unity or on natural disasters such as the potato blight. Also, three-fourths of the members of the Frankfurt sessions were ex-university students, fifty-seven of them then employed as schoolmasters and forty-nine as university professors. They passed a guarantee of the freedom to emigrate and banned emigration taxes, but they spent most of their time on weightier questions of the governance and divisions of power in the newly united Germany struggling to be born. It may have been "the most highly educated parliament in constitutional history," as it was often described, but it could not speak knowingly of the problems faced by the almost three-fourths of the population dependent on agriculture. When the Frankfurt Parliament was finally determined to be powerless and King Frederick William of Prussia spurned its offer of a crown, large numbers who had once been driven to consider emigration were now forced to bring the idea forward again, for the future seemed uncertain and life bereft of its anchors.

They left in droves as congregations, as individuals, but mainly in family groups. While all areas were represented, this *Auswanderung* was strongest from the heavy potato-growing areas of west and south Germany, districts marked by intensive agriculture and tiny plots. Farmers trying to save their meager holdings had mortgaged all, but now the notes were falling due and could not be paid. In Württemberg, foreclosure auctions had averaged one for each two hundred fifty families during the 1840–1847 years, but now the rate jumped to one for each seventy-six families in 1850–1855. "Former proprietor" was a common description of these emigrants.

The failure of the revolution was like the collapse of a dam. When a Baden organization began in 1849 to provide information and assistance to prospective emigrants, it was besieged with 3,000 inquiries within a few days. And soon after the revolution ground to a halt and its supporters were hunted down, 976 of the 4,089 residents of St. Blasien left for America, an exodus repeated frequently across the region. All Germany west of the Elbe seemed on the move—most seeking salvation in the city, certainly, but enormous numbers opting instead to begin anew across the sea, in an attempt to avoid further declines in position, holdings, and standard of living.

These *Auswanderers* flowing into the United States and the Upper Mississippi Valley in the late 1840s and 1850s were part of a stream of Germans that had been flowing for decades. Benjamin Franklin, concerned about the predominance of Germans in many areas of Pennsylvania, estimated in 1766 that they numbered perhaps 110,000, a third of the colony's population. When the Americans broke with Britain a decade later, the German total for all thirteen states was put at 225,000, mainly along the frontier. A sharp increase followed the abortive 1830 revolt, however, when the total immigration from the German states rose dramatically to 152,454 for the decade, up from 6,761 in the 1821–1830 period.

From 1841 through 1850, as the revolution developed and then failed, the total climbed to 434,626. But in just three years from 1852 through 1854, the immigration of Germans into the United States topped half a million, reaching 215,009 in the single year of 1854. The decade total for 1851 through 1860 was 951,556 Germans.

To state that these *Auswanderers* were fleeing deteriorating, hopeless conditions at home is to tell only a half-truth. Emigration has always involved a complex of dreams, frustrations, falsehoods, might-have-beens, adventures, and blind faith. Many were driven from home, but it is also true that leaving Germany became increasingly easy as the 1840s wore on. The pioneers of the German exodus of earlier decades had been forced to submit to numerous indignities from local civil and religious authorities, then traipse long distances on foot or in ox carts, braving robbers and weather as they sought out ports along the English Channel or North Sea.

But the coming of the steam engine, especially the development of the screw-driven propeller, changed this. Soon the steamers were providing cheap travel, on the Weser by 1844, and in 1847 the Düsseldorf Steamship Company began transporting eight hundred emigrants a week down the Rhine to Arnhem to board ships for America. Railroad mileage in Germany almost doubled in 1846–47, while the territories of neighboring countries were crisscrossed with rails that served to ease the way of Germans to other ports. These shipping and rail lines were not content to wait for passengers but began to seek out customers through agents spread across Germany. The Union Steamship Line of Liverpool and Philadelphia had twenty-one men scouting passengers in Württemberg, a total exceeded by several other agencies. As noted in regard to the Irish emigration, shipboard conditions began to improve near the end of the forties, helped by both British and American laws of 1848 and 1849; even stronger measures were passed in 1855 and remained in force for years.

A flood of publications helped convince the wavering. An 1858 listing found more than one hundred travel books published in Germany since 1815, most as emigrant guides and almost all favorable to the idea of moving to America. Foremost among these was undoubtedly Gottfried Duden's *Bericht über eine*

Reise nach den westlichen Staaten Nordamerikas...in Bezug auf Auswanderung und Übervölkerung, published in numerous editions from the 1830s on and providing a romantic picture of life in the primeval forests of the Mississippi Valley. Duden went to Missouri in 1824, ultimately locating on 250 acres near the Femme-Osage River west of St. Louis in what is now Warren County. Unlike almost all of those who both preceded and followed, Duden was able to hire men to clear his land and plant and harvest his crops, while he traveled and penned descriptions of frontier life.

Newspapers and journals carried the message of the New World opportunities into German homes. Two periodicals aimed specifically at the potential emigrant were the *Allgemeine Auswanderungszeitung* of Rudolfstadt and *Der Deutsche Auswanderer* of Frankfurt. With articles bearing such titles as ''The North American Freestate of Illinois'' and ''On the Upper Mississippi,'' and with reports on available land, prices, and taxes, the emigrant journals told of a bountiful land where rich soil, minerals, forests, and jobs seemed abundantly available. Their pages were filled with advertisements for tickets that would provide full passage all the way from a German village to the interior of the United States, backing up a shipping agent's claim that a man could board a ship in Bremen on January 1 and be working on his new farm in Wisconsin one month later. German-language pamphlets and newspapers from America made their way to Germany as well, and when American Catholic leaders held a conference in 1856 to promote immigrant colonization in the West, its sessions were widely reported by European Catholic journals.

Personal letters filled in many of the gaps in printed reports but often seemed little removed from Duden's romanticism. These missives were frowned upon by German authorities and sometimes confiscated in earlier years, when the emigrant was considered to be anti-German. Prussian police in 1836 were instructed to watch for American letters because of the antagonism these might excite in the local population. Governments soon began circulating counteraccounts that painted America in darker tones than the emigrants used. It is not difficult to comprehend the authorities' anxiety over reports such as this from Iowa, sent in 1851 by a former Mecklenburg resident who had moved to the ''prairie, near Davenport'':

"One-third of the people [of Davenport] are German, and in the country perhaps one-half of the people are Germans. One hardly realizes that one is in America because one hears German spoken everywhere. German laborers are given the preference; German girls find ready employment. In general I would advise all my countrymen, who like to work...to come to our beautiful and free America....Here people are not divided into classes as in Germany. One person is as good as another."

It was the contrast between Germany and America that drew attention: abundant land in the Great Valley; cheap living, not burdened by heavy taxes; and a lack of controls. While many Germans were forced to seek official permission to travel, Americans could—and did—go everywhere, diverted only by their own or nature's whims. Soldiers were not in evidence in the new republic; churches did not receive tax money; voting was open to almost all white males (several western states let aliens vote and reduced the residence requirement to one year or less); and everywhere abundant resources waited only for the laborer to extract them. This was the land that awaited the *Auswanderer*.

A leaflet circulated during the heady days of 1848 and purportedly written by an emigrant pointed to these contrasts. "How kindly [America] allows free movement," it argued, while Germans were bowed by compulsory military training, their farmers treated like domestic animals, their workers forced to pay backbreaking taxes to support "paid scoundrels." The citizen of Germany, the author charged, "allows himself to be treated as a contemptible lowbrow by any little official." The leaflet concluded: "GERMANY, BECOME PRACTICAL. Do your duty, strike away, tear up the fetters that hold you, and hopefully and confidently look to us. We hate aristocracy and the bourgeoisie, and we burn with the desire to bear the victorious flag of our republic toward you in the battle of freedom."

Many did not need leaflets scattered on the street to prod them on their way to America. In this number were several varieties of assisted emigrants, such as the 224 paupers whose trip across the Atlantic was paid by town officials of Schwenningen, in Württemberg. The community decided to appropriate 20,000 gulden to be rid of the wretched creatures forever, rather than continuing to feed them in the village soup kitchen. In some other villages the entire population was sent to

German shipping advertisements by 1851 showed how cheaply the immigrant could travel to the Upper Mississippi country, via *"dampf-schiff und canal"* (steamboat and canal) after crossing to New York, taking a steamboat up the Hudson, going by canalboat to Buffalo, then steamboat again on the Great Lakes, or *"eisenbahn und dampfschiff"* (railroad and steamboat).

Allgemeine Auswanderungszeitung, June 24, 1851, p. 292. Commerz-Bibliothek, Hamburg, West Germany.

Allgemein

...en wird über ... von Theil ausgereisten Zeilen aus Peritschrift kostet 14 ... oder 5 ... von 3 bis 4 Zeilen 27 ... oder 7½ ... Ueber diese
... jede ... ... besonders berechnet. Für Depeschen, welche von der Expedition an beliebig ihr aufgegebene übersende
... mit nur 7 ... oder 3 ... pr. Abrede

---

[5] **Wm. Rischmüller,**
General-Agent für
Eisenbahn und Dampfschiffe,
befördert Passagiere und deren Gepäck, Güter und Gelder
auf dem schnellsten, sichersten und billigsten
Wege nach allen Theilen der Vereinigten Staaten, Cali-
fornien, Canada, nach und von Europa ꝛc.
Bureau № 104 Greenwich-Str.
Newyork.
Inland-Passagepreise pr. Eisenbahn.

			Doll.	Cts.
Von Newyork nach		Buffalo	4	37½
"	"	Toledo und Detroit	5	56¼
"	"	Erie, Cleveland Sandusky	5	31¼
"	"	Chicago, Milwaukie (über Beaver)	7	
"	"	Pittsburgh	6	00
"	"	Cincinnati	8	69
"	"	Louisville	9	38

Die Office des Hrn. W. Rischmüller befördert vorzugs-
weise pr. Eisenbahn, und nur auf ausdrückliches Verlan-
gen des Reisenden wird ihm Canal-Passage zu dem von
den Comm. of Emigration vorgeschriebenen Preisen gegeben.
Curtius B. Michaelsen,
Agent in Bremen.

[6] ### Danksagung.
Die unterzeichneten Passagiere des am 1. Juli d. J.
von Hamburg abgegangenen, dem Rheder Herrn R. Slo-
man angehörenden Schiffes **„Franklin"**, bezeugen
hiermit gerne und der Wahrheit gemäß, daß sie über
die Behandlung auf besagtem Schiffe während der Fahrt
nach Newyork nicht nur nicht zu klagen gehabt, sondern
sich von Seiten des Herrn Capitäns Knudsen der be-
sten, sorgfältigsten und humansten Behandlung zu erfreuen
gehabt haben. Namentlich mußten sich die Kranken die-
sem wahrhaft menschenfreundlichen Manne, für die ihnen
zu Theil gewordene liebevolle Pflege verpflichtet fühlen,
so wie alle Passagiere für die geschickte und sorgfältige
Führung des Schiffes.

Expeditionen
über
... PEN UND **BREMEN**
... anderen nord- und südamerikanischen Seehäfen durch die
... Z DESSAUER in Aschaffenburg.

... der neuen amerikanischen Postschiffe der **new line**
... Einrichtungen mit zweiter Cajüte, wie durch pünktliche

[2]
„...OFFNUNG."
... Bureau für Auswanderung
nach Amerika
... Havre & New-York.
... über **Havre** nach **New-York** sind hinläng-
... Einrichtungen ... Erklärungen bekannt. — Mit dem Monat
... Havre und **New-Orleans**, und expedire ich:
... 1500 Tonnen, am 11. Septbr. ab hier,
am 18. " ab Havre.
... Emerson, 1200 Tonnen, am 25. Septbr.
... Fahrt ab Havre.
... Tonnen am 10. Octbr. ab Havre,
... erster Classe. Jede Auskunft wird meinen Rei-
... HAVRE und **NEW-YORK** unentgeldlich er-
... Agenten zu den billigsten Preisen abge-
... 1851.
J. M. Bielefeld.

Ein Bote
zwischen der alten und neuen ...

Fünften Jahrganges 2. Semester.

Preis: halbjährlich 1 ... Rg. oder 2 ... ...

Bestellungen sind
nicht beim Verleger unmittelbar
sondern
bei jeder nächstgelegenen Post oder Buchhand...
in BREMEN und HAMBURG bei
den Fürstl. Thurn und Taris'schen Postamt
anzubringen.

Rudolstadt, den 23. Septbr....

Erklärung der Abbreviaturen: ...
...

Inhalt. Nicaragua. Von ...
in Neu-Seeland. — Liverpool: ...
land. Neue Dampferlinie. — Granada ...
und Kerr. — Rio de Janeiro: ...
Schiffsnachrichten. — Briefkasten. — ...

Nica...
Bericht aus Granada vom 8. Juli

Unter den Bemerkungen, welche ...
... zu machen habe, stehen die ...
... Beziehung auf die Gesundheit fremder

A Bremen agent sought passengers for railroad
and steamboat lines running from New York to
the Ohio and Upper Mississippi country, charging $7 to Chicago or Milwaukee.

Allgemeine Auswanderungzeitung, Sept. 23, 1851,
p. 448. Commerz-Bibliothek, Hamburg, West Germany.

America by landlords who had bought all their individual and communal land holdings. Communities vanished from the map.

If German towns were disappearing from Germany, they were often reappearing on the map of the United States. One result of the ease of emigration was that more and more Germans had already settled in America, forming clusters that served as magnets and bases for later arrivals. Dunkel's Grove was a German settlement near Chicago by 1825, and in the following decade many farmers and laborers from Hesse, Westphalia, and Hannover followed Gottfried Duden's guidebooks to settle near the Missouri River not far from St. Louis. Others came in later years, until both sides of Missouri River for some 125 miles were German territory—St. Charles, Washington, Hermann, Warrentown, Boonville, and other outposts. Germans also settled early in Perry County in southern Missouri. These swelling totals would provide the state with 45,319 Germans by 1850 and 88,487 a decade later, at which time St. Louis's 50,510 Germans made up almost one-third of the city's population.

This influx gave St. Louis a German coloration, first softening and then obliterating the French hues that had characterized the city from its early days. Although musical activities were slight among the English-speaking majority, the Germans by the 1840s had their *Singverein* and Singing Academy as well as debating societies, library, mutual benefit groups, and similar organizations. In 1835 the *Anzeiger des Westens* began publishing, reporting St. Louis events from the viewpoint of liberal Germans; soon German parochial schools were operating as well.

East of the Mississippi, St. Clair County was becoming the major German center of Illinois, the goal of large numbers of Germans arriving from the early 1830s on. Charles Dickens encountered "an encampment of German emigrants carrying their goods in carts" as he crossed the Looking-Glass Prairie near Belleville in 1842. The country around Belleville featured a strip of fertile upland some one hundred miles long and six to ten miles wide. The incoming German farmers appropriated it quickly. All of Belleville's town officers for years were Germans, and one of the community's most renowned leaders was a young radical who had been forced into exile after being wounded in the fighting of 1833. He was Gustave Koerner, born in 1809 in Frankfurt, who fled Europe in 1833 and reached Belleville soon thereafter. By 1840 he edited a German-language campaign newspaper. In 1842 voters sent him to the legislature, and three years later he was appointed to the state Supreme Court as he continued his rise in state politics.

Several other Illinois cities developed into German centers as the post-1848 immigration swelled, including Quincy, Alton, Peoria, Springfield, New Trier (where the bishop reported "all Catholics of this district are Germans" in 1850), McHenry, Galena, and Peru, which by 1854 had 1,000 Germans in a population of 3,500. Germans numbered 22,230 of Chicago's 109,260 residents in 1860, the largest group among the 54,624 foreign-born in the city. The state of Illinois had by then 130,804 Germans, 7.65 percent of its total population.

Germans reached the Iowa prairies by the early 1830s, and in 1836, the same year the territory was officially created, Davenport received the first representatives of the influx that eventually made the city a major German community. In 1842 the St. Louis newspapers announced that 529 steamboats had arrived during the first three months of the year, with more than 30,000 passengers bound for Iowa. Many of these probably were Germans, for German communities soon began to dot the Iowa landscape, including New Vienna, Dubuque, Guttenberg, and a cluster around Daveport: Avoca, Minden, Walcott, Wheatland, and Dewitt.

Germans settled along the Mississippi in Iowa during succeeding years, providing Clayton County with 13 percent of its population and prompting the state legislature to print documents in German as well as English. By 1860 the census reported 38,555 natives of the German states within Iowa's foreign-born population of 106,081; the total Iowa population that year was 674,913.

Wisconsin began adding large numbers of Germans to its population by mid-1830, and by 1840 Milwaukee was receiving up to three hundred German immigrants a week in the summer, jumping to over a thousand weekly four years later. In addition to the *Alt Lutheraner,* several other German religious groups targeted on Wisconsin—Evangelical Lutherans from northern German districts in 1843, Reformed groups coming in the late forties to Sheboygan and Manitowoc counties, and large numbers of Catholics encouraged by the Milwaukee diocese.

"Panoramic view of Milwaukee, 1854."

Milwaukee became a German city during this era, with Germans first challenging and finally moving into dominance over Yankees and Irish. This 1854 chromolithographic reveals a busy, prospering city with ships entering the harbor and river and with solid, substantial buildings rather than rough-hewn pioneer structures.

Courtesy of the State Historical Society of Wisconsin.

These groups helped in the creation of the vast German infrastructure that developed in the territory in those years, a German literary society and music groups by the early 1840s, protective *Volksvereine,* the territory's first German newspaper in 1844, and a total of twelve journals launched by 1854. Wisconsin was an early favorite of Germans seeking to create an all-German state in America, a dream nourished by some despite the fact that it had been rejected in 1837 by a German immigrants' national convention in Pittsburgh. Wisconsin also worked harder than its neighbors to attract Germans, naming a commissioner of immigration in 1852 and sending an agent to New York City, advertising in Europe, and countering the claims of other locales.

Milwaukee burst forth as one of the country's most German cities in these pre-Civil War years, developing a "German Town" where visitors encountered German signs, German architecture, German faces, German newspapers, "and many Germans...who never learn English, and seldom go beyond the German town," a European observed. On the contrary, many Americans there took it upon themselves to learn German, an immigrant wrote in 1850, and he noted other evidence of the position his nationality had gained in Milwaukee: "You will find inns, beer cellars and billiard and bowling alleys, as well as German beer, something you do not find much of in this country. The Dutchman (the Americans call the Germans this name by way of derision) plays a more independent role—has balls, concerts and theaters—naturally not to be compared to those in Germany and has even managed to get laws printed in German. His vote carries a heavy weight at election time. You will find no other place in which so much has been given the Germans." By 1860 the city had 15,981 Germans, slightly more than a third of its total population.

Only California ranked above Wisconsin in percentage of foreign-born in 1860—48 percent for California, 35.7 percent for Wisconsin. Germans numbered 123,879 in 1860 in Wisconsin, 16 percent of the state's total population and many more than the second-ranked group, the Irish with 49,961. Minnesota received its German influx later, due to the movement of the line of settlement as well as that territory's greater transportation problems. Some Germans settled early at Henderson on the Minnesota River, and in 1854 a group of Chicago German workers established a settlement at New Ulm.

Several colonization efforts were part of this movement into the Mississippi Valley; most were led by Catholics. Such Illinois communities as St. Marie (1837), Teutopolis (1839), and Columbia (1849) began with groups of Catholic Germans, under a priest or organization, first selecting a site, dividing lots, and constructing a church. Most of the first settlers had lived elsewhere in America for some years. Their colonies then became havens for those arriving later from Germany. In Missouri, New Westphalia was launched in 1838 because of a priest's concern that dispersal of Catholics over the state's central region would result in a weakening of the faith. His response was to organize communities composed of immigrants from the same districts of Germany to prevent discord. An attempt to launch a large-scale western colonization movement for Catholic immigrants was scotched when an 1856 convention in Buffalo ran into opposition from the church hierarchy. Catholic colonization efforts in Iowa involved Irish rather than Germans in this period.

As the trickle enlarged to a torrent, this German immigration into the Upper Mississippi country at mid-century assumed such proportions that all the institutions of society were forced to take it into account and to react in some way. ''The Germans are becoming so numerous in this part of Iowa,'' reported a Davenport preacher in 1848, ''that it is a serious question with us, what can be done for their spiritual benefit?'' Several denominations aided the Germans, and Catholic Archbishop Peter Richard Kenrick of St. Louis set aside various churches for the use of German inhabitants ''and for these alone.'' He also pleaded with the Catholic hierarchy elsewhere that the next appointee as bishop of Chicago ''ought to speak German and French as well as English.... Germans constitute the principle portion of the Catholic population in northern Illinois.'' By 1847 Chicago's city councilmen finally decided to employ a German interpreter to help collect the street tax.

If all Germans had fitted smoothly into existing Protestant or Catholic classifications, their adaptation and acceptance in America might have been accomplished more easily than was the case. But there was a complicating factor: large numbers of Germans, including many who ostensibly belonged to regular churches, were rationalists, estranged from many of the era's religious beliefs and practices. Many early arrivals from Germany were of this category, and in St. Louis, Wilhelm Weber's newspaper *Anzeiger des Westens* in the 1830s and Paul Follenius's *Die Waage* in 1844 promoted rationalism. In nearby Hermann, *Lichfreund,* edited by Eduard Mühl and Friedrich Münch, took similar stands promoting liberalism, anticlericalism, and antislavery.

Soon revolution in Germany provided a more forceful impetus for rationalism. The revolutionary elements of 1848 took note of the reactionary attitude of the state-supported churches, the clergy's furtherance through pulpit and school of what the revolutionists considered the worst aspects of Germany's problems, and the links between religious and political leaders. These developments drove many of Germany's radicals of the 1840s into forthright opposition to all organized religion; they became "free thinkers" or supporters of similar groups.

When the famous migration of "Forty-Eighters" began to flow into the Mississippi Valley after the revolution was defeated in Germany, dissension over religion became more frequent in the German immigrant communities. The rationalist philosophy appeared even within Protestant and Catholic churches, leading to the appearance of "free and independent Catholic" congregations and of Lutheran churches "composed much of German rationalists," as one critic described a church in Belleville in 1851.

Belleville became a center for the Forty-Eighters, as did Davenport upriver and Milwaukee. At the time Gustave Koerner settled in Belleville, the community was already nurturing elements cordial to revolutionary philosophies. Belleville became known as a "Latin settlement" because of the numerous scholars who settled there, men more conversant with Latin and Greek than with running a farm or shop. Friedrich Hecker came to Belleville after his escape from an abortive *putsch*, in which he and a small group of young radicals had proclaimed a German republic before the Frankfurt Parliament could act. Hecker, who once had trumpeted that he would create a republic in Germany with the aid of a portable guillotine, soon became a leader among Belleville's rationalists and ex-revolutionaries. A Catholic historian later charged that the aim of this group was "to bring about a universal anti-Christian state" in America.

In Davenport the Forty-Eighters held firm control of city affairs for at least a generation. Many came from Schleswig-Holstein in far northern Germany, in-

Davenport street scene, circa 1860.

Davenport became a predominantly German city during the antebellum era, with refugees of the 1848 revolutions providing leadership and stimulation. German singing societies, literary groups, and physical culture clubs abounded.

Courtesy of the State Historical Society, Iowa State Historical Dept.

cluding three who had been officially chosen to represent that state in 1848 before the court of Denmark. In Davenport these Forty-Eighters soon developed the variety of *Turnverein* groups, musical societies, debating clubs, and other organizations with which Germans, and especially the liberal Forty-Eighters, became identified in America.

Milwaukee was also heavily influenced by this group, whose members published the *Humanist,* formed a *Freie Gemeinde* (free congregation) and the *Verein freier Maenner* (Society of Free Men), and provided the major stimulus for the *Turnverein,* with its emphasis upon German language and culture. As in Davenport, from these organizations came much of the city's leadership. Carl Schurz, the most famous of the Forty-Eighters, settled in nearby Watertown, Wisconsin, and quickly became involved in politics. Not infrequently these Forty-Eighters argued with the older liberals of Gustave Koerner's generation, calling them *die Grauen* (the Grays). The newcomers in turn were nicknamed *die Grünen* (the Greens), and on occasion they tried to instruct the older Germans on the proper course to follow in America. The advice was not always welcomed.

The presence of rationalist elements was disturbing to many religious Germans as well as to native-born clergy in America. A German Evangelical pastor in Belleville complained that the Germans there were "most all infidels or rationalists calling the Bible an old rusted book." An American preacher agreed that the German church in Belleville was "almost entirely made up of skeptics and loose moralists," and he told of offering to sell one of them a Bible. The German responded, "I want no Bible; I have the great book of the world. I want to know nothing about Jesus Christ; I have the guide of my own reason." In some St. Louis German congregations, according to another American preacher, "believers and infidels are joined together as one mystical body of Christ," and they seemed bound to "continue in the old German system."

The Germans and Irish whose migration paths crossed and mingled on the prairies of the Upper Mississippi country thus had several basic similarities and dissimilarities. Both groups came from lands where agriculture and the land question were at the focus of turmoil, where peasants for generations had been forced onto smaller and smaller landholdings that by the 1840s were being taken away by wealthy landlords. Capitalism and efficiency were basic ingredients of the new agriculture in both lands. Because of this, a contemporary's charge that the growth of large farms in Germany was "like a colossal conspiracy of greedy wealth against the small proprietors" could have been delivered against Irish landlords at the same time. Heavy dependence on the potato permitted families to survive on smaller and smaller plots of land, but when the potato failed, the small plots of Germany and of Ireland were inadequate, and they were incorporated into larger holdings.

The economic transformation of Europe affected both Ireland and Germany in similar ways, making travel easier and cheaper but throwing local farmers into competition with distant producers while destroying local artisans' monopolies. This meant that many persons of some standing and accomplishment were hurt in both Ireland and Germany long before the potato blight, and these families often had money for emigration, especially after selling their land and homes. They were "those who had something to lose," and their presence loomed large in the emigration from both lands.

One other similarity linked the Irish and Germans; tales reaching them from America were numerous, were in their own tongue, and were overwhelmingly favorable to emigration. By 1840 several thousand Irish and Germans had gone to America. Many of them wrote travel books for the home market, and all formed a new base or haven for the next traveler. Home remained the tie. This aspect of the New World continually surprised those who had feared they would see familiar faces no more. This was the experience of a German from Freienseen when he arrived in Chicago in 1855 and set out the first morning to investigate the neighborhood. "As I was coming back from the bridge," he wrote, "all at once a girl stood before me with a basketful of lettuce. I knew her at once as the daughter of Loui Steuernagel from our village." It was an experience to be repeated hundreds of times as the communities of the Rhine and Weser, County Kerry and Bantry Bay yielded their excess population to the land across the sea.

If religion was extremely important in the backgrounds of both Irish and German immigrants, the fact remains that Germans emerged with much more extensive infighting among their religious groups. Irish Catholics battled Presbyterians and Anglicans but usually fought them as part of the attack on everything connected with the British. However, when the *Alt Lutheraner* resisted merger with the Reformed church, and when German Catholics locked horns with rationalists, they were struggling against neighbors and fellow Germans, whose ideological roots ran back generations. The fervency of these beliefs was carried intact across the ocean with as much care as the goods in their America chests. When these groups reached the Upper Mississippi country there were many within the immigrant clusters who sought to retain their German identity.

Many others began to merge into American life, of course, but for some the change was traumatic. A preacher in Joliet, Illinois, said that he could not form a Presbyterian church there "because the German Protestants of the place will not assume the name of Presbyterians, there being no such denomination in Germany.... They therefore wish to be called Evangelical Protestants, that is, they wish to effect a union of the Presbyterian and Lutheran, forming one church." Denominational lines, it was soon clear, did not blur in transit, at least at the outset. Watertown, Wisconsin, was half made up of immigrants by 1857 and had an Irish Catholic church, a German Catholic church, three German Lutheran churches, a German Moravian church, and a German Methodist church. (Americans attended the Congregational, Methodist, Episcopal, or Baptist churches.)

The two groups' experiences with government were somewhat at odds. Irish people generally considered Britain an occupying power, and its policies during the famine years only confirmed this view. Hatred of a system that represented another religion and another land increased amid Ireland's travail of the forties. Many of the German authorities, however, sought to alleviate famine suffering; for example, the south German governments bought food and sold it on credit to communities, and power in the individual German states was generally wielded on the side of the religion practiced by most of the inhabitants.

In one regard the Germans and Irish seemed cut from the same cloth; by the 1840s and 1850s they had the feeling that as nations they had been held back, frustrated by history, blocked from reaching a place in the sun. It is significant that "Young Ireland" and "Young Germany" movements appeared in their respective lands at the same time, stimulated by revolutions, and met the same fate. This spirit remained strong among those who crossed the ocean, and the fact that these newcomers "were not the kind to surrender or become indifferent" led to confrontations in America that would not have occurred if the incoming Irish and Germans had been meek, defeated, humiliated groups.

These proud immigrants came at a crucial point in American history, when the land they and others coveted in the West seemed threatened by slave power. Land, they quickly found, was also at the focus of America's growing discord. If southerners generally seemed cool to many of the newcomers from Europe, it was also true that many persons in the North were perplexed by these immigrants, even frightened. Employers, on the other hand, often welcomed them as ready laborers at low rates.

All this lay in the future, as the "former proprietor" on the Upper Rhine dreamed of a new home in the Upper Mississippi country. The letters he read emphasized how the distasteful burdens of Germany were absent across the ocean. An immigrant in Waukesha County, Wisconsin, wrote home: "There are no dues, no tithes here, no taxes (there is taxation, of course, but compared to yours they amount to almost nothing), no community dues, no dog license...no [mounted] police, no beggars, no skinners." And how could German enthusiasm for that region be dimmed when *Der Deutsche Auswanderer* carried letters asssuring that "the land is so 'fat' that the laborer can always count on a good harvest. There are so few workers that they have to pay them well....The paradise of America is Illinois."

4. Needed: Laborers

"I was creditably informed, a few days since," a correspondent wrote to Illinois Governor French late in 1851, "that General Pickering, the indefatigable proprietor of the Mt. Carmel and Alton Rail Road, in his zeal for the completion of his favorite work, has actually hired an Irishman and set him to work on it, he (the general) acting as superintendent."

Both the general's zeal and his choice of a workman were representative of the "Age of Internal Improvements," a movement, a desire bursting across America from the 1820s on, promoting roads, bridges, harbors, canals, and railroads, directing the entire vision of society away from primitive reality and toward a wondrous future. This spirit was not long in reaching the frontier of the Upper Mississippi. By the time it arrived in the West, it had a legacy from the East that included the Erie Canal and a host of lesser arteries of commerce that helped tie the regions of the young republic together. As in Europe, these internal improvements stimulated mobility and eased the way for persons wishing to move to new homes.

Transportation was at the hub of this era's transformation in the Upper Mississippi as elsewhere. The steamboat was the initial vehicle of change, although it was limited to existing routes—oceans, rivers, lakes—but dreamers ashore were soon planning other enterprises that would compete with more traditional forms of transport. As early as 1836 Beardstown on the Illinois River reported 450 arrivals and departures of steamboats, and three years later a steamboat captain said that he had carried some 10,000 passengers in his vessel's fifty-eight trips from St. Louis up the Illinois River to Peru.

Suddenly people could think only of future greatness for every port and every town existing on the map or only in the minds of land speculators. The spirit was especially strong in Illinois. A canal official in 1848 noted the previous twenty years' changes along the Illinois River and forecast that, for improvements of the next two decades, "the most extravagant estimate at this time would be too low." There was no dearth of extravagant estimates, especially as projects moved off the drawing board in the 1830s and 1840s and construction began. The plan to build the Illinois and Michigan Canal was hailed as "one of the greatest and most important, in its consequences, of any age or nation," and the governor of Illinois asked, "What patriotic bosom does not beat high with a laudable ambition to give to Illinois her full share" of such internal improvements?

Contemplation of these future wonders affected more than speculators, especially as talk of the Iron Horse raced through the region's new urban centers. Politicians, including Stephen A. Douglas and Abraham Lincoln, doted on the theme. One Illinoisan assured the governor that the riverboats' business would soon all be transferred to the rails: "We will have a railroad world yet in a few years.... Every body, and every thing, will yet go to every point on railroads." This possibility seized the imaginations of communities previously doomed to low status. "A ray of light" came into Port Byron in Rock Island County, Illinois, with the report that St. Louis entrepreneurs had applied to construct a rail line to their vicinity. At Carlinville in Macoupin County, a clergyman wrote of "great excitement here about the railroad terminating here or running this way." Land in the area, he added, was suddenly "not to be had without almost covering it over with money." Another minister at Galena in far northwestern Illinois reported on "flattering" local railroad plans and said the area would soon be "so threaded with R. Roads" that every acre would be "within six hours of as good a market as New York" and each resident within fifty hours of the East Coast. "What numbers of villages and cities will start up as if by magic," he added. An easterner looking for engineering work on the proposed railroad quickly wrote home to Boston for money to purchase land when he realized what the Iron Horse would do for farming on the prairie. The Vandalia region of Illinois, he informed his father, "has had heretofore no advantages of a market. It is seventy to eighty miles to St.

Steamboats were the first major transportation improvement to throw open the midcontinent to settlers. Galena, in Illinois's northwestern corner, was the major center of the lead region and attracted a thriving steamboat trade into the railroad era.

Courtesy of the Illinois State Historical Library.

Louis, the only market in this vicinity, and although corn may be worth there from 30 to 50 cents, it will only sell here from 15 to 20" due to hauling costs. The writer assured his father that he knew the best spots to purchase "even if it were not almost impossible for a man to miss making a good speculation in any event."

Cairo, at the southern tip of Illinois, became the state's "great city of prophecy" in a region which was raising itself up on prophecy. It was a natural site for greatness, a funnel-spout for the Old Northwest, the obvious port for boats traveling the Ohio and upper and lower Mississippi, the rail center for trans-shipment from the prairies to the south (or vice versa) via riverboats or a planned southern railway. A neighbor watched the workmen building the Cairo levee and wondered at how great a city the convergence of railroad and steamboat routes would produce: "Can anyone be extravagant in his estimate of the amount of business that must concentrate on that spot?" The town site affected visitors that way and the enthusiasm seemed contagious. A Chicago newspaperman who stopped over asked, "What is to hinder Cairo from speedily becoming a store-house, a granary, and a shipping-place of the whole West?"

The experience of states to the east provided enough examples to nurture these dreams. The Erie Canal's commerce "quadrupled every five years since it was completed," it was claimed, and once quiet eastern hamlets had suddenly risen to wealth and importance with canal and railroad connections. This seemed to be happening in the Upper Mississippi Valley. A traveling missionary in Illinois encountered the town of Sheffield, which he said had been "called into being by the rail road." "One year ago last summer it was a cornfield," but by 1854, when he happened by, it had a hotel, several stores, three taverns, and some twenty houses. The opposite effect was experienced by the river town of Albany, which was apparently beaten by its rival Fulton City in obtaining the railroad and an eventual bridge over the Mississippi. An Albany clergyman described the people's mood as "unsettled and discouraged." Many had already left, and he said, "if this town does not go down, there is not much prospect that it will grow."

Small wonder that tiny settlements sent swarms of delegates to the offices of the railroad companies or that the legislative sessions were inundated with hopeful agents. Communities offered companies free rights of way and liberal city franchises, and some even went to court to block their rivals. Springfield became so overcrowded during legislative debates on railroad charters that one visitor could obtain bedding space only on a cot installed in the U.S. circuit court chambers at night. A pleading resident of Nashville in southern Illinois urged the Illinois Central Railroad president to build a station at Ashley ("bound to be the largest place in our county") because if the station were built instead at Dubois the company "will lose ten times as much as all the land around Dubois is worth." From across the Mississippi, delegations of Missouri and Iowa men pleaded for connections with the railroad net then forming in Illinois, and one such prayer from Dubuque assured that "the united energies of the people of northern Iowa are directed to this cherished enterprise, which nothing can now thwart or seriously impede."

Small wonder, also, that the entire population became absorbed in this topic of such widespread concern or that the preacher in a tiny, isolated village in western Illinois urged special prayers for the success of a railroad project, "that through its accomplishment the 'rest of mankind' might have access to Jerseyville." From all parts of the Upper Mississippi country the call went out: "Hurry up the railroad!"

But more than hope or great expectations were required before the campaign for internal improvements could erect monuments across the region. Labor and capital were necessities and both were needed in vast quantities. But while hope was a bumper crop, the supplies of labor and capital remained at famine levels.

Labor shortages had seldom been absent from the moving frontier, and farmers settling on the newly opened sections were generally not available in large numbers for regular outside employment. The Upper Mississippi's single other major economic activity was mining in the lead regions. But the mining industry had no surplus workmen to serve as a ready source of labor for the numerous canal and railroad projects starting to twinkle in the eyes of entrepreneurs. Nor were adequate amounts of capital available locally from the mines, farms, and steamboat enterprises.

This was painfully evident by the late 1820s, when Illinois officials finally convinced Congress to donate land for a canal to run from Chicago to La Salle, connecting Lake Michigan with the Illinois River, a route so obvious that it had occurred to explorer Louis Jolliet in 1673, and so tantalizing that its promoters had been pestering federal officials for years. The land provided by the 1827 law consisted of alternate sections one mile square arranged checkerboard fashion in a belt extending five miles from each side of the proposed route of the Illinois and Michigan Canal. But difficulties in raising money for the project limited it to dreams until 1836, when a third canal commission was finally able to borrow money and turn the first shovelful of dirt on the Fourth of July. Some 350 laborers were working on the project by the closing weeks of that year, and their number swelled to nearly 1,000 the following autumn. But even this crew was obviously too small, and this was among the factors blamed for the delays of those early months.

The east provided the example for the canal builders at this crucial juncture. When the Chesapeake and Ohio Canal was started in the late 1820s, its planners advertised for workmen in newspapers in Ireland. These notices stated that canal workers would have "meat three times a day, plenty of bread and vegetables, with a reasonable allowance of liquor, and eight, ten, or twelve dollars a month for wages." This pattern was continued on other eastern projects, with some 5,000 Irishmen eventually working on the Erie Canal and nearly 2,000 on the Wabash-Erie Canal in Indiana in 1835. This gave canal entrepreneurs valuable experience in labor recruitment, and it provided precedents eagerly adopted by the hard-pressed officials of the Illinois and Michigan Canal.

Soon Irishmen and other immigrants recruited in Canada and the eastern states were appearing along the canal line, some 200 in La Salle and Peru, hundreds more in other communities along the canal, and many more in Chicago, where the Catholic population swelled to 1,000 (in a population of 8,000) by 1838. Housing for the Irish laborers came in the form of makeshift shanties; other needs were not met so readily. An Irish Catholic contractor at the La Salle end of the canal line requested that the bishop of St. Louis send a priest to serve the area's Catholics, who totalled 2,000 Irish, French Canadians, and Germans by 1838. When two priests arrived from St. Louis the evening of March 29, 1838, they were escorted into La Salle by a large procession with fife-and-drum accompaniment playing the Irish tune "Garry-Owen," the marchers' path brightened by five hundred torches.

The opening of the Illinois and Michigan Canal in 1848 made the travelers' way much easier, stimulating town formation as well as farming in interior regions.

Courtesy of the Chicago Historical Society.

FOR LASALLE, PERU, ST. LOUIS,
And all Intermediate Landings on
ILLINOIS RIVER.

TWO DAILY LINES OF
U. S. MAIL PACKETS.

PRAIRIE STATE,	Capt. J. E. Vedder.
ST. LOUIS,	" A. S. Wiggins.
LOUISIANA,	" Fred. Reed.
NEW ORLEANS,	" C. H. Wheeler.
CHICAGO,	" N. M. Wheeler.

One of the above boats will
leave the Packet Boat Dock on Washington street, every morning at 8, and evening at 5 o'clock, connecting at Lasalle with a line of First Class Steam Packets, on Illinois and Mississippi Rivers, also with Stage to Dixon, Lamoil, Princeton, Burlington, Rock Island, etc. These boats are expressly for Passengers, and are as comfortable as a Canal Packet can be made.

For Passage, apply to the
Captain on Board, or at the Office on Washington street.

SEATON & PECK, Printers, (Argus Office,) Chicago.

When the parade arrived at its destination, the crowd gave a thundering cheer to the missionaries, who were forerunners of the army of Catholic priests who arrived in waves over the succeeding years to serve the thousands of Catholic immigrants of the Upper Mississippi Valley.

But even recruited Irishmen were inadequate to keep canal construction moving at the rate desired. The project was lagging in late 1837 when it encountered another problem: the other crucial factor—capital—suddenly evaporated in the national financial panic that year. The State Bank of Illinois suspended specie payment, the legislature failed to provide funds for continued canal work, and contractors and laborers were forced to abandon the project. Deteriorating channels stood for nearly a decade as testimony to the financial poverty of the frontier. Illinois's situation had fallen so far by 1842 that the state treasurer refused to accept payments in anything but gold and silver.

The collapse of canal funding hit workmen even harder. Wages had already been cut from $26 a month to $20 by late 1837 before the panic, and contractors found they had to raise the charge for board above the stipulated $2 per week. At that point many workmen went on strike, and the state was coming to the rescue with funds when it was forced to abandon support due to the financial panic. A "superabundance" of small-denomination Michigan bills appeared along the canals in early 1838, when contractors used them to pay off workmen. The canal company treasurer admitted that use of this form "falls particularly hard upon the laborers upon the canal, who experience great difficulty in converting it into provisions." But contractors had no other small bills and no coins available.

Chicago's mayor led the campaign to provide relief for sufferers caught in the financial panic, and a newspaper reported that those applying for relief "were principally from the canal." Canal scrip was also issued by the canal directors with the same immediate result. Workmen were unable to cash it for full value and so took a reduction in real wages. The state finally agreed to accept this scrip as payment for state land, and many Irish contractors and laborers used it to purchase acreage along the canal, further establishing the Irish as a permanent feature of the northern Illinois landscape.

A vigorous governor and a new group of promoters renegotiated the loans by 1845, putting up canal property as collateral. Construction contracts were let again, and soon the Illinois and Michigan Canal was again under construction. But the former workmen were gone, having drifted away to other jobs or other climes. Once again the search for laborers became a major activity. "I hope that Mr. Leavitt and yourself will make an effort to have a strong reinforcement of men sent us as soon as practicable, else we shall all be disgraced," a canal official wrote desperately in July of 1846. But even as he wrote, former and potential employees were reported en route to "visit the 'Halls of the Montezumas,'" as war loomed with Mexico over the question of Texas annexation.

This increased the labor shortage, and the canal secretary was soon calling for hiring agents "to go thro' New York, and among the emigrant ships" to secure 1,000 more laborers as well as running advertisements in New York, Boston, and Montreal newspapers. "Something must be done," he pleaded. These efforts brought in hundreds more workmen, with 2,000 employed on the eastern (Chicago) end of the canal alone by late 1847. Many who came from the East were not hired, however, and had to return home. Evidence indicates that Irish continued to predominate, and the canal company secretary observed during a late December squall, "we have quite a storm of rain, but as it is holyday week, and to be kept sacred by the Pats, it is of less consequence as to interruption of the work."

Conditions and wages ultimately became more distasteful than many of these workmen could stand. In July 1847, a group of workers, apparently Irish, petitioned for a shorter workday, a wage increase, and less hard-driving bosses. They described workdays lasting from 4:30 A.M. until 7:45 P.M., "in a hot climate in a sickly state," under harsh foremen who paid them $1 per day. In their tortuously written petition they appealed to Colonel Oakley, the resident canal trustee, because they considered him "both human and gentlemany. Beside being an independant, born American, who should abhor oppression in any form." They called on him to take over their direction "so as not to have white citizens drove even worse than common slave negroes." They offered to work for $1.25 per day, from 6:00 A.M. until 7:00 P.M.

The strike lasted two weeks, company records indicate. One official opposed any compromise, "for where would this end?" Other contractors would then be forced to pay more, this official argued, and in the end his view apparently prevailed. Whether many of the striking "Pats" continued to labor at such wages when local farmers were paying a dollar per day plus board is questionable. One official reported soon afterwards that "several hundred" canal men had gone to farm work, but it was also noted that hundreds more were being recruited in Buffalo and New York.

And finally the Irishmen's labors drew to a close. The canal secretary wrote to another official in late February 1848: "The next time I make my mark as deep as the above, I shall have the pleasure of telling you that the big ditch is dug." A line of boats was soon plying the sixty-foot-wide canal's waters, pulled along by mules on the towpath, with up to two-and-a-half days required for the round trip between Chicago and Peru. The canal received some $88,000 in tolls the first year as lumber from the north woods and manufactured goods from the East came to the prairies. The canal's major impact was in turning the marketing of farm commodities, especially corn and hogs, to Chicago and away from St. Louis. As people continued to surge into the Upper Mississippi Valley, it was the new city sprouting on Lake Michigan's shores that received the lion's share of trade and people, and the canal was a major factor in its midcentury rise.

Other types of internal improvements were being discussed during these years, spurred by the successes of eastern railroads as well as by the frustrations of Illinois canal builders. Hope, capital, and labor were still prerequisites, but by the time the Illinois and Michigan Canal was operating the latter two were in better supply across the region.

The railroad craze paralleled the canal craze throughout the Upper Mississippi region for several decades. In the 1835 Illinois legislative session, when canal building received its major impetus, twelve railroads received charters. While Irishmen were scraping and shoveling for the canal in 1837, the first railroad tracks in Illinois were being laid on a Quincy-to-Springfield line. But the end-of-decade panic stalled the railroad as it did the canal, and while part of the Northern

Canal boats line the docks at Ottawa, Illinois, loading grain for shipment to Chicago. The Hossack elevator was built by John Hossack, a Scot who labored to build the canal and then became a wealthy grain dealer by locating his elevator beside the new waterway.

Courtesy of the Illinois State Historical Library.

Cross railway was in operation by 1839, the line was not finished to Springfield until 1842. Numerous railroads were launched on paper in the following years, although in Wisconsin and Iowa the rush waited until the 1850s. Railroad meetings blossomed across the landscape, and salesmen scattered to buttonhole prospective buyers of railroad stock. They found eager buyers, for men chafed under the transportation difficulties that blocked large-scale farming on the prairies. Despite setbacks, many of the promoters' plans eventually rolled on to completion, resulting in four cross-state Illinois railroads south of Chicago, as well as the Chicago, Alton, and St. Louis line to connect central Illinois with the Mississippi and a multiplicity of shorter operations. It has been estimated that, if the network had been laid down according to the hopes and plans of the would-be entrepreneurs, all parts of Illinois would have been within two to five miles of a railroad track.

One of the most publicized early lines was William Ogden's Galena and Chicago Union Railroad, which opened for business in 1848. Ogden built a Chicago depot with a tall tower from which he peered through his telescope and called down arrival times to the passengers waiting below. When Ogden took a group of civic leaders for an introductory ride on the line in November 1848, carrying them in a baggage car equipped with seats, two alert passengers sighted a farmer transporting wheat and hides to Chicago with a wagon and a pair of slow-moving oxen. The train stopped, the pair purchased the farmer's load, and Chicago received its first freight by rail. The *Gem of the Prairie* editor was ecstatic with his introductory trip: "We took a seat on the Engine car yesterday morning, and in a few moments found ourself traveling westward, ho!...at the rate of sixteen miles per hour. The track is completed about five miles, and in less than twenty minutes, we were at the end, away out on the prairie, where the fences do not mar the beauty of the landscape, and Chicago, with its church spires, and the masts and flags of shipping in the harbor, looked dim in the distance. The hands are also taken out and brought back, morning and night."

Other railroads were taking shape in these years, bubbling from the minds of the state's "progressive" element, who saw future greatness if prairie farmers could only reach markets cheaply. The most titanic in scope was the plan for a central railroad to run the north-south length of Illinois, ultimately to reach the Gulf of Mexico. It emerged from legislative and congressional debates in the frenzy of internal improvements of the 1840s and took final shape in 1850 with a congressional land grant. This provided a rail line from Chicago along the Mississippi Valley to the Gulf of Mexico, part of Senator Stephen A. Douglas's grand plan to unite the nation economically as a counter to worsening sectional divisions. The state of Illinois received alternate sections of land for six miles on each side of the Illinois Central, plus a hundred-foot right-of-way. This land was to be given to the company selected to construct the line. The charter required that the main line be completed within four years and branch lines within six years; costs were estimated at $16.5 million.

This was the Illinois Central, to comprise seven hundred miles of track, including the line between Chicago and Cairo and routes connecting with Galena and running along the eastern side of the state. It was quickly championed as the region's major project and hailed as the longest railroad in the world, the largest "single private undertaking" in the nation's history.

Ground-breaking day for the Illinois Central was December 23, 1851, at the southern end in Cairo and the northeastern end in Chicago, and was celebrated with cannon salutes, the ringing of bells, and speeches. The line had twelve construction divisions of fifty to seventy-five miles each, with bids let for grading and bridge construction. The company itself laid the rails. Local economic activity was stimulated immediately as contractors arranged for purchasing various items. By the spring of 1852 contracts were made for delivery of 20,000 ties ("of good white or burr oak") at Bloomington and 10,000 at La Salle.

Cheers for railroad ground-breaking echoed across other states in the region during these years. Wisconsin's first track was laid in 1850 from Milwaukee to Waukesha, and crowds hailed the "brave little engine" as it roared into Waukesha at ten miles an hour on February 25, 1851, to open the state's railroad era. Iowa's first lines also appeared early in the decade as eager promoters sought to extend Illinois routes westward, continuing the Chicago and Rock Island across the river as the Mississippi and Missouri Rail Road. Construction began in September of 1853 following a course directly from the Mississippi at Rock Island to Iowa City and thence to Council Bluffs on the western border. A race with the competing Iowa Central Air Line Rail Road stimulated a rush across the state before the lines were completed in 1855. The first railroad bridge across the Mississippi was erected at Davenport, and the first locomotive crossed the great river on April 21, 1856.

Such activity may have helped local economic enterprises, but towns and villages were as poorly equipped to provide laborers and supplies as they were to furnish investment capital. The *Charleston (Ill.) Courier* noted in mid-1852 that one of the contractors "has arrived at the eastern end of the line with his engineers, tools and laborers, all which he has brought from the East." This became the pattern for goods and workmen, and steamers carrying workmen also brought English railroad iron.

Satisfying the enormous labor needs of railroad construction proved to be a challenge seldom met satisfactorily across the region. The Illinois Central's chief engineer estimated early in the company's operations that no more than a quarter of the thousands of workmen needed could be recruited within the state. He stationed agents in St. Louis and Chicago, and contractors tried local advertising, such as the plea carried in the *Galena Jeffersonian*:

TO LABORERS.

The subscribers will require from 200 to 300 able bodied laborers, to work on their Railroad Contract, about five miles from Galena. The locality is healthy and there is an abundant supply of excellent water.

Parties having good second hand CARTS to dispose of, will do well to apply. Also, wanted a few good work Horses.

CARTER & SAMPSON.

Soon the call went out to distant climes, with Irish newspapers reporting the need for "10,000 laborers at wages of a dollar a day." These reports assured Irish readers that, while the work was "no doubt, very laborious," it was "not much harder than that of draining" (a common activity on the raindrenched farms of

Enormous demands for construction crews kept the Illinois Central and other railroad companies busy in the 1850s. Recruitment reached as far as Europe. This advertisement was run in the Irish newspaper *Western Tablet*, published in Chicago.

Western Tablet, Aug. 20, 1853, p. 7. Courtesy of the University of Notre Dame Archives.

Ireland). One of Germany's leading emigration newspapers also reported this need for railroad laborers, specifically mentioning that Illinois railroads were recruiting 6,000 workers in the East, "and they offer very good wages." The Illinois Central in 1853 contracted with a New York firm for 1,500 German emigrants. Recruiting was also carried on within Ireland. Other dealings with emigrant-aid societies were in the wind, and the company sent agents to meet boats in New Orleans and New York as well as running advertisements there.

Railroad agents did much of the recruiting. One of the Illinois Central's most active was Henry Phelps in New York. His contract, on file with the railway's papers, indicates that from August 4, 1853, onward he would receive "one dollar for each and every laborer that he shall deliver on the twelve divisions" of the line by the end of the year. The Illinois Central would pay passage from New York to Kankakee for each man hired at a charge of $4.75. It has been estimated that from 5,000 to 10,000 laborers were recruited for the Illinois Central alone from 1852 to 1856. Although this seems a massive number of workmen, it proved inadequate because of the constant turnover among the crews. Some estimates put 100,000 men at work at some time during the fifties for the Illinois Central. By August 1852, the Cairo division had 800 to 1,000 hands employed at various times and was seeking 3,000 more. The entire line had 6,000 to 8,000 working during the following winter, and the total swelled to 10,000 by the autumn of 1853, when Phelps's recruits were arriving. These were largely foreign crews, aliens in a sparsely settled land. When the Northern Cross, one of the early Illinois lines, was started in the late thirties, a Protestant minister complained that the work "is bringing large numbers of German and Irish Catholics; their priests are also to be seen in our streets, and the bishop has been here laying his plans." A missionary Italian priest at Galena reported in that period that Irish and German Catholics "generally perform the most laborious work of the nation," including in the lead region where he served. This trend continued during the boom of the fifties, when the total of Irish people in Rock County, Wisconsin, suddenly rose from 900 (4 percent of the population) to 3,300 as the railroad work began. But this was a highly mobile group as seen dramatically in nearby Waukesha County, where the 500 Irish railroad laborers present in 1850 suddenly dispersed when wages were not paid as promised. An Iowa editor confronted the reality of this foreign-born labor force as he traveled into Illinois in 1855 and encountered "another engine working its way west assisted by a hundred Irishmen."

This brought the "monster emigration" into the Upper Mississippi country, overloading housing and leaving clergymen frustrated over meeting spiritual needs. "We are already beginning to be embarrassed in this region with the great and constant influx of population," one preacher lamented, and another noted with exasperation that a new railway was approaching his community: "And what shall we do when it arrives?"

Its impact was seen in myriad ways. Catholicism soon spoke in German and in Irish-accented English across the region. By 1853, when a traveling Irish priest reached La Salle, he found there a "Catholic atmosphere" with "many Catholic farmers" and a large congregation that donated $344 to aid a Catholic university in Ireland. He obtained "nothing from Germans," however. Bloomington, Illinois, by 1860 had "perhaps, two thousand or more, of foreigners, who had come to stay," heavily Irish, brought initially for railroad construction. Germans by that year had become the major purchasers of farmlands from the Illinois Central, although Irish remained numerous on farms along the canal and were found as residents in large numbers in the railroad centers.

This labor—shoveling, grading, working in junglelike summer heat and frigid winters—formed the entry to American life for thousands of European immigrants in the antebellum decades. Canal and railroad experiences became part of the song and story of these men, to endure for generations as they and their descendants harked back to the pioneer days.

But other facets of canal and railroad labor emerged, too, and many were less heroic than track laying or blasting hillsides. The famed $1-a-day yielded to higher rates as labor shortages developed, with ordinary workmen demanding and obtaining $1.50 because of competing employers or defaulting contractors. Such problems vexed railroad officials, and a worried letter to New York told of fears that one contractor would have to be removed because "they are quarreling among themselves and doing very little work." A protesting contractor pleaded that his delays south of Bloomington had "been beyond the control of man," and included about a 50 percent rise in labor costs (going from $1 up to $1.50, with track layers getting an increase from their previous $1.75 to the new $2.50), similar increases for provisions, and frustrations over lack of iron, chains, and grading that had to be completed before track-laying could begin. As a result, he had had to let his crew go, "besides after a gang is broken up and scattered it is no small matter and attended with no small expense to get up another gang and break them in." Furthermore, the onset of summer meant that "I have been obliged to increase the price of my men as the warm weather made its appearance." (Labor shortages affected other employers, too: farmers by 1857 were forced to pay $2 and $3 a day for harvest hands.) Board was sometimes obtained by the railroad laborers from nearby farms, at $2.50 a week.

Newly hired Germans pleased onlookers as they marched to work in Galena singing "some lively airs," and observers were impressed with the work organization, an editor noting that it proceeded with "every man knowing his place and having a part to perform in the economical arrangement." But industrialization possessed underlying problems not always visible to outsiders, including wage disputes that provoked protests on several occasions. These marked another episode in the coming of the Industrial Revolution to the prairies.

Soon after railroad construction began in the Galena area, it was reported that workmen who were willing to labor for 87½ cents a day "were forced to quit in consequence of threats of violence made by those on adjoining jobs, who are demanding a greater compensation." This occurred among railroad construction crews in the Milwaukee area when German workers drove off the Irish, whom they charged with accepting low wages.

Strikes, or "turn-outs," continued sporadically along the railroad lines during the first half of the fifties, as they had along the canal lines earlier. Men working on the Rock River Valley Union line in southern Wisconsin struck in 1853 to raise their 75-cents-a-day wages to $1 and paraded through Janesville led by "a couple of fifes."

But often the strikes erupted over a more basic question; not wage levels, but whether the wages would be paid at all. "When the old Watertown R.R. started I went to work on the road until the company bursted'' still owing him $300, a Milwaukee Irishman later recalled. It became a frequent story across the region, a foretaste of labor's woes on a frontier where money came from the East or Europe and where contractors had an easy time eluding their employees. At Hannibal, Missouri, an observer noted that ''not 10 cents has been paid'' by investors on their subscriptions for a new railroad, with the result that ''the hands at work upon the railroad are leaving, on account of not being promptly paid.''

Men building the Northern Cross extension in early 1853 through Decatur, Illinois, woke up one morning to learn that their contractor had fled, owing them and Decatur merchants some $2,000. An Illinois Central contractor in that area absconded at the same time, ''deeply indebted to our citizens'' it was reported. When a contractor on the La Crosse railroad tried to postpone payday in July 1853, his largely German crews marched into Milwaukee and stormed the line's offices demanding their pay. The mob, numbering between three and four hundred, argued with city aldermen, the mayor, and police and finally fought with firemen sent to hose them down in ''a general melee.'' The mayor issued a proclamation in German assuring that they would be paid, and a subcontractor who was assigned the project eventually gave the men their wages of several weeks. The Wisconsin legislature in 1855 finally held railroad companies responsible for labor, rather than allowing contractors to hold final responsibility, and then required contractors to provide bonds covering wage payments.

Added to wage problems was the disagreeable reality of working up to twelve hours a day pushing a canal or railroad line across the steamy, unshaded prairie. Going south from La Salle over the ''grand prairie,'' a visitor noted that for much of the distance ''not a fence, a house, tree, or bush can be seen.'' While such a landscape could be inspiring to farmers for its lack of trees to remove, it left slight refuge from the elements for workers. Summer temperatures of 90 degrees and above, with humidity to match, were common on the prairies and contrasted with the cooler, milder climate of Ireland and much of Germany. This made for a difficult transition. ''The men do not work harder here than in Ireland,'' an immigrant wrote home from Ottawa, Illinois, ''but the weather is so hot it [is] more severe on them as you can hardly thin[k] but the perspiration will be running down your body."

Intricately connected to the problem of excessive heat were the dangers from disease and accidents. The former were often linked to sanitation and housing, both notoriously inadequate in immigrant districts. A missionary priest concluded as much in his visit to workmen's dwellings along the railroad lines near Galena: the houses, he said, "consisted of one room of planks where thirty or forty of them slept," their bedding of straw. The census taker in Dodge County, Wisconsin, simply wrote "shanty" to indicate the real estate held by the Irish railroad laborers in his district.

From such conditions came health problems, with sporadic flareups of devastating diseases. Ague, a form of malaria, was prevalent throughout the Old Northwest and was widely believed to arise from gases released by plowing the previously unopened soil. Unaware that the real culprit was mosquitoes breeding in the swampy prairies and bottoms, pioneers came up with a variety of cures for "the ager." Canal company ledgers reveal that laborers received large amounts of quinine, the preferred remedy for malaria.

But a more destructive killer arrived in the Upper Mississippi just in time for the great influx of immigrants in the 1830s and 1840s—cholera, carried from Europe on an emigrant ship to Quebec in 1830. It traveled up the rivers and overland with the tide of immigrants, reaching the region in 1832 with troops arriving to fight in the Black Hawk war. The death toll began to rise so rapidly in Chicago that a federal official there reported all families had fled, "gone in different directions to escape from this malignant disease." Cities took on a funereal tone as houses were draped with black crepe.

The suddenness of cholera's attack was terrifying as it swept along the canal and railroad lines. A La Salle priest reported that "twenty-four hours was the term set down by the destroyer," and perfectly healthy persons suddenly felt uneasiness, followed by internal burning and a craving for cold drinks. Then came vomiting and intestinal spasms, giving way to slowness of circulation, sunken eyes, cold skin, and finally collapse. The canal company gave ninety-day extensions to contractors in 1845 because of the time lost to the disease.

The search for a cause found many possibilities, as had been true with ague. A Chicago newspaper offered the explanation that "the miasmatic poison which is supposed to be lurking in the system, when cholera is epidemic, is brought into vigorous action by the quickened circulation which alarm produces." Trepidation, therefore, was not advised. Camphor doses were widely recommended as a cure. Belleville and other communities burned huge piles of wood during the summers to purify the atmosphere. The low-hanging smoke of those sultry days became linked with memories of the cholera years. Sanitation was crucial in the spread of the disease, but canal crews lived almost exclusively in swampy, often fetid areas along the river bottoms, where sanitation was poor and water supplies were frequently polluted. Cholera found them there, destroying them in their shanties. "The plague-stricken region was, with hardly an exception, Catholic," a La Salle priest lamented. Soon canal construction was at a standstill; fluctuations in numbers of workmen were dramatic, "attributable mainly to the severe sickness of the past season, which still confines one hundred at least to their shanties," a canal engineer stated in late 1838. Another official said that many employees remained along the line, but "have not yet recovered their strength sufficiently to labor."

Beyond this, the canal's chief engineer noted that the summer illnesses "discouraged laborers abroad from coming here (for exaggerated reports of the unhealthiness of the country were everywhere circulated)" as well as driving off men already hired. To recruit adequate numbers of laborers, the chief engineer urged efforts to obtain employees "from a distance," and campaigns "to correct the misrepresentations that have been made in relation to the sickness, to show the liberal wages uniformly paid upon this canal, and the advantages that this country presents over most every other for the investment of their earnings."

Although the chief engineer closed his annual report in December 1838 with the hopeful explanation that the sickness "from whatever cause it may have proceeded...was unusual, and it will not likely occur again," the record of the following decades showed cholera rampaging sporadically through the region, especially among immigrants. It laid low hundreds of canal employees during the project's rebirth in the mid and late forties and stimulated campaigns to build a hospital in

La Salle and an orphan asylum in Ottawa. In St. Louis, Catholics pledged to erect a monument to Saint Joseph if, through his intercession, they were left untouched by the cholera epidemic. Although the parish had been the site of up to twenty-five funerals a day during the outbreak, it was later claimed that no one was stricken after signing the pledge, and the resulting Shrine of Saint Joseph is still standing. By late 1845 the continuing reign of illness caused the Illinois and Michigan Canal secretary to blame "the excessive insalubrity of the season" for lack of progress, and a year later he reported that "more than three-fourths of the officers and men on the line of the canal have been prostrated for most of the last two months."

Cholera, ague, and other diseases knew no occupational limits. From Marshall, an Illinois community near the Indiana line, a clergyman reported in 1851 that "there has been a great deal of sickness through this whole region, and more deaths than I have known any season since I have been in the West." In Chicago the following year, a Norwegian pastor said that although the cholera toll was less severe than in 1848, there was "much more among the emigrants than for the past two seasons," and he was forced to convert his home into a hospital. Another Illinois clergyman's letter, in 1854, noted the swift attacks that made cholera a dreaded word around the world: "In Greenwood we have had some experience on a small theatre of the fearfulness of that mysterious scourge the cholera. Five persons in two families died in a few days. They would be well one day and dead the next.... They were Norwegians but had been seven or eight years in the country.... On Friday [a Norwegian woman] had buried a son; on the Sabbath her oldest boy a lad of thirteen had harnessed up his horses and started alone with his father's corpse at twilight to go with it three miles to the grave. Monday this lad was taken low."

The immigrants who arrived to build the prairie railroads in the 1850s had ample warning of the illnesses that awaited them. The *Allgemeine Auswanderungszeitung,* a German emigrant newspaper, informed its readers in 1851 that cholera was abundant in Illinois and Missouri "with many victims." Such reports prompted the Illinois Central to use recruiting advertisements that promised "permanent employment in a healthy climate." Cholera quickly numbered many of the newly arrived railroad workers among its victims, and a Freeport man wrote that "twenty-four men who had been working on the railroad took dinner and ate very heartily—being to all appearances sound in health. When lo ere the sun had set all had closed their eyes in death—cholera was the cause." Most of the diseases' victims thereabout, he added, were "among railroad hands and foreigners."

Up and down the Illinois Central cholera spread its toxic web, back and forth along the crisscrossing lines that formed a network of rails throughout the Upper Mississippi region in the 1850–1855 period. Because many of its victims were at the bottom rungs of society, their deaths tended to be ignored despite their numbers. "There have been a few deaths from cholera," a young engineer in Alton wrote to his father, "nothing however to excite alarm and mainly among new emigrants, laborers on the rail road."

The stories multiplied. Over and over, the victims of cholera were railroad laborers and immigrants. A Peru work gang lost 130 to cholera in two days, and construction of the bridge over the Illinois River at nearby La Salle was repeatedly delayed in the summer of 1853 due to cholera, until a large force of men was added in the fall. A similar problem occurred that year where the Illinois Central crossed Salt Creek, south of Bloomington. "Some delay has been occasioned by severe sickness among the laborers during the past summer," it was reported. According to a story handed down in that area among members of the Funk family, a mass grave in Funk's Grove cemetery contains remains of fifty-two construction laborers who died of cholera while building the Mississippi and Chicago line nearby in 1853.

Farther south, in the Illinois Central's construction division near Cairo, a contractor lamented in 1854 that "sickness broke out among Burk's men—and my men all left." Cholera still retained its virulence by 1855, as construction was finishing on most of the major lines. At the Terre Haute and Alton road's crossing over the Okaw River near Shelbyville, "fifty died of it and the work has been stopped," an Illinois Central official reported, adding that "it is very healthy along our line and I hear of no sickness of any of our men." But the town of Shelbyville itself lost 200 from its population of 1,600 to cholera that summer of 1855, lending some credence to the tales circulating in the East that life expectancy in Illinois was no more than six months. At least that was true for some.

The immigrants died of more than disease in this early foray by the Industrial Revolution into the American frontier. The work was dangerous, involving as it did new machinery and unfamiliar processes as well as excessive heat and cold. Despite the fact that conditions were widely recognized as new and unprecedented, the legal environment remained tied to centuries of common law precedents, doctrines leaving workmen with little support in case they were injured on the job. Cave-ins repeatedly claimed victims among the railroad construction crews. A typical incident occurred when a thirty-foot bank suddenly gave way as workmen were digging south of Bloomington and three shovelers were buried. One was quickly freed, but the others were reached two-and-a-half hours later—Duffenbah, a German, and Kelly, an Irishman. "They were followed to the grave by a large number of their comrades," the local newspaper reported. When a passenger train crashed into a construction train, the *Chicago Tribune* announced in a relieved tone that "to the surprise of all it was found that only one man was killed and comparatively few were injured."

A paradox soon appeared, because passenger accident liability on the railroads was changing quickly in this era. Everyone could see that the railroad was a totally new ingredient in daily life and large numbers of innocent people—the passengers—could be killed or injured by the negligence of someone else. The Illinois legislature in 1853 set $5,000 as the amount a railroad would pay as compensation in fatal accidents where the company was careless or reckless. But liability for work accidents was not modernized so easily. The common law remained the ruling doctrine and was mainly on the side of employers. The workers assumed the risks inherent in the job. Any negligence by employees removed all company liability, and negligence by a fellow worker freed the employer from all liability also. Companies could, and did, provide payments to some victims of job accidents, but during the railroad-construction era the injured could count on little. Survivors' benefits were also limited, as a widow found when she received only $300 from the Illinois Central "for the loss of Frederick O. Leffingwell, her late husband, from injuries sustained by him while in the employment of the said Company, upon their Railroad, and resulting in his death." It would be almost another half-century before juries, judges, and legislatures would carry out a revolution in this area of the law.

This was the less-publicized underside of the internal improvements frenzy that swept across the Upper Mississippi country in the antebellum decades. More than the region's physical appearance was changing when the last spike was driven on the Illinois Central on September 27, 1856. Customs, economic procedures, and attitudes were also being transformed as the immigrants ended their initiation into American life.

To be sure, the physical changes were extensive. By 1854 Chicago had seventy-four trains a day—thirty-seven each way—run by ten railroad companies. This was just one outward sign of the economic transformation resulting from the fact that more than 1,750 miles of track had been laid in Illinois during the hectic 1853–1855 period; Wisconsin had 750 miles of track by 1858, and Iowa and Missouri were enthusiastically entering the railroad era.

The exciting prospect of new goods and new markets was hailed in mammoth celebrations whenever lines or even sections of lines were completed. The pounding of the "last spike" became a common celebration in those years. As the Illinois Central put down its final rails into Cairo in 1854, large crowds pressed near, "the men dressed in their snuff-colored jeans, and the women with gaudy-colored calicoes, check aprons, and big sun-bonnets." A new world was being created, and they wanted to witness its birth. At Union Grove, Illinois, a pastor enthusiastically reported that the coming of the railroad "has greatly increased the business in this region—many families have moved in—property has increased in value—all the available land has been entered on the line of the rail road and society is rapidly changing." The economic impact was enormous. By 1858 only one-sixth of the grain receipts in Milwaukee still came by team. The rest now entered the city by train as rail connections touched the Mississippi River at Prairie du Chien and La Crosse. Recognition of the economic value to Iowa was seen when residents of Iowa City gathered to help crews finish the railroad through to their town in late 1855, even though this meant the city would have to provide the $50,000 promised to any line reaching there before 1856. The citizens' efforts paid off. At midnight

"On the Chicago-St. Louis Railroad."

Franz Holzlhuber, a German artist, traveled throughout the United States and Canada in the 1850s. He was entranced by the vast prairies and once witnessed an Iowa prairie fire. In this 1859 watercolor, Holzlhuber used his imagination to show the railroad crossing the prairies.

Courtesy of the Glenbow Museum, Calgary, Canada.

on December 31 the engine crawled on temporary rails into Iowa City to win the prize and open the railroad era for Iowa.

New towns were born, but others died. Illinois jumped from eighteenth in the nation in railroad mileage in 1850 (when it had 111 miles of track) to second in the nation in 1860, by which time it had 2,790 miles of track, exceeded only by Ohio's 2,946 miles. Wisconsin's limited rail mileage remained concentrated in the southern counties until after the Civil War, and the newly launched railroad eras of Iowa and Missouri also waited until the postwar era for boom times.

Their labors on the canals and railroads ended, the immigrants moved on to other places, joined the rush for California, or settled on farms and in cities of the region. Although conventional wisdom has it that the Irish did not become farmers, census materials and other evidence make it clear that large numbers settled on farmland across the Upper Mississippi region. Many Irish canal workers took this step after the scrip with which they were paid was ruled acceptable for purchasing land from the state. An historian of Illinois settlement has noted that "as a consequence the farming population of that part of the state immediately bordering the Illinois River from Peoria northward and along the Illinois-Michigan canal is composed largely of Irish." Another study claims that "in the farm belt, about one-third of the Irish were engaged in agriculture" by 1850. Former congressman John Wentworth recalled covering his eastern Illinois district in the early years and often encountering a lone Irishman tilling the soil, but on a second visit, "I found more Irishmen there, or else the original one had gone." For the immigrants, this much-criticized "clannishness" was one means of protection, and it produced hundreds of heavily Irish or heavily German communities.

Most railroad companies, but especially those given large land grants, worked diligently to settle farmers and build communities along their lines. The Illinois Central, with its enormous land donation, was a leader in this, although the 1856 land grant for four trans-Iowa rail lines stimulated the advertising and recruiting in that new state. After the Illinois Central was warned in 1854 that it was losing newcomers to Iowa and other areas because it lacked a German-speaking agent to meet immigrants in New York, the line launched a vigorous campaign in both Germany and the eastern United States that helped bring thousands of Germans to settle on the company's Illinois lands.

Experiences of the immigrants in these early years of settlement had not always been favorable for the development of amicable relations with other regional and national groups in their new homeland. These immigrants received several lessons while aiding the spread of industrialism. One of the first, most unavoidable lessons was that canal and railroad construction work was extremely difficult and unhealthy, and it fastened on the laborers a rank far below that of other occupations. An Irish immigrant facing poverty lamented, "I suppose for the purpose of earning clothes [etc.] I shall have to go (greatly against my will) to work on some canal or railroad amongst the wicked, ignorant, profligate dregs of society."

It was a common attitude. "Railroading steemboating and canaling ruines a great portion of our fine countrymen," an Irish immigrant wrote home from Peoria County, Illinois, in 1854. Railroad labor, contended an Irish priest writing on the plight of Catholic immigrants, "is undoubtedly the worst description of work, either as regards their temporal comforts or spiritual welfare." And another Irishman warned his uncle that employees in America "have to work more steadily and more lively than you do in Ireland." After ten or twelve years of such labor, he added, the employee "is of very little use afterwards—he becomes old before his time, and generally dies unheeded." These stories became part of the legacy of the canal and railroad era, considerably at variance with the hope and exuberance with which the projects were launched across the Upper Mississippi Valley.

It became evident to immigrants that they were often victimized in their adopted land, whether by falling for "a Yankee trick" that left them broke after a presumed friend had absconded or by the frequent cases of wage delays or cuts, unannounced layoffs, or desertions by contractors. Even a new Catholic church for the Irish canal workers in La Salle fell victim to this when the local banker who had donated land for the structure ran away, leaving the canal workers $9,000 short and the church without title to the land.

The immigrants' condition was never so demoralized as to stop them from organizing to protect themselves, however. Out of the early troubles with foremen

The railroad quickly tied in with stagecoach lines and canalboats to offer transport across the region. This 1856 poster proclaimed the Illinois Central's many connections.

Courtesy of the Chicago Historical Society.

ILLINOIS CENTRAL

RAIL ROAD

CONNECTING

CHICAGO WITH CAIRO, ST. LOUIS AND GALENA:

The most reliable and only continuous Railroad communication between these places and Chicago.

362 MILES AIR LINE.

TRAINS LEAVE CHICAGO [WELLS STREET DEPOT:]

St. Louis and Cairo Express, at - - - 8·45
every evening (except Saturdays,) arriving at St. Louis at 4.30 P. M., and at Cairo at 8.30 P. M. Passengers for *Springfield, Jacksonville* and *Naples,* take this train and arrive early the following morning.

Amboy & Decatur Accommodation at 9.20
A. M., every morning. (except Sundays,) connecting at Mendota with trains North to Amboy and stations above, and at Decatur with trains of Great Western Railroad.

Galena Express at 9·45 A. M. & 4·10 P. M.,
every day (except Sundays), arrives at Galena at 6.00 P. M. and 1.15 A. M.

PASSENGERS TAKING EITHER THE

ST. LOUIS AND CAIRO NIGHT EXPRESS,

OR THE

AMBOY & DECATUR ACCOMMODATION,

Connect with trains at Mendota, for all Stations on the Main Line and Galena Branch of the Illinois Central Railroad.

FOR NEW ORLEANS

AND ALL PLACES ON THE

OHIO AND LOWER MISSISSIPPI RIVERS

AND THEIR TRIBUTARIES.

No Steamboat passes Cairo, going either up or down, without stopping and

FROM CAIRO,

The most favorable opportunities are presented to passengers to take Boats either for the

PRINCIPAL CITIES of the SOUTH WEST,

Or less important places.

THE ONLY DIRECT ROUTE FOR GALENA, DUBUQUE, ST. PAUL AND MINNESOTA.

Both Galena Trains connect with Steamboats at Galena, daily, for the whole Upper country.

THROUGH TICKETS can be had at the M. C. R. R. Ticket Office, S. W. corner of Lake and Dearborn Sts., and at the WELLS STREET PASSENGER DEPOT.

and employers came protests and "turn-outs" that provided the germ for an eventual union movement of considerable strength in the region, especially in Chicago and Milwaukee. The first strikes in the Chicago area came among the canal workers during the late 1830s, and strikes erupted again in 1847 when the workers demanded more agreeable foremen as well as a wage raise. These struggles were lost, but in their defeat the immigrants gained valuable experience for the coming years as the foreign-born continued to provide the nuclei for labor organization. After the Icarians (French utopians who followed the Mormons to Nauvoo in 1849 and remained through the mid-1850s), the major radical critique of capitalism in the region was advanced by the German-language *Der Proletarier,* published in Chicago from 1853 on. Chicago Germans sent representatives in 1858 to a New York convention of the *Arbeiterbund* that called for the right of revolution and the right of labor to organize, protested the treatment of labor by capital, and urged workers to elect their own candidates to office. One year later the *Arbeiterbund* transferred its executive offices to Chicago.

Such moves further separated immigrants from the native population, laying the groundwork for the later stereotype that all labor radicals were of foreign origin. These early leaders of labor protest collided with the philosophies of a rural, preindustrial society and were criticized by those who had little familiarity with wage labor, digging a canal, or grading a railroad line. "These misguided men are led by a few fanatics and agitators," the *Western Citizen* stated in 1853 when reporting a strike by Chicago laborers seeking a shorter Saturday workday. The editor charged that the protest's leaders "assume to regulate all the business affairs between workmen and their employers, and pretend to be the true friends of the laborers." These "strikers and unionists" were headed from "one folly to another," the editor added, "and it is difficult to tell where they will stop."

As well as organizing to further protect themselves in this threatening environment, the Europeans also brought their churches, their festivals, their day-to-day customs, such as a glass of whiskey after work or a Sunday afternoon visit to a beer garden. And they spoke proudly of the monuments they were creating. This was the theme of Thomas D'Arcy McGee, a famous Irish patriot, immigrant, and writer, who pointed with pride to the structures created by his compatriots as they worked westward on public projects in America. A touring Irish priest lectured in Chicago in 1853 and impressed one of his countrymen when he "told the Yankees what the Irish were." To hear this priest talk, the listener added, "You would think it was the great sinewey arm of the Irishman done everything in America, made their rail roads dug their canals stopped the great Mississippi—in fact it was they done everything."

Many of the native-born watched this immigrant influx with apprehension. A transplanted New Englander, Fletcher Webster, son of the Massachusetts senator Daniel Webster, wrote home as canal construction was beginning at Peru, Illinois, that "we are surrounded by Irish—More than half of the Col's tenants and all his workmen and women are from Green Erin." He added disparagingly, "They steal from us by the wholesale. I hope a few years will make a great change in the population of Peru and Salisbury." But such a change toward Webster's preference did not occur, for Peru and adjacent La Salle became among the most immigrant of cities in a region swelled by the "monster immigration." To many native-born Americans of Webster's background, these newcomers were strange and unwelcome, with habits and activities that boded ill for the future, for the immigrants' activities and beliefs often clashed with the traditions and dreams held by many New Englanders and other eastern Protestants, who were also flocking into the Great Valley of the West.

5. Saving "This Dark Valley"

The Iowa missionary was desperate as he sent his quarterly report east late in 1841. "Now is the seed time of this territory," he pleaded. "Now, the people every where want and demand the Gospel. Preachers of some kind, they will have—Mormons, Catholics, Campbellites, or followers of Kneeland." True religion, he stressed, must not miss this opportunity.

The analogy of seedtime was used repeatedly as settlement rolled into the Upper Mississippi Valley. It carried echoes of the missionary impulse present among westering peoples since Columbus was authorized to save Indian souls and the Puritans came to New England to create their City on a Hill.

As the frontier churches appealed for help in the 1830s and 1840s to save "this dark valley," they were spurred on by a mounting sense of urgency. Foreign influence, infidelity, and the power of competing religious groups were all described in fearful terms by missionaries who realized it was now or never. The region was filling up. The Great Valley "if *once* lost, will be lost *but once*," they warned. There would be no second chance.

The presence of Catholics in this rush of settlement added to the desperation of Protestant missionaries to be first to "plant" their brand of religion in the region. "Already almost every spot of promise in the West is more or less preoccupied" by Catholics and infidelity, the *Home Missionary* asserted in 1839, so that "what is done in this cause must be done quickly." But Catholics felt the same urgency. Noting Peoria's rise in importance in the late 1830s, a Chicago priest wrote to his bishop that "it is now the time to plant." Expanding on this theme, the leading European Catholic missions agency called it "bad economy to delay the establishment of Christian institutions where the land belongs, so to speak, to the first occupant," and in this way first occupancy became the desire of Catholic missionaries and Protestant circuit riders as well as pioneer farmers.

The churchmen's way was difficult, for thousands of settlers lost their religion while moving west, and many others were thrown into situations where traditional ties were weakened. Some saw opportunity in this, for the Upper Mississippi Valley was in a "forming condition," as a religious leader argued in 1839. "Hundreds of communities are now in an elementary state. The concretion of the materials into permanent forms is but just commencing." Similarly, a German Catholic leader urged increased missionary work in the West, partly because that region had "most Germans and the least priests," but also "because there affairs are still developing and the church ought not to be without its influence thereby." Other religious leaders from non-English-speaking lands stressed the need to preserve their native language among immigrants as a means to retain religious faith. This thrust another ingredient into the vortex of religious controversy as the missionaries followed the settlers westward.

The focus of their energies in the 1830–1860 years was primarily upon the Upper Mississippi Valley, although it turned sporadically westward to Texas, Oregon, California, and Kansas as events brought those areas to national attention. Church leaders were further stimulated to action as they realized that America's center of power was shifting westward with the masses of new settlers. An estimate made in 1839 was that the Great Valley would contain 200 million people when the nation's total population reached 300 million. Just one year later, as a result of the 1840 census, the eastern states lost thirty representatives in Congress while the West gained twelve. The development of a western majority seemed a certainty. Where would the West's affinities lie then, "with the boisterous blasphemer, the duellist and the assassin"? If so, "the wave of ruin will roll over all that is fair in the land of the Pilgrims, quenching the fire on their altars, and sweeping away the monuments reared by the fathers' piety and toil." And so the missionary movement did more than follow the sons and daughters of the East—it sought to shape the developing lands. The eminent theologian Lyman Beecher, especially concerned over rising Catholic immigration, called the struggle in the new regions "a conflict of institutions for the education of her sons, for the purposes of superstition, or evangelical light; of despotism, or liberty."

While showing apprehension over the West, missionaries also devoted much oratory to the subject of America's future greatness, in which the West figured prominently. Although Calvinist predestination for individuals was losing favor on the frontier, a parallel belief in predestination for the nation seemed to be developing. This idea gained followers as the United States surged westward in the pre-Civil War decades, first expanding into Texas with the migration of American settlers, then moving on to the Oregon country, and finally winning the Southwest with the Mexican War. As the nation acquired these territories, the American people seemed participants in a divine plan, and Catholics as well as Protestants, immigrants as well as native-born, were infected with the fever of exultant nationalism. Father Boniface Wimmer, a German Catholic priest active in the West, proclaimed in 1848 that "here if anywhere, the destiny of the Catholic church, yea of the whole world, will be decided." The "young eagle of the free union has hardly begun his practice-flights," he added, and it was already clear that America would someday dominate the world. If this was certain to occur, Father Wimmer asked, "is it therefore indifferent which principles become dominant here?... What will happen if those [Protestant] fanatics obtain the control of the government?"

But patriotism was often mingled with anti-Catholicism, and the combination nettled Catholic missionaries who might otherwise have joined the hurrahs for national expansion. Abbé Cretin, traveling from Dubuque to Boston in 1846 as the United States and Mexico prepared to clash over Texas, wrote that the American government saw the conflict "as a war of religion.... There are already rumors of sending five or six thousand yankees to Mexico to civilize that country, that is to say, to Protestantize it." Americans, he added, are becoming proud, and "they pride themselves particularly about their railroads, about their steamships, at the sight of these large cities which seem suddenly to spring from the earth." Such people were to be handled delicately, "like puffed-up persons," the Catholic leader added.

The missionary impulse came from several sources. One of the major centers was New England, from whose seminaries the spirit of missions went westward with its people, ideas, and institutions into western New York state, along the Erie Canal, through the Western Reserve of Ohio and Indiana's rolling lands, and finally onto the fertile prairies that reached to the Mississippi and beyond. One estimate puts the total New England exodus at 800,000 between 1790 and 1820, principally in a band westward toward, and later including, Iowa. This emigration included Methodists and Baptists as well as the dominant Congregationalists and lesser numbers of Presbyterians.

Few groups in American history migrated with more consciousness of their roots. When New Englanders floated down the Ohio River to found Marietta in 1788 they traveled in a flatboat named the *Mayflower* and reenacted the Pilgrims' landing at Plymouth as they stepped ashore at their new Ohio home. In the New England-dominated settlement of Freeport in northern Illinois, participants in the Fourth of July celebration in 1845 included lineal descendants of Pilgrim fathers William Bradford and William Brewster. A banner was paraded that had been formed from "a yellow satin coverlet, brought over by Governor Bradford, in the May Flower, 1620."

By 1847, when Wisconsin held its prestatehood constitutional convention, twenty-four of the sixty-nine delegates were New England natives and five more were of New England stock. In Illinois at least twenty-two communities by mid-century had started as colonies originating in New England or New York (which in many ways mirrored New England). Chicago's leadership was heavily dominated by men of that section, with nine of the city's first ten mayors coming from New England or New York. The New England Society became a prestigious Chicago organization, annually commemorating the anniversary of the Pilgrims' landing. At the group's 1849 celebration, the choir "sang the old Pilgrim Song, so familiar to all New England ears, with fine effect, calling up a throng of early memories and patriotic emotions in the breasts of all present who hailed from the fatherland."

Representing several denominations, many of these New Englanders sought to continue—not escape—the all-pervading religious presence of their native region. In 1831 the group that formed Princeton, Illinois, stated before departing from Northampton, Massachusetts, that members were seeking to improve their living standards, "provided the privileges of a social, moral, and religious character which they now have and which they highly value, can be made secure to them in their future home." Upper Mississippi settlements with large numbers of New Englanders were soon marked by the presence of public schools, libraries, and a proliferation of temperance and other reform groups, as well as a climate of fervent religious interest.

These activities did not necessarily betoken a powerful clergy. One of the recurring themes in antebellum history is the apparent decline in influence both of New England as a section and of the New England clergy. At the end of the American Revolution the Congregational church (the Puritan church of New England) was America's largest religious body, ensconced in both state legislation and the popular mind as arbiter of moral issues across a large part of the North. But gradually the New England states had ended government aid to the Congregational church, while the denomination's influence was steadily eroded by secularization and the success of outside proselytizers. Also, the New England clergy generally opposed American entry into the War of 1812, an unpopular stand that speeded the decline of their prestige.

As the eastern tide of emigrants into the Great Valley encountered that originating in Ireland and Germany, the New Englanders discovered much that needed reforming, much that made them hark back to earlier times. Lyman Beecher contended that Americans were once "a homogeneous people," and he took fright at the influx of strangers. These foreign immigrants were "unacquainted with our institutions, unaccustomed to self-government, inaccessible to education," and open to intrigue. He raised the possibility that European potentates were purposely sending their paupers to the United States to help the princes seize power. This theme of the need to protect democracy appeared frequently in New England missionary writings. The American Home Missionary Society resolved in 1848 that "the thorough evangelization of the masses of the people is the only guaranty of representative democracy." To save the nation, then, it was necessary to create a replica of the land of their childhood. "Here, fifty years hence, will be another New England in the West," a clergyman predicted of Minnesota in 1854. Church colleges and architecture, and even entire communities were compared hopefully to those of New England; a Beloit College graduate described the school as "truly the child of New England Puritanism as though its walls were standing on Plymouth Rock." The nearby Rock River Valley was praised for its "New England look," and a missionary at Upper Alton, Illinois, who saw his congregation losing members to the westward migration, wondered "why may not the Pacific slope be made another, even a better New England?" Looking at his own somewhat discouraging field of operations, a transplanted New Englander suggested that, if "a few New Englanders" could be brought to southern Illinois, "that portion of our state would soon be more sought after than the North."

Southern Illinois especially appeared as a barrier against the spread of New England influence. Missionaries sent to Illinois by the Congregationalists or their allies, the Presbyterians, found little fertile soil for their brand of Christianity once they headed south from Springfield. "At the present time, there is scarcely a bright spot in the Egypt of Illinois," a New Englander reported from Perry County in 1855, and others sent back reports of loose living, a lack of religious interest, and a contempt for reforms. "The people are principally from the southern states and therefore a long way behind the times in all the reforms of the day." Worse, the Illinois Egyptians were found to be ignorant on religious subjects; one missionary encountered over 50 percent adult illiteracy "and not one in fifty can repeat the Ten Commandments." A traveling agent of the American Bible Society discovered also that a third to a fifth of the people he had visited during the previous year "were without a whole copy of the Bible!" All seemed to agree that southern Illinois was "a hard field" for the New England missionary.

Beyond this conflict in Egypt, New Englanders ran into frequent opposition because of their own origins and education. Frontier settlers everywhere often viewed New Englanders and New Yorkers as a bit too smart, a bit too crafty, perhaps a bit too much the "Yankee peddler" (the character long known in frontier folklore as a sharp trader). This feeling surfaced in Iowa, where a New England missionary told of encountering prejudice because "I am an eastern man and am called an educated man and a Presbyterian." He reported that following one of his sermons an elderly member of his congregation had remarked, "I understand he is a college larnt chap, and they generally talk so you cannot understand them." Clergymen were not the only targets of this prejudice. A Springfield resident bolstered his application for a position with the Illinois Central Railroad by stressing that he was a western man and so would not need to devote half or more of his energies to keep down "the prejudices that exist here in the West against eastern men, eastern capital, etc."

These themes of antimissionary feelings, of desperate concern for the future, of the absence or weakening of churches were all part of the fabric of a tumultuous era of American religious history. Church records, newspaper accounts, and other documents of that period show a society in flux—forming, breaking apart, joining again—and churchmen had to compete for the loyalty of a population turned loose in this swirl of ideas. This was especially true on the frontier in the early decades of the nineteenth century, when old-style Calvinist predestination began to erode rapidly under the revivalistic onslaught of Arminian ideas, ideas that stressed the individual's ability to be saved for Christ by his own free will, rather than being eternally blocked from salvation by a previously decided divine plan. The Arminian philosophy was visible in the declaration of faith voted in 1851 by the annual session of the Nine Mile Baptist Association, covering five counties in southern Illinois:

VI. Of the Freeness of Salvation.

That the blessings of salvation are made free to all by the Gospel, that it is the immediate duty of all to accept them by a cordial and obedient faith; and that nothing prevents the salvation of the greatest sinner on earth, but his determined depravity and voluntary rejection of the gospel, which rejection will submit him to an aggravated condemnation.

Sects multiplied under the impact of Arminian thought and the belief that individuals should interpret the Bible for themselves. Preaching often took on an ecumenical aspect, however, as most denominations found much in common, but there was still a wide-ranging sense of competition. The way lay open for religious groups to gain adherents if they could somehow find the key to success in this new environment.

This was a strange world for many who were accustomed to the steady, seemingly unchanging nature of churches in the East and, especially, Europe. The bishop of Vincennes warned in a letter to clergy in Ireland in 1843 that "the habits, customs and manners of the people" in the frontier areas were so different from those of Europe that prospective missionaries needed a year or two of American residence "in studying the moral habits of the people" before beginning their life's work. In Protestant congregations the heterogeneity had a similar impact on some newcomers. One missionary reported eighteen ministers of various denominations working within seven miles of his little village in Illinois. An Iowa minister described the eleven members of his Knoxville church, who had come from seven states and two European countries: "Three were originally Congregationalists, two were Associate Reformed Presbyterians; one a Lutheran; two Methodists; two Cumberland Presbyterians, and one person reared under Presbyterian influences." Lack of religious training was also abundant, and a Missouri minister reported sadly that members of his church at Deep-Water were "so unaccustomed to attend on the means of grace, their minds so little cultivated, their feelings so blunted" that he sometimes felt he was in "a land of darkness and death."

This conglomeration of listeners called forth varied preaching styles. Peter Cartwright, a Methodist circuit rider who became the most famous frontier preacher, held that westerners would respond only to extemporaneous speaking. He typified the Upper South and older frontier in religious style. Cartwright once traveled on circuit with an educated eastern Presbyterian minister, who, he said, had transported west "a number of old manuscript sermons, and read them to the people; but as to common sense, he had very little, and he was almost totally ignorant of the manners and usages of the world, especially this new western world." Unable to adapt to western ways, the easterner became discouraged and left.

Chicago's principal exponent of the arm-waving and pulpit-thumping style of preaching in the mid-1840s was Reverend W.M.D. Ryan, a Methodist. His first sermon there impressed one witness, who wrote, "He pounded the Bible, he flew from side to side of the old box pulpit, he exulted, and exclaimed, and harangued, and aroused, melted to tears, and exhilarated to shouts the vast throng." In later sermons the Reverend Ryan "would sometimes reach over the pulpit and opening the doors of the lower world would let his congregation have such a vivid sight of the damned they would quiver." But then he would show heaven "with the overflow of glory" and the people "would shout for joy."

Flavel Bascom, a Congregational missionary in Illinois, told of the distaste he felt in sharing a pulpit with such a preacher, who began his talk with indiscriminate and unconnected Bible quotations: "Thus he went bellowing and blowing through the Bible shedding no more light upon the passages quoted, than the roar of artillery does upon our Declaration of Independence." Bascom conceded, however, that as he walked to his horse and buggy after the service he heard two women contrasting the styles of preaching. Of the "pioneer" preacher's presentation, one said she "allowed that was the greatest sarmon ever preached in that house." "Yes," said the other, "but I don't like these Yankee preachers, they are always proving things, just like lawyers."

Catholics looked with disgust and occasionally with a twinge of jealousy at such unfettered practices. They noted that the Protestants could travel freely, unencumbered by sacred vessels or ritual, preaching from tree stumps in the open air. Father Samuel Mazzuchelli, who came west in 1830 and served for several years in Galena, complained that the Protestant preachers "have very scant doctrine" and "do not study any theology." The eloquence of the Baptists and Methodists, he asserted, "consists in much loud speaking, in quoting the Bible in every sense that may suit them, in pronouncing the name Jesus innumerable times, in violently censuring sinners, inviting them to conversion through simple faith in the Savior, praising the word of the Gospel, and readily promising Paradise to their followers." But nowhere, Father Mazzuchelli lamented, was

**Father Samuel Mazzuchelli, O.P.
(1806-1867).**

An Italian, Father Mazzuchelli came to the United States in 1828 and reached Mackinac in 1830. He served a church at Green Bay in 1834, then traveled to Galena the following year, working for several years in Iowa and in the lead region of southwestern Wisconsin and northwestern Illinois.

Courtesy of the State Historical Society, Iowa State Historical Dept.

there a place in frontier Protestantism for penance, restitution, unity of faith, obedience to the church, or the necessity of the sacraments. On the contrary, these preachers attacked the Catholic church to cover their own lack of religion, and they had the art to "weep at will and to pass from gravity to gaiety with the utmost facility and swiftness."

Freewheeling revivalism lay at the base of the difference in religious approach that typified the frontier and more settled regions. Although most often connected with Methodists and Baptists, in truth all Protestant denominations used revival meetings at times, joined in them, and sought to add members through them. Peter Cartwright recalled that he had been converted in a campground, and during his life as a circuit rider spent from two to three months each year preaching in camp meetings. Through such events, he added, "the word of God has reached the hearts of thousands that otherwise, in all probability, never would have been reached by the ordinary means of grace."

The shouting, "jerks," and wildness characteristic of frontier revival services offended some newcomers, and nowhere was the gulf between native-born and immigrant more evident than in the disbelief, bewilderment, and revulsion shown by the latter to the frantic jumble of the camp meeting. Gustave Koerner, who came to Illinois from Germany in 1833, once attended a Methodist camp meeting at Shiloh. Some fifty families camped in their covered wagons, while the Koerners and several hundred others rode in from nearby areas. Koerner described the service: "After painting hell and its tortures in the most vivid colors, he invited the sinners to come forward to the anxious seat. Some women did come, mostly Negroes, and they howled like mad.... The most ridiculous thing was his calling for a vote. 'Is anyone here opposed to the Lord? Let us take a vote; those who are for the Lord, will hold up their hands!' Of course, most hands went up. 'Those who are against Him will hold up their hands!' Of course, nobody did. There was howling in every corner of the building; women cried; one negro woman repeatedly jumped up several feet high, and finally fell down. Some of the converted also commenced preaching from the anxious bench. Some tried to sing hymns at the same time.... A good many spectators were laughing and cracking jokes, others courted the girls in the tents and booths."

Father Mazzuchelli visited an eight-day Methodist revival in Burlington, Iowa, which featured numerous ministers preaching several times a day; and said, "They pray, they sing, in no particular order, just as the Spirit moves the minister or the congregation," and some women fainted and remained like corpses for hours.

The importance of revival meetings in the spread of Protestantism during the antebellum years has been stressed repeatedly by historians, some of whom have termed revivals "the core" of that era's Protestantism, a development that helped basic unity evolve through "muddling" distinctions between denominations. Revivals are credited with stimulating lay leadership, emphasizing "the primacy of ethics over dogma," and weakening Calvinist notions of predestination. From the first large-scale camp meeting at Cane Ridge, Kentucky, in August 1801, where attendance was estimated at up to 25,000, through the 1858 resurgence of revivalism that reached eastern cities, vitality pulsed through the denominations with the people's outpouring of energy and concern over leading Christlike lives.

Excited over the impact of this movement upon the Whetstone Creek Freewill Baptist church in Coles County, Illinois, the church clerk was moved to pen his comments in the church minute book:

> I feel it duty to say something about the revival in the Feb. commenceing about our regular monthly meeting—it was the powerfuest Time I ever saw amongst the Baptist about 48 additions at the meeting House & about 29 West of this at a School house near Brother *John Halls* about 3½ miles, makes in all about 77 amost all new converts. I suppose thare has been over 100 new converts since near last Christmus in a smal section of this Country. The Lord Should be Praised. The above written the 10th day of April 1860, by me James Rennels Clk.

Revivals spread widely despite immigrant and eastern criticism. The American Home Missionary Society lashed out at the use of "exciting means" and cautioned its missionaries that it was their duty to "*mould*, rather than to be *moulded by* the tastes of the new settlements." The revivalistic Cumberland Presbyterians originated in a dispute with the Presbyterian Synod of Kentucky, largely over the Cumberland group's flexible approach to licensing preachers and its emphasis on free-will doctrines, both stemming from revival influences. But a few years later, when the Upper Mississippi Valley experienced the boom in immigration, many regular Presbyterian ministers in the region participated in revivals and omitted talk of predestination.

This in turn pointed toward one of the fundamental developments in American religious history during the first half of the nineteenth century: the creation of a general "evangelical united front" joined by the vast majority of Protestants. This was reformed in its foundations, Puritan in outlook, and moving rapidly away from presdestination to Arminianism, that is, to free will. This broad unity developed despite the multiplicity of sects that grew and thrived with the freedom of Biblical interpretation, groups such as the Millerites, who waited for the fast-approaching end of the world, Universalists, Spiritualists, Mormons, and others.

The four major Protestant bodies most active in the Upper Mississippi country were the Methodist, Baptist, Presbyterian, and Congregational churches. They had few major disagreements beyond form of baptism and church organization, although to some these could be crucial. They often worked together, for all stressed regeneration of the individual as a prerequisite for salvation and believed it possible for God's world to be created on earth. From this came their support for both "Immediatism" and "Perfectionism" in the spreading reforms of the antebellum era.

When it came to founding churches in the heterogeneous frontier society, religious groups frequently followed different paths and used different methods. The most structured and most closely tied to strict ritual and doctrine were the Roman Catholics. The most flexible in methods were the Baptists and Methodists, while the Presbyterians, Congregationalists, Lutherans, and smaller denominations fell in between.

Baptists came in various subgroups by the time the tide of settlement reached Wisconsin, Illinois, Iowa, and adjacent areas. With some overlapping, there were Regular, Separate, United, General, Particular, Primitive, "Two-Seed-in-the-Spirit Predestinarian," and Free Will Baptists. They moved out of the East in two major streams: one from Virginia and North Carolina, where they had struggled with the Anglican establishment, and the other from New England and the Middle Atlantic states. New Design, Illinois had a Baptist church by 1796; Missouri, by 1804.

By 1855 this previously small church was the second-largest Protestant denomination in the United States, with more than 1.1 million members. It developed rapidly on the frontier with its use of the self-supporting farmer-preacher, which meant that whenever there were a few Baptists there could be a Baptist church. No waiting for a circuit rider or a missionary from the East was necessary. Most Baptists supported the broad doctrines of the "evangelical united front" while emphasizing adult baptism by immersion. However, some, such as the "Separates," were unhappy with the use of missionaries; others, including the Primitives, had not shaken off Calvinism.

The major Baptist groups were eager supporters of missions. A Massachusetts Baptist organization launched in 1802 to send missionaries to the frontier had evolved by 1832 into the American Baptist Home Mission Society. A year later it dispatched Allen B. Freeman to Chicago in response to a petition from Baptists there, and two months after his arrival, the Chicago church was organized and conducting baptisms in Lake Michigan. The denomination's *Missionary Herald* stated in 1845 that the American Baptist Home Mission Society was active in eighteen states, Canada, and Texas; "the valley of the Mississippi is, however, its principal theatre of action." By 1851 it boasted of 140 active missionaries, including 32 in Illinois, 21 in Wisconsin, 14 in Iowa, 3 in Minnesota, and 1 in Missouri.

John Mason Peck became the best-known Baptist missionary on the Mississippi Valley frontier, gaining fame for his emigrant books that depicted the abundance awaiting settlers. Peck was a New Englander who became a Baptist in 1811, volunteered for western missions in 1817, and was sent to the St. Louis area. In 1822 he moved across the river to St. Clair County, Illinois, and began an active missionary career that had as its legacy numerous Baptist churches, one seminary (Rock Springs, later moved to Alton and a predecessor of Shurtleff College), and a newspaper, the *Western Baptist*. Peck also became known for his opposition to slavery.

John Mason Peck (1789-1858).

The most important Baptist missionary in the region was John Mason Peck, who left the Congregational church of his native New England and came west in 1817. He wrote eight books, launched a newspaper which became the *Western Baptist,* and founded Baptist churches and a seminary.

Courtesy of the Illinois State Historical Library.

An offshoot of the Baptists known as the Christian church, or Disciples of Christ, was also aided in its spread by a lack of complex requirements for either joining or preaching. Led by Alexander Campbell, immigrant son of a Scotch-Irish seceder family from Ireland, the new church was formed in 1811 and supported baptism by immersion. It developed a theology based on the belief that Old Testament law had been abrogated with the coming of Christ. The Sabbath was therefore not holy and paying tithes was no longer required. The Disciples, also referred to as the "Campbellites," grew to some 118,000 members nationwide, and within Illinois the number of Disciples of Christ congregations jumped from 69 in 1850 to 148 in 1860.

The ease of entry into Disciples membership annoyed clergy from stricter denominations, such as those joined in the American Home Missionary Society. In Manchester, Illinois, in 1839, the Campbellites and the Methodists formed the town's largest congregations, each with a hundred members. The AHMS missionary there charged that "the most abandoned wretch in the world can become a member of [the Campbellite] church without a change of life, and yet practice no deception." The Reverend Asa Turner, a Congregational minister in Denmark, Iowa, complained that all the labor of developing Christian beliefs in children and helping them grow in faith was done away with under the Campbellites. "All they have to do," he wrote, "is to take a man and wash him, and he comes up out of the water, pure as an angel." Despite such criticisms the Disciples continued to spread across the region.

The Methodists were similar to the Campbellites in their appeal to a broad spectrum of national, regional, and economic groups, and in the rapidity with which they spread on the Upper Mississippi Valley frontier. They employed the circuit rider system to cover sparsely settled areas and to plant churches early. By 1855 they formed Illinois's largest denomination, with 178,450 members in 405 churches, compared to the second-place Baptists, who had 94,130 members in 282 churches. Nationwide, the Methodists had also become the largest Protestant denomination, a startling change from the time of the American Revolution, when the church ranked as one of the least significant in membership and influence. But the Baptists and Methodists showed a ready adaptation to frontier conditions, and by 1855 they, together, made up 70 percent of Protestant membership nationwide.

How did they do it? The circuit rider was the crucial difference, providing the Methodists with a built-in missionary association that made a separate missionary institution unnecessary. Chicago was included in a circuit before 1831, and in 1834 the town's Methodists built their first church structure. A Presbyterian writer observed enviously in 1843 that "the whole land is covered with a network system of [Methodist] stations and circuits, and the Gospel is carried into thousands of the most remote as well as the most secluded and thinly peopled neighborhoods." This system of circuits operating in annual regional conferences set the Methodists apart from the Baptists, although becoming a Methodist preacher was not difficult in terms of training. A license to preach and organize classes was given to members who felt a "call" and could preach effectively; college or seminary training was generally not discouraged, however.

The Presbyterian and Congregational churches, which joined their mission operations in the West in 1801, had several differences from the Baptists and Methodists. Much more tightly rooted in New England and requiring extensive education for their clergy, the Presbyterians and Congregationalists established colleges and seminaries all along the moving frontier—Illinois College, Grinnell, Beloit, McCormick, Blackburn, Chicago Theological, and others. The two groups tended to seek out New Englanders or the Scotch-Irish to form congregations, rather than rushing to convert all residents of an area. Congregationalists and Presbyterians were usually cool to the emotionalism and free-will philosophies they saw developing around them in other denominations.

These characteristics sometimes worked against the success of the agents sent by the American Home Missionary Society, the two churches' joint organization. "The Presbyterian minister is a very poor preacher for one who has spent eight or nine years learning to preach" was a complaint overheard by an AHMS minister in Pekin, Illinois. Small wonder that Congregational and Presbyterian congregations

Peter Cartwright (1785-1872).

The rapid growth of Methodism on the frontier can be traced through the work of Peter Cartwright, a Methodist circuit rider. He left Kentucky in 1823 and settled in Sangamon County, Illinois, the following year. After fifty-three years of preaching, Cartwright concluded that "the most successful part of my ministry has been on camp-ground." By the 1840s, just sixty years after his church had first broken off from the Episcopal church, Methodists had become America's largest Protestant denomination.

Courtesy of the Illinois State Historical Library.

in such surroundings could become isolated and known as the aristocratic churches, attended by business leaders, and pronounced in their social and economic influence but limited in mass appeal.

Presbyterians in America had developed initially on the frontier and were in a strong position to spread westward after the American Revolution. But their New School-Old School schism, largely over adherence to Calvinist views on predestination, weakened the denomination, as did its frequent repudiation of the revivalists' emotionalism. Old School Presbyterians in particular refused to go along with the joint missionary efforts of the AHMS. They divided with the New School in 1837 and did not rejoin until 1869.

Congregationalists, with their emphasis on the power of the local church, faced enormous hurdles in becoming an active mission church. One congregational leader later concluded, "Our system, as bequeathed to us by the early fathers of New England, was poorly equipped for anything beyond parish-work in that section [New England] of the land." The Plan of Union with the Presbyterians helped overcome some of the structural difficulties, but the Congregational church grew slowly in the Upper Mississippi country, often yielding to the Presbyterians with their supportive denominational structure. (Under the Plan of Union, Congregational and Presbyterian settlers in a frontier district could combine and employ a minister from either denomination. When it came to choosing church affiliation, the local majority ruled, regardless of their minister's denominational loyalty.)

The AHMS's activity across the region was far from minor, however. In 1836, Iowa received its first AHMS missionary, who went to the Dubuque region only to find a Methodist ahead of him. The most famous group of AHMS missionaries in Iowa was the "Iowa Band," eleven Andover Theological Seminary students who agreed in 1842 to serve as missionaries there. In Wisconsin, 121 of the 135 Presbyterian and Congregational ministers active in 1851 had been aided by the AHMS. By 1852 the joint organization was sponsoring 1,065 missionaries, half of them in the West, including 119 in Illinois, 72 in Wisconsin, 41 in Iowa, 29 in Missouri, and 4 in Minnesota. The AHMS said in 1856 that it had planted 400 churches within 150 miles of Chicago. By 1873 the Presbyterians estimated that nine-tenths of their churches west of Pennsylvania and New York had been organized by home missionaries; Congregationalists put their proportion at four-fifths.

The Lutheran church was torn by debates that were sometimes akin to the New School-Old School schism within Presbyterianism, but the sources lay on different ground. Early in the nineteenth century Lutheranism in America seemed to have embarked upon a journey into Americanism, taking on more and more Puritan characteristics while dropping the German language inherited from its German founders.

In 1807 the Lutheran Ministerium of New York switched its official language from German to English. Then came the enormous influx of Germans from the 1830s on, and in 1837 the New York body reversed that 1807 decision and readopted German as the official church language. This was a bow to traditionalist leaders, who viewed the German language as connected to German culture, which rested on the true Lutheran faith.

The Americanization group within Lutheranism made repeated efforts to wrest control from the rising German group, sending bilingual missionaries to the West, espousing the use of English, "free communion," and "new measures" and even instituting the mourners' seat identified with frontier revival meetings. But they were blocked in the late 1830s and again in 1855 when they sought to delete portions of the Augsburg Confession, Lutheranism's basic doctrinal statement.

These reformers of Lutheranism were too late, defeated by the sudden increase in German immigration. But they had not missed by far, for reports of the 1830s show that German preaching was rare in the West. One itinerant German preacher who toured the Upper Mississippi country in those years told of desperate immigrants who promised to divide all their belongings with him if he would remain as a permanent clergyman. Some immigrants traveled up to twenty miles to attend services performed by visiting German ministers, and one family went fifty-four miles to hear an Easter communion service in German. A group of German-speaking Swiss at New Aargau, Illinois, pleaded for a missionary with the argument that they had been without the services of a minister for seventeen years. Soon there were German-speaking Lutheran pastors in bountiful numbers,

Rev. Carl F.W. Walther (1811-1887).

Leader of the Saxon Lutherans called *Alt Lutheraner,* who began arriving in St. Louis in 1839, the Reverend Walther insisted that parochial schools spread with the church. The organization's formal name soon became German Evangelical Lutheran Synod of Missouri, Ohio, and Other States, but it was known as the "Missouri Synod."

Concordia Historical Institute.

arriving with the cresting immigrant tide. The *Alt Lutheraner,* coming in the late 1830s, large numbers of confessional Germans, arriving during the following decade, and the new *Kirchenverein des Westens,* arising in the region from 1840 on, provided clergy either through immigration or through recruitment and training in America.

European aid was important for the growth of Lutheranism. As early as 1835 a group of Connecticut nativists sought missionary aid from the Basel Missionary Society to block the spread of Catholicism in the West. The Basel society responded by dispatching two missionaries, and other help came from such German and Swiss Lutheran missionary organizations as the Evangelical Society for North America in Berlin, the Langenberg Mission Society, and groups in Bremen, Barmen, Hermannsburg, and Neuendettelsau. With such aid it became possible to set up training centers on American soil, as at Gettysburg, Pennsylvania.

Various branches of German Lutheranism appeared, some forming before, some after, the crossing to America. The *Deutscher Evangelische Kirchenverein des Westens* was formed in 1840 in Missouri, and in 1866 it anglicized its name to German Evangelical Synod of the West (it would eventually merge with the Reformed church to form the Evangelical and Reformed church).

Similar offshoots developed among the incoming Norwegians and Swedes, although their numbers were relatively few in the period before 1860. Norwegian dissenters against the established Lutheran church arrived in Wisconsin in the 1840s, forming the Evangelical Lutheran church in America at Jefferson Prairie in 1846. The Norwegian state church lived on, however, in congregations started among Norwegians in Muskego, Wisconsin, in 1843, and across Wisconsin and other states of the region in ensuing years. Many Swedes joined these Norwegian churches, as when the Evangelical Lutheran Synod of Northern Illinois was launched in 1850 by one Swedish and two Norwegian pastors. In 1860 forty-nine congregations came together at Clinton, Wisconsin, to form the Scandinavian Evangelical Lutheran Augustana Synod.

Iowa's new capital of Iowa City had its first Roman Catholic mass celebrated in the home of a German mechanic one day late in 1840. The Holy Sacrifice was first

Rev. Hendrik Peter Scholte (1805-1868).

Leader of the Dutch Free Calvinists who founded Pella, Iowa, in 1847, the Reverend Scholte
became involved in territorial politics. He convinced the Iowa legislature to permit the Hollanders to vote for township officers even
though they lacked the five years' residence required, and he fought Whig and Republican attempts to put through a Maine law.

Courtesy of the State Historical Society, Iowa State
Historical Dept.

offered the next morning in an Irish family's log cabin. Both services were conducted by an Italian missionary priest, who had rushed to the city to beat out Protestant groups in obtaining a choice lot for a Catholic church in the capitol environs. These incidents pointed to major factors in the spread of Roman Catholicism into the Upper Mississippi country; it was based on the immigrant and directed by missionaries sent from the outside, and it struggled in an atmosphere of vigorous competition.

The Roman Catholic church in America found itself in a new era, "almost a second history," after the American revolutionary era. Accustomed to the protection of European kings, the church in the United States saw its traditional bases among the French and Spanish suddenly transformed under a Protestant-directed government in a nation marked by vigorous denominational challenge. "No longer could the papacy depend upon the governments of Europe for its sacred work," one author has remarked. That drastic break with centuries of traditional organization threw up barriers in the church's path. These called forth innovation, and one by one the barriers were overcome; by 1850 Roman Catholics were the largest single church group in America, numbering 3.1 million members.

The growth was spectacular. Some seventy years earlier, Roman Catholic membership had stood at 24,000, mainly in Pennsylvania and Maryland, and these communicants were served by fewer than thirty priests. Many of these early members were English Catholics, who soon moved westward, establishing Catholic churches in Kentucky; some eventually headed on to the Mississippi Valley.

The church was then forced to adapt to the midcontinent frontier. Roman Catholicism had already made some operational changes in America, however. Early intracongregational disputes between French and Irish in Boston and other eastern cities gave rise to the concept of the national parish. The church proclaimed its universality, but the besieged bishops agreed there could be, for example, German parishes located within the geographical area of an Irish parish and vice versa, each serving only those of its own nationality.

Widely held American beliefs in local church self-government collided at this point with Roman Catholic traditions of obeying higher-level authority. This was seen most vividly in the struggles between trustees and priests for control of church property, disputes which appeared in various forms in the West as well as in eastern cities.

Several Wisconsin communities were torn by intra-Catholic feuding due to the spirit of lay domination present among immigrants from Baden, Rhenish Bavaria, Hesse, Trier, and Rhenish Prussia. The Bavarian parish at East Bristol, Wisconsin, opposed clerical control so fervently that the pastor left after being confronted with armed demonstrations. During a visit by Bishop John Martin Henni the opposition yelled, "Down with the bishop!" but his efforts ultimately brought peace. A similar conflict developed in Quincy, Illinois, when Bishop James Oliver Van de Velde ran into a storm of petitions and complaints from German Catholics on the issue of controlling church property. Quincy's Catholics had elected trustees on their own, and these dissidents flocked out of a "beer house or tippling shop" and "came to annoy" Van de Velde. They did not win their fight. A Chicago quarrel over control of church property prompted the bishop to have the church edifice raised four feet off the ground, blocking attendance and frustrating the trustees. A priest who was severely hamstrung by an anticlerical faction at New Westphalia, Missouri, became so frustrated that when he left the community in defeat he attached a notice in Latin to the church door. The statement, as translated, could have come from many priests attempting to deal with the Upper Mississippi Valley's independent-minded and unruly Catholic parishes: "Why should the man who covets hardships hie him to the dusky Indies? Let him come to Westphalia and he will find hardships aplenty."

The trusteeship controversy pointed to an underlying premise of the era; America stood for self-government, so congregational control of churches, as provided in Protestant denominations, was therefore an American solution. Churches that did not permit this were not American. This was hinted when the *Daily Democratic Press* of Chicago argued that the only practical way to settle the trusteeship matter was to let the members of the congregations rule: "It is not a theological question, but one of natural and political right.... Men, in becoming Catholics, are not curtailed of their privileges as citizens in any respect; and while they feel that they as well as the clergy are a part of the church, and contribute largely to its support, they will as a matter of course assume some control over church property—over the edifices where they worship, and the grounds where their bones are to rest."

By this time the Catholic church in the Mississippi Valley and the nation was, even more than the Lutherans, almost entirely an immigrant church. When Bishop Van de Velde wrote to Europe in 1852 of his progress in Illinois, he reported that in three years he had built some forty churches: "among these new churches are nineteen exclusively for Germans; six or eight for mixed congregations; two for French Canadians; and the remainder for those who are Irish or American." Many Protestants noted this direct relationship between immigrant settlements and Catholic churches. One was the AHMS missionary at Tivoli, in Dubuque County, Iowa, who said there were four Catholic churches within eight miles, "one German, one French, and two Irish." It was an oft-repeated story.

To counter this foreign image, Catholics missed few opportunities to appear to be an American body. Bishop John England of Charleston, South Carolina, was one of the early Catholic leaders concerned over this issue, and he warned that the church would have to adapt its outward character so "as to appear indigenous." This meant giving attention to patriotic activities: the bishop reciting the Declaration of Independence at the community Fourth of July celebration, Catholic parochial schools emphasizing American orations for students, and church hierarchy being selected with an eye to nativist criticisms. "Show your attachment to the institutions of our beloved country," urged the American Catholic hierarchy, in their First Plenary Council in 1852.

The church required builders and organizers as it moved onto the American frontier, erecting dioceses at Bardstown, Kentucky, in 1808, St. Louis in 1826, Detroit in 1833, Vincennes in 1834, Dubuque in 1837, Chicago and Milwaukee in 1843, and Quincy in 1853. It also required an abundance of priests who could operate in this religious no-man's-land where Europe's shield was absent.

Perhaps if the Roman Catholic church had been confronted in America with an excess of priests serving a small number of church members, a missionary crusade to convert the heavily Protestant frontier population might have been attempted. But the opposite was true: there existed a spiraling European immigration that constantly threatened to completely overrun all attempts to meet its religious needs or even to sustain its Catholic identity. Converting Protestants was not the top priority in such a setting. Father Mazzuchelli realized this in Galena and decided it was "much more important to call back to a Christian life those who, by the divine mercy, had already received the faith than to turn one's energies toward the person without that light."

There were additional reasons for concern over lost sheep. As Catholic immigration doubled each decade after 1820—almost tripling between 1830 and 1840—church leaders came upon disheartening clues that many former European members were finding themselves in a dangerous position in America. As with Protestants heading westward, the Catholic religion in many cases did not "bear transportation." Lack of clergy worsened this condition. An 1832 report to a European missionary society told of at least 1,000 German Catholics without a German-speaking pastor in New York, and two years later it was stated that the 500-mile Erie Canal-Hudson River zone "was almost entirely without the care of a priest" despite its heavy Catholic population. German priests visiting in frontier cities were considered "a curiosity."

Illinois had no priests in 1830, the bishop of St. Louis complained, and Iowa reported only a single resident German priest from 1840 to 1848. Expansion came as new dioceses were formed, but the supply of priests was never enough to keep up with demand. Bishop Simon Bruté of Chicago wrote in 1837 that he heard "nothing spoken about except the emigrants and the cry for priests that goes up on every side." One town called for a priest to serve its 2,000 Catholics: "What shall we do, especially as our French priests are, many of them at least, still quite too weak in English? And as for German priests—alas! where shall we find them?" As late as 1851 a priest at Iowa City told of finding children of Catholic parents who, at age sixteen, were "ignorant of the first principles of Christianity," and of meeting Catholics who were preparing to move away to avoid raising their children to become infidels or Protestants.

Some reports claimed that not only the German-speaking church, but also the Catholic faith in general was losing adherents by the thousands in America. Bishop England of Charleston, South Carolina, asserted in 1836 that there were fewer than 1.25 million Catholics in the United States out of 5 million residents who had had Catholic upbringing. One Catholic missionary estimated that for every hundred Indians baptized as Catholics, "a thousand Catholics fell away from the faith," while in St. Louis it was claimed by a Catholic spokesman that large numbers of lukewarm German Catholics were joining with German Lutherans or German rationalists.

This concern was heightened in 1842 by the publication in Europe of *Meine Reise nach Nordamerika im Jahre 1842*, by Canon Salzbacher of Vienna, who merged his descriptions of travels across America with poignant tales of Catholics isolated from the church. Included were the experiences of a Catholic missionary who encountered Germans "scattered through the land in groups of two, five, eight, ten, or twelve families. Often they see no priest, attend no mass, hear no sermon for many years." Older members of these families retained their Catholic identification, Canon Salzbacher wrote, but "the young people generally became Protestants after the death of their parents." And when a German Catholic immigrant arrived in Kenosha, Wisconsin, in 1847, he wrote of "sad experiences... we found in Wisconsin neither church, school nor priest. This pained me more than anything else."

The increased Roman Catholic missionary efforts followed several routes. Bishop John Martin Henni of Milwaukee became a leader in campaigns to establish seminaries in the West to train German-speaking priests. His efforts brought creation in 1845 of a seminary in Milwaukee, but it struggled along with closings and reopenings for years with only moderate success. Bishop Mathias Loras had a "grand design" to establish Catholic colonies in Iowa, each with its accompanying European priest, but while several were attempted, the total number of people involved was small. Meanwhile, various Catholic orders in Europe were sending members to the United States, and many of these ended up in the Upper Mississippi country. They included the Ursuline nuns from Oedenburg, Austria, who arrived in St. Louis in 1848; the Benedictines, who launched a center in Minnesota in 1856 (it became Saint John's Abbey); the Capuchins, who came to Wisconsin in 1857, and others. Catholic clergy made forays back to European Catholic centers in their desperation to obtain priests. Francis Xavier Weninger, who eventually established some two hundred fifty parishes and one hundred Catholic schools in the United States, was recruited through an advertisement in a German Catholic newspaper.

The most famous program to supply priests for America was launched in Drumcondra, a section of Dublin, Ireland, in 1842. All Hallows Seminary was created expressly to prepare priests for America and other foreign missions. In its first century a thousand priests left its halls to serve the church in the United States. This included some two hundred sent in the 1842–65 period, many of whom headed for the Upper Mississippi Valley. Irish Catholic leaders considered themselves particularly blessed with this opportunity, for their English-language background prepared Irishmen for service in America, Australia, and other areas where "there may be said to be no hope of salvation unless in the charity of the Irish people." Such missionaries gave an Irish coloration to the Catholic church as it developed in the United States in the nineteenth century.

Catholics on the Continent also responded with funds under a variety of motives: to help establish Catholicism in America, of course, but also to block the spread of the church under control of a rival European power, to enhance the prestige of a particular national mission organization, or to aid emigrants of a specific nationality. The Society for the Propagation of the Faith was the first such group, organized in France in 1822 and soon sending a generous portion of its funds to Catholic bishops in America. Its treasury was continually replenished with penny-a-week donations from thousands of French Catholics, who were also expected to offer daily prayers for its success. While not itself recruiting or training missionaries, the society sometimes paid their passage to foreign mission posts.

As news spread of the dangers from Protestant proselytizers in America, the concern of European Catholics mounted. "The amount of money employed [by Protestants] in this ceaseless campaign against the Christian faith is almost incredible," an Irish Catholic report on Protestant missions warned. A traveling American bishop, Father Frederic Rese of Detroit, cited another reason to be concerned. He told King Louis I of Bavaria that English Protestant activities in the United States should stimulate renewed European Catholic activity in America

Bishop William Quarter (1806-1848).

William Quarter, first bishop of Chicago, typified the new era of the Roman Catholic church in America. Born in Killurine, Ireland, he came to the United States in 1822 and received church leadership training before the vast influx of Irish and German Catholics arrived in the 1840s and 1850s. Bishop Quarter faced enormous problems in meeting the needs of the rapidly growing Catholic immigrant population while mediating between nationality groups and local parish lay leaders demanding more power.

The Archives of the University of Notre Dame.

"lest perhaps the balance existing in Europe between the different confessions be disturbed too much by new acquisitions and our negligence be punished by various evil results." Austrian and German donations for missions increased after reports circulated that German-speaking Catholics were being poorly served or ignored by Irish and French Catholic clergy in America.

These frightening tales from America soon prompted the creation of two other major European missionary societies: the *Ludwig-missionsverein,* initially organized in 1827 in Bavaria but not given royal sanction until 1838; and the *Leopoldine Stiftung* of Vienna, which received legal standing in 1829 and existed exclusively to aid the church in the United States with funds collected within the Austrian Empire. Both were responses to complaints of neglect of German immigrants and of real or supposed machinations of the French in America through their Society for the Propagation of the Faith.

Aid from these three organizations flowed into the Catholic dioceses of America—$700,000 for the 1832–1841 decade, $1.3 million from 1842 to 1851, $1.55 million from 1852 to 1861, and continuing through the end of the century. "What these three societies did for the Catholics in the United States has never been fully told," one writer contends. He asserts that "the very immensity of their charity" and cooperation has "loomed so large...that no American historian has had the courage to canvass the social and religious facts" that their reports "contain for our history." Abundant evidence remains today in diocesan records of the variety and extent of this aid, such as building a seminary in Missouri or German churches in Chicago, sending funds to Iowa to "be employed for the churches of the German Catholics," helping establish a monastery at Sac Prairie, Wisconsin, and a Benedictine center in Stearns County, Minnesota, and supporting the education of German seminarians in Illinois. The bishop of Vincennes explained in 1843, "I have no other pecuniary means but that portion of the alms of Catholic Europe, which are, every year, granted to me by the Society of the Propagation." His comment was echoed frequently in reports of Catholic leaders across the Upper Mississippi country.

Backed by the European missionary societies, the Catholic church began to spread. Chicago had five Catholic churches by 1847, with a heavily foreign membership. In 1853 the Chicago diocese employed twenty-nine Irish priests, twelve from Germany, seven from Alsace-Lorraine, three from France, two each from Scotland, Switzerland, Belgium, Canada, and Italy, and one each from Spain and the United States. Catholicism, as one historian concludes, "was not so much founded in this country but rather transplanted to its soil."

Growth brought problems, however. Language disputes jarred Catholic unity in many communities as various nationalities long separated in Europe suddenly came together in the same church building. Irish Catholics chafed at French sermons in St. Louis as early as the 1820s, demanding English-language sermons at Sunday mass; they got their wish in 1841. At Teutopolis in Effingham County, Illinois, the congregation erupted when the new priest spoke in High German rather than the Low German they were used to. The priest eventually went home to his native Alsace. Irish-German disputes over the use of English or German in Catholic churches flared in several cities, especially among the Burlington, Iowa, Germans who refused to give time or money to the church as long as the Irish priest preached only in English. The Burlington Germans eventually chose what became the customary course in such cases: they built their own church, permitted under the "national parish" system.

Continued use of native tongues became a key factor as well in the question of immigrant adaptation to American life; to outsiders it was simply an attempt to avoid becoming American, a way to cling to Europe and its old-fashioned ways. But many German leaders worried that once the German language was lost among their countrymen emigrating to America, German culture would quickly be forgotten and the German Catholic faith would be weakened. Their motto in America was "Language Keeps Faith," and this was adopted by German Catholic missionaries and their European supporters. King Louis I of Bavaria argued that "religious and school instruction in the German language" in America would always be needed "for the continuance of the German spirit."

But this way was fraught with danger. Divisions appeared quickly over the issue, for Irish and English priests were calling for "one people, one language," urging the German immigrants to learn English. But an Austrian Jesuit disagreed. "One people, one language," Father Xavier Weninger wrote, would be acceptable if most of America's population were Catholics. But most were Protestants, he said, and English-speaking German girls frequently married Protestants and lost their Catholicism. Citing Pennsylvania districts where the loss of German language among immigrants had opened the door to Protestantism, Father Weninger contrasted that situation with Wisconsin districts of five or six hundred German Catholics where German was retained as the language and Catholicism remained strong. "Therefore," he concluded, "whatever is done for the Germans here in America is done at the same time for the interests of holy faith."

Driven on by a variety of motives, Protestant and Catholic missionaries poured into the Upper Mississippi Valley to plant churches in the antebellum era. Their coming was not always welcomed in the region's mushrooming communities, for many settlers came to America to escape religious controls. And there were mixed feelings among some European and eastern church leaders, who feared the weakening of religious dedication that always seemed to accompany emigration. New York's Archbishop John Hughes in particular attacked the "dangerous" idea that settlement in the West meant improvement for the Irish, who were "entirely unfit" to settle there.

The rush to save the immigrants and the native born across the Great Valley thus became a mosaic showing dedicated service, narrow nationalism, and most of all desperate attempts to hold on to tradition. For, to many Protestant missionaries Christianity also meant Americanization, and it was soon evident that not all newcomers wanted to be Americanized when this meant deserting the religion of their fathers. This refusal or reluctance in turn raised questions among the native born, already discomforted over the sudden rise of such previously insignificant groups as the Catholics and Lutherans, both largely alien in makeup. At that point the region needed little prodding to become torn by controversies growing out of religious and national differences.

6. A Land without a Sabbath

The Fourth of July, 1858, left bitter memories for many native-born Americans across the Upper Mississippi Valley. The problem was that Independence Day that year fell on a Sunday, a day that reformers believed should be reserved each week for quiet dedication to religion. In Barton, Washington County, Wisconsin, the Reverend J.S. Lord was barely able to conduct his church services, what with the din of the Germans marching by in their rollicking, noisy parade. Their gambling, drinking, and hilarity went on for hours that Sabbath day, and the hills around the small eastern Wisconsin community echoed with the clangs of an anvil "purloined from a blacksmith shop," as well as the blasts of firecrackers. All this was produced by "a motley group" of Germans "who never had a single drop of the blood of our forefathers in their veins," the Reverend Lord reported. "I see nothing encouraging in our German population," he added, "unless it be in the rising generation." It was a day of bitter memories.

Farther south, at the German center of Belleville, Illinois, Independence Day brought a similar clash of philosophies that year. The *Belleville Advocate,* the voice of the English-speaking portion of the community, instructed the local Germans that "those who deem Sunday a suitable day for the celebration of our national independence...have yet to learn what are the elementary principles of American liberty and good government." In nearby Chester, the *Herald* joined in censuring the immigrants' "desecration of the Christian Sabbath." The local Germans refused to take such criticism silently. The *Belleviller Zeitung* spat back that Germans should celebrate Independence Day on the fourth despite the fact that it was also a Sunday. To do otherwise, the newspaper proclaimed, "would be a disgraceful yielding on the side of the German enlightened morality, to the long-faced standard of the Americans.''

Disagreements over the Fourth of July on the Sabbath in 1858 epitomized the clashes erupting across the region during much of the period after 1830—some of them brief and without serious consequences, others searing in their implications for the future. So frequent and serious were the disagreements between the native-born and the immigrants as to what was moral or sinful, patriotic or alien, that some Americans grew apprehensive for their country's future. They saw the Sabbath, the common schools, the very coherence of communities increasingly in jeopardy in this region. Their uneasiness marked a reversal. Once the advent of steamboats and railroads and the onrush of settlement had seemed to open the way to a millenium in the Mississippi Valley. Its denizens were to be the Chosen People of a New Eden. Then came disputes such as those of the Fourth of July in 1858.

Basic to the conflicts was the fact that the immigrants arrived simultaneously, often on the same steamboats or trains, with the bearers of the most widespread, numerous, and fervent reform movements in the nation's history. The era was accurately described in 1841 by Ralph Waldo Emerson: "In the history of the world, the doctrine of Reform had never such scope as at the present hour.'' The various reform movements touched most aspects of life, combining a reliance on moral arguments and voluntary choice with a belief in the perfectability of the human race. And the reformers who believed people to be perfectable were soon calling for immediate change. Why tolerate the continuance of sin when it could be ended? Why compromise when utopia was possible? Why merely tinker over minor improvements in a bad situation when the Bible had commanded, "Be ye therefore perfect even as your Father which is in heaven is perfect.''

Former New Englanders were the main source of this reform spirit in the territories and states of the Upper Mississippi, and New England generally served as the model for western reformers. Presbyterians, Congregationalists, Methodists, and some Baptist groups were the major religious denominations passing on the torch of reform, but others picked it up at times, and even the Catholics had a

Belleville became known for its homes of local brick, constructed by the mushrooming German population. This house was on North Illinois Street.

Courtesy of the Historic Preservation Commission, Belleville, Ill.

temperance movement of some note. The clergy of these denominations were the most respected persons in many communities, and armed with the zeal of righteous causes they sought to reform the frontier settlers during the "seed time," concentrating on individuals first and hoping to change communities and regions soon thereafter.

Just as the clergy sought to regulate all aspects of the lives of church members, the reformers quickly turned their burning gaze on everything in society, from food and dress to economic systems and slavery. It was a "sisterhood of reforms," and few crusaders labored on only one. A minister in Charleston, Illinois, reported in 1838 that he had formed a county temperance society in the winter, and a county Bible society in the spring, and by the following autumn he was distributing literature on various reforms put out by the American Tract Society. One anti-slavery newspaper in Chicago in the late forties reported extensively on campaigns against Catholicism and alcohol, and for cheap postage, a holy Sabbath, and free land for farmers; it also ran numerous articles attacking slavery. Groups fought dueling, prostitution, card playing, dancing, and tobacco. The Wesleyan Methodist Conference, meeting at Mushawanago, Wisconsin, in late 1852, resolved that tobacco's use "is one of the most palpable violations of physical law that can be performed, and as such should be opposed by all Christians and Christian ministers." Some groups championed women's rights.

The reform spirit was on the rise, its legions growing as they marched toward perfection. The steady expansion of this spirit may be charted within a variety of institutions, such as the several Iowa constitutional conventions. In 1844 the delegates indefinitely postponed a proposal to open sessions with prayer, and in 1846 the convention heard a prayer only at its opening session. But by 1857, when the third Iowa constitutional convention met, it hired a chaplain, voted to open each day's session with a prayer, and banned smoking in the chamber.

Each reform generally was supported by a separate voluntary organization, such as the American Bible Society, the American Sunday School Union, or the American Anti-Slavery Society. Most of these major reform groups were linked by a series of interlocking directorates into a form of "benevolent empire," in which leading Protestant clergy directed American reform. The same situation prevailed within many communities.

The immigrant was often, though not always, an outsider in these activities. Indeed, he was frequently the target of the reformers' wrath. The newcomers from Europe were numerous, often clustered together, spoke and dressed differently from the native-born, attended their own churches, and had their own lodges and other organizations. They also seemed immune to change. Reports soon circulated about the practices of some of these strangers: they threw Bibles (donated by the American Bible Society) into the flames; they bought out Americans so they could live together and retain old customs; they fought with local citizens; they sold their votes to politicians. At Oconomowoc, Wisconsin, foreigners were blamed for a wave of murders and lynchings in the early months of 1856, and a local minister lamented that "the influence of our emigrant population upon the public morals is well known to be deplorable." But it did not take mayhem to lead Americans to such conclusions. In Belleville, for example, the proprietor of a natural history collection was frustrated by the barbarism shown by Irish railroad laborers, who had encountered the skeleton of a mastadon while excavating for the rail line: "I went down to see what could be done about getting the bones, but found that the d——d fool Irish work hands had destroyed the greater part of the bones with their picks. The teeth which could not be disposed of in this way were turned over to the stone masons, who cracked them as they would rock....All I could do was to get the upper part of a thigh bone, partially petrified and with several pick holes in it. I would not have gotten hold of that, even, if it could have been destroyed."

An Illinois Baptist committee agreed that Germans were "an interesting and useful class of people" but cautioned that they were "quite different in their habits from Americans." To Germans, the Baptist report stated, the Sabbath was "a day of hilarity and recreation"; their drinking houses were destructive to morals. Worse, "in our sense of the term, they are an irreligious people." Similar reports abounded, and a German Methodist leader admitted that his compatriots needed to be "Americanized" before they would improve. Small wonder that when Germans sought to join with Americans in church and school, many Americans held back. "There is not that sympathy for the foreign population that there ought to be among our eastern Christians," one American pastor admitted. Among many determined reformers the anti-immigrant feelings ran even stronger.

As the bustle of railroad construction crews approached each town, some reformers had second thoughts about the benefits credited to the Iron Horse. For many the worst aspect of the railway was not the Sunday business it encouraged among Americans or the Sunday labor it often required, but the "demoralizing influence of the class which is always drawn together by such works," that is, the foreign-born workmen. A missionary in Vandalia, Illinois, watched with mounting concern as Catholic immigrants came to push the line onward, until he finally unleashed his thoughts in a letter attacking "the 'Man of Sin,' who has been pouring his representatives in among us by scores, bringing with them drunkenness, profanity, Sabbath-breaking, midnight reveling, licentiousness, and every abomination."

The Irish tended to be dismissed out of hand by some reformers. As a group almost totally identified with Roman Catholicism, they were given little chance of ever turning from their sinful ways. To a larger extent than other groups, they seemed to cluster in the liquor-infested shanty towns of canal and railroad projects, while large numbers of Germans escaped these hovels and settled on farms.

Further, many Germans were Protestants and this led some reformers to labor long and hard in German communities, whereas less effort was made among the Catholic Irish. But even German Protestants were found sadly lacking. An Illinois missionary reported that in his village, where Germans were "perhaps the majority," efforts continued to enroll German children in Sabbath school, distribute German-language tracts, and so forth. But "on account of their drinking, dancing, profligate religious teachers, Roman Catholic and Lutheran; their habits, their prejudices against American views; our ignorance of their language, [etc.], we can accomplish but little for them." Another missionary found German Protestants deceitful, for they pretended to agree with evangelical doctrines but soon revealed different beliefs, "taking advantage of a language which is little understood." But although filled with "deep depravity," the Germans were not without hope, the missionary said, and added, "A more needy people are not to be found in the West."

German communities suffered under an additional burden in the eyes of many reformers; they were frequently torn between vigorously competing denominations of Protestants, Catholics, and nonbelievers (often called rationalists or infidels). Refugees from Germany's 1848 revolution were often found in the latter group, and the resulting feuds added to the impression that dissension was typical among immigrants. Much of this strife was also turned against the native born, as occurred in a series of outbreaks between Germans and Americans in Washington County, Wisconsin, during the mid-1850s. As the conflict spread, the German majority in West Bend closed the schoolhouse to American Protestant worship services, and the American preacher reported being stoned several times while crossing the street. Many other heavily German and Irish communities witnessed similar violence.

Even where such open conflict did not occur, the mere presence of Catholics stirred the reformers' ire. Prepared by centuries of antipopery and the patriotic fervor of colonial-era conflicts with the French and Spanish, American anti-Catholicism was already virulent before the large-scale arrivals of Catholic immigrants fanned it to a white heat. The era was marked by a spate of widely circulated sensationalist books filled with lurid tales of Catholic horrors, such as Maria Monk's *Awful Disclosures of the Hotel Dieu Nunnery of Montreal.* Incident built upon incident. These years witnessed the Presbyterian General Assembly's decision to create a committee on the "Prevalence of Popery in the West"; the uproar among nativists over the Baltimore Council of American Catholic hierarchy in 1829; and the launching of several nativist organizations—the American Party in 1843, the American Protestant Society the following year, and the Know-Nothings a decade later.

Most of this represented homegrown nativism and a search for scapegoats, but European conflicts were transferred to American soil as well. Orangemen and Corkonians who battled in green Erin were capable of resuming hostilities on the richer turf of the Mississippi Valley. An Irish Presbyterian minister who relocated in Iowa City complained of his struggles building a church while all around him new Catholic edifices were springing up. "If Rome is losing ground in Europe," he wrote to his brother in Dublin, "she is moving heaven and earth to plant and cultivate her heresy in America." He marveled at the Catholics' ability to build "fine chapels—cathedrals—convents, and schools wherever she needs them in this country, whereas Protestants can't always do so." Why, the Reverend Allen pondered, "should not truth be as well supported as error?"

But the bulk of the struggle against immigrants and their sinful ways was conducted by native-born Protestants, such as the Chicago minister in 1834 who prayed each night in front of the city's lone Catholic church that "no evil should come to Chicago from its presence." It was predictable that reformers who ventured into the canal and railroad towns of the Upper Mississippi country would be repelled by the actions of the Catholic immigrants there. The Reverend J.G. Porter, who settled in Lockport on the Illinois and Michigan Canal, was especially downcast by the scene. The majority of the people in that heavily Catholic community, he wrote in 1840, "are living without God and without hope in the wish." They presented "a sad sight; they fight, and swear, and drink and murder." Most rejected his offer of a free Bible. To reformers from New England and elsewhere, such persons constituted an immense profane barrier to the spread of Christian perfectionism across the Upper Mississippi country.

German rationalists were only slightly less detested by the reformers, but then they were not so numerous as the Catholics. Part of the broad movement against the European church establishment, Lutheran as well as Catholic, rationalists were generally drawn from the most educated groups in the German exodus, a fact that helped propel them into public affairs and controversies. Rationalism and popery, "the extremes of servile superstition and atheistic recklessness, blend in dreadful harmony in German infidelity," the *Home Missionary* asserted, and Protestant reformers were soon fighting running battles against both groups.

A Swedish writer who visited the Upper Mississippi country in 1849 reported that Scandinavian immigrants often held to the belief that the state church and religion were identical and interchangeable, so that when they came to America they not only left behind the state church but also discarded religion. In Belleville, a German preacher admitted sadly that many of his immigrant countrymen yelled "liberty" but meant by it that "in this country they were free from God and his word." Another found that "all the rankest forms of error" in Belleville had "open advocates and partizans." Not surprisingly in such an environment, church services were sometimes invaded or disrupted. The story was told that a veteran of the German revolutions offered a reward to anyone who would break up the Presbyterian services at nearby Dutch Hill.

When the papal emissary, Archbishop Gaetano Bedini, was attacked by a mob in Cincinnati, the rioting was led by the German rationalists' society of *Freimänner*. Open antagonism by rationalists led Bishop Henni in Milwaukee to advise a community of nuns to avoid installing large windows in their planned chapel because free thinkers would smash these if the designs had an ecclesiastical look. A group of Milwaukee anticlericals even baptized a cow beside the walls of a convent to ridicule church rituals.

Across the Mississippi in Iowa, the German Catholic missionary Francis X. Weninger also encountered bitter opposition from his anticlerical countrymen. He was once the target of a thrown bottle of nitric acid, and he received a warning that the new cross erected outside a church in Fort Madison would look better "if we would nail that missionary to it." When Father Weninger walked through the streets one day a horseman attempted to ride him down, yelling "*Reit doch den Pfaffen nieder!*" (Ride down that papist!) The horse swerved a moment before it would have hit Weninger.

German rationalists were especially provoked with one of the major American reform drives of the era—the attempt to maintain a quiet and religious Sabbath day. Their opposition was only more vociferous—not unique—when compared to that of the bulk of the Germans, the Irish, and other European immigrants. These newcomers all carried with them the traditions of a "continental Sunday," in which visiting, singing, dancing, drinking, and other forms of conviviality were welcomed. Church services had their place on Sunday, but they did not dominate the day's activities.

Immigrants moved quickly to organize their own societies for social, educational, and increasingly for political reasons. The *Turnverein* movement, because it drew Germans together, frequently served all three purposes.

This 1857 photo shows the *Turn Halle* in Davenport, Iowa.

Courtesy of the State Historical Society, Iowa State Historical Dept.

This continental Sabbath was rejected by American reformers. They had seized upon the quiet and religious Sabbath as a new cause early in the century, at that time opposing the U.S. government's Sunday mail delivery and the Sunday operation of steamboats. In 1828 they launched the General Union for Promoting the Observance of the Christian Sabbath, and in 1843 the American and Foreign Sabbath Union was founded. A year later a National Sabbath Convention met in Baltimore with 1,700 delegates from eleven states led by ex-President John Quincy Adams. The movement was underway with vigor.

Sabbatarians argued that Sunday should be a day apart, a day to characterize American civilization as Christian. It was heralded by reformers as a God-given day of rest—people should stop work and had a Christian duty to avoid worldly amusements. Like backers of other reform movements, many Sabbatarians saw their cause as the magic key to a utopian future, as evidenced in the Illinois Methodist General Assembly's proclamation that "so long as Sabbath violation exists, there will be drunkenness, gambling, uncleanness, quarreling, murder and every other crime; but induce all to stop, and 'Remember the Sabbath day to keep it holy,' and the Grand Jubilee of earth may be proclaimed."

Frontier America seldom showed much sympathy for such a Sabbath. While there were many among the native-born who disagreed with Sabbatarianism, the settlers of southern Illinois became especially infamous among reformers for the extent of their Sabbath breaking. As one missionary reported, "the largest collections were always found around a whiskey barrel" on a Sunday in Egypt. A Baptist committee in Perry County, Illinois, found local residents cutting firewood on Sunday, traveling to and from market, visiting and "conversing upon matters of worldly interest." A Cairo preacher similarly told of young men playing marbles and grown men playing "town-ball" on Sunday mornings, while the local stores were open for business as usual.

Some areas also produced numerous reports of hunting on the Sabbath. At La Harpe, Illinois, a man even "fired his gun under the [church] window during public worship." Rockport in Pike County, Illinois, was alleged to be a "Sabbath breaking community," where even ex-New Englanders joined the irreligious activities on the Lord's Day. A missionary described the town as "a rendezvous for

Sabbath breakers all over the country, for fishing and hunting. They come in wagon loads—sometimes on Saturday afternoon and sometimes on Sabbath morning—with fishing tackle, rifles and dogs, and of course are joined by all the idlers of the village....The Sabbath is also the day for social visiting."

River towns, such as Warsaw and La Salle, Illinois, Davenport and Council Bluffs, Iowa, and of course, St. Louis, were moral disasters for Sabbatarians. Business seemed, if anything, to concentrate on Sunday in such towns, and selling town lots was a fever that brought out large, jostling crowds. A missionary at Council Bluffs described his frustration when, after preparing most of the week for Sabbath day services, he discovered on Sunday that "something has called away the congregation. Perhaps boats are at the landing; merchants are there receiving goods, teams are busy moving them, and the pleasure-loving are there for recreation." In his church, meanwhile, "the seats are almost empty."

It was the immigrants, however, who came in for most severe criticism from reformers, for they often revealed a complete lack of interest in upholding the Sabbath. Many were armed with ready arguments to throw back at the reformers. The Catholic Irish, in particular, had already fought out the Sabbath desecration issue with their Protestant enemies across the ocean, and as a result they were impervious to the pleadings of American Protestants on the topic. Their groggeries in the canal and railroad camps thrived on the Lord's Day. In Belleville the Germans **treated the** Sabbath as a festive holiday and once even held a boisterous **Sunday funeral** parade, with colorful band, for a deceased fireman. The fact that **the Fourth of July** fell on Sunday in 1858 only gave an extra reason to celebrate. Chicago on fair summer Sundays witnessed a massive, one-day exodus of thousands of Germans, who traveled to beer gardens and carousels at nearby Cottage Grove and Holstein. Attempts to have these events declared nuisances failed. Sunday dancing as well as drinking were featured in various parts of Milwaukee, with many Americans joining the Germans. Wondering at the extent of Sabbath breaking at Okaw, Illinois, a missionary learned that a nearby German preacher had stated to his congregation that "the Sunday is not established from God, but from the government. Therefore if we have been in the church, we can do any work on Sunday." From Missouri, a missionary was surrounded with similar problems when the Germans in his community opened a new dance hall near the church, "and on last Sabbath they commenced their orgies." After the crowd gathered, the dancing, drinking, "whooping, yelling, and all other such demonstrations" continued for hours. Disheartened, he labeled it "a land without a Sabbath."

The role of the immigrant in ruining the holy Sabbath could no longer be missed as the decade of the 1850s began. A resident of the town of Camanche in Clinton County, Iowa, contrasted the Sunday activities of the natives and the foreign-born: "While the native looks upon Sunday as a divine institution, appointed by God as a day to be observed above all others in prayer and praise to their Almighty Father, the Germans look upon it as one especially adapted and intended as a gala day.... I was strongly impressed with the contrast Sunday evening in a walk through town, by passing first a prayer meeting; a short distance further a dancing house with all the necessary fixtures in the way of music, and something to rouse the spirits up."

Churchmen had little trouble turning their wrath upon this "infidel emigration" over the issue of Sabbath breaking. The Illinois General Council of Methodists set the tone in a resolution at its 1848 meeting, asserting that "the ideas of our foreign population in regard to the Sabbath must be revolutionized."

Local petitions sought similar ends. A broad 1839 Wisconsin law banning business and amusements on the Sabbath was widely ignored by Milwaukee Germans, so reformers in 1852 gathered 1,400 signatures on a petition calling for an end to "Sunday orgies and excesses" in the city. This prompted a vigorous response from German newspapers, one of which countered: "Let us not take our liberty, in a free country! We will not obey the *Pfaffen*" (bad ministers). The Wisconsin Freemen's League, a German rationalist group, attacked Sabbatarian statutes as a violation of equal rights that in reality raised the views of individual sects to the status of "a universally binding political law."

Sabbath desecration was attacked in Menasha, Wisconsin, in 1856, although the campaign aimed mainly at those who went hunting on Sundays. "This practice, confined mostly to our foreign population, became a source of serious annoyance to the religious portion of the community," a missionary affirmed.

"Saint John's Cathedral, Milwaukee."

Father John Martin Henri laid the cornerstone in December 1847 for Saint John's Cathedral, major church for Milwaukee's German Catholics. This watercolor, believed to have been painted by William Thomas Saul in 1860, shows the church as a stunning example of European architectural style in the midst of an American frontier city.

Courtesy of the State Historical Society of Wisconsin.

Despite having signatures on the petition from "the best and most substantial men of our community," the matter failed to win the Menasha city council's approval. At a massive Sabbath convention in Chicago in 1854, delegates urged prayers for the "vast influx of immigrants," who had learned in Europe to hate established religion "and the Sabbath law as made a part of it." Specific Sunday legislation was sought by Iowa Methodists, who passed resolutions in 1849 and 1854 calling for the government to take steps to secure "the proper sanctity of the Sabbath" within the state.

If the immigrants were attacked for ignoring the Sabbath, they were invited, lured, and cajoled into the common (public) school movement then aborning. The school system was a logical vehicle for reformers, for by catching children early, little feet could be placed upon the correct pathways, leading them away from the influence of erring parents and European traditions. This was the hope of a missionary in the strife-torn German community of Barton in Washington County, Wisconsin: "[Children of the troublesome Germans] will be a different class. Though now under a German influence at home, yet, as they live with us, go to school with our children, and attend our Sabbath schools, they will gradually become more and more Americanized."

Horace Mann, the Massachusetts reformer who became the most famous proselytizer for public schools in the nation and world, shifted his focus away from reforming adults to educating the young, because "men are cast-iron; but children are wax." Schools, he stressed, were "preventive" rather than "curative" devices, for if successful they could stop the growth of the evils besetting society. Both stimulating and riding the crest of common school reforms, Mann and his Massachusetts friends carried the movement westward. The American Education Society, formed in New England in 1816, had an Illinois branch by 1832, by which time a group of emigrant New Englanders had already lobbied a common school law through the Illinois legislature. But reformers did not rule the region. Southern Illinois politicians were strong enough to eviscerate the 1825 measure during the following legislative session, and Illinois had to wait until 1855 for a workable public school law. Iowa and Wisconsin had similar fits and starts in achieving effective public school funding during the pre-Civil War years.

As with other reformers, partisans of the common school regarded utopia as assured if their schemes were carried out. They argued that by mixing children of rich and poor together, common schools would raise the lower classes. School attendance would make each child a "moral and intelligent" citizen, thereby helping banish crime, poverty, and war. Such improvements were dire needs on the frontier, the reformers held, because there a nation was being "born in a day." The Reverend Lyman Beecher, in his *Plea for the West,* warned also that Catholics would provide the schools if Protestants did not. These sentiments were echoed by one of the Illinois leaders of the common school campaign, who asserted that to "see our free institutions perpetuated and America happy" education must be brought to the thousands of immigrants who arrived illiterate and "ignorant of our free institutions."

It was to be a Protestant education. This was dictated by tradition and by the fact of an overwhelmingly Protestant population as the common school movement began to form across the region. In 1833 the Western Baptist Educational Association called for schools to preserve basic freedoms but stressed that classes should be "under the guidance of approved teachers" who could demonstrate the "bright example of moral and religious worth." For Protestants, the legacy of the Reformation called for literacy and education so that individuals could read and interpret the Bible themselves.

As in the East, new public schools in the Upper Mississippi region often merged with existing private Protestant academies. When Chicago city officials allocated the first public funds for education in 1834, these went to two schools already operating in the Presbyterian and Baptist churches. In another era this act might have led to disputes between churches, but Protestant interdenominational strife seldom occurred in the region as church-connected academies converted to public-supported schools. General agreement among the major Protestant groups and realization of the need for unity against Catholicism helped stave off such divisions.

The New England school reformers who led the way, including the "Yale Band" in Illinois and the "Iowa Band" in Iowa, had little trouble agreeing with the general views of a united Protestantism. These transplanted Yankees created the organization, did the lobbying before legislatures and village boards, and promoted the rallies to convince taxpayers that public money allotted to education was well spent. John Mason Peck, a Baptist New Englander, was one of the movement's main spokesmen in Illinois, lecturing widely on the New England and eastern school system and its adaptation to frontier conditions. Soon New Englanders were recruiting New England girls as teachers for the schools of the Upper Mississippi, stirring southerners in the Illinois legislature to warn of the danger that "these selected emissaries of abolitionism would try to convert the youth of Illinois into the likeness of 'canting' and 'freedom-shrieking' New England demagogues." One wealthy citizen donated a building for his community's schoolhouse, with the provision that no instructor from the East should teach in it. And in Pinckneyville, Illinois, anti-eastern sentiment reduced the local school to ineffectiveness after the teacher, "a young lady from eastern New York," severely beat a stubborn boy with a rod until he was rescued by his aunt.

But the Presbyterian and Congregational missionaries labored on, helping form school organizations in most communities where they settled. At La Salle, Illinois, the Congregational minister took the lead in soliciting community pledges of over $4,000 for a school, while his counterpart upriver in Joliet formed a board of school trustees, helped obtain a classroom building, and sent a plea to the East for a qualified teacher "who has the spirit of missions in the cause of education." An agent of the American Home Missionary Society contended in 1848 that he knew of no Illinois community that lacked a day school and Sabbath school within one year after the arrival of an AHMS missionary.

The influence of this type of leadership by New Englanders was evident in the activities of the Reverend Hope Brown of Naperville, Illinois, who was president of the local board of school trustees and commissioner of the county school board. Reverend Brown said he was endeavoring "to make the schools in this county like those of Massachusetts, which I formerly had under my supervision." In an 1853

**Beecher Hall, Illinois College,
Jacksonville (1936).**

Proclaimed to be the oldest college building in Illinois, this 1829 edifice reveals the classic New England architectural style. Like the reformers who erected it at Illinois College, the building represented an outside influence in the region.

letter he elaborated: "This office imposes some extra labor and some extra responsibility on me, but it at the same time gives me access to all the schools in the county.... I have never met with any opposition to my preaching or praying in any of our school houses.... [On] one occasion I refused fifteen applicants who applied for certificates of approbation as teachers, some of whom had been teachers for years, and one of whom had been and is now a missionary under the patronage of the 'North Western—or Free Missionary Society.'"

Besides the opposition of southerners, resistance to these school plans came mainly from European immigrants. By 1849 Chicago's public school population was 39 percent children of the foreign-born, raising the question of reforming immigrants to new importance as part of the common school campaign. But it was increasingly evident that not all immigrants were eager to join this movement, at least in the manner prescribed by the New Englanders. A grade school started by a Wisconsin missionary, a German working under the aegis of the American Home Missionary Society, ran into opposition from German "humanists" (probably rationalists), who won a community vote forbidding him to teach there. As in Pennsylvania, where German communities often supported public schools but demanded local control over teaching content, immigrant settlements across the Upper Mississippi frequently chafed at reformers' educational blueprints. Germans in Elk Grove, near Chicago, followed the call of their Lutheran minister in 1851–52 and voted down a tax to build a schoolhouse. They wanted German children taught only in German schools where they could learn church doctrine. "The fear is that in English schools this end could not so well be reached. The children might be corrupted," a reformer reported. Finally, the American element in Elk Grove united and convinced enough Germans to go along with the tax so that it passed, over the "embarrassing narrowness, ingratitude, or bigotry" of the immigrants. Elk Grove was not an isolated case.

The question of maintaining foreign languages complicated the school campaign. The reason was not obscure: both immigrants and reformers considered the immigrants' continued use of a foreign tongue as a way to retain European beliefs and traditions. While many immigrants—certainly a majority—agreed that learning English had first priority, some rejected this view. To some immigrant clergy, the retention of the mother tongue was crucial for the faith. Also, many immigrants wanted schools taught in their native language as part of their broader support for physical culture clubs, musical organizations, and other groups working to retain traditions and unite folk of the same country or region. But to reformers the use of foreign languages in the classroom frustrated the basic purposes of common schools.

Language, culture, and religion were entwined in this broad controversy. When a group of German Lutherans in Union County, Illinois, appealed in 1825 for ministers from the North Carolina Lutheran Synod, they called for men who could preach in German as well as in English, so that German schools could be established, "and the German language be retained." Without German teachers, they foresaw dire consequences "to them and to their children." But the plea for German instruction was not limited to church schools. A group of Germans in Chicago issued a call in 1849 for a school "in which both the German and English languages and the elements of the most needful sciences shall be taught." St. Louis Germans, who had more political power, successfully pushed through the board of education a rule in 1860 that a teacher competent in German be hired for Lafayette and Clay schools, despite protests from those who argued that since the nation's laws were in English, the public schools' instruction should be also: "The sooner the German and all other naturalized citizens learn and adopt our vernacular tongue the better, it is believed, for all concerned."

In Wisconsin, with its heavily foreign districts along Lake Michigan's shores, public schools conducted in German, Norwegian, or the Belgian dialects were numerous. At the second Wisconsin constitutional convention late in 1847, a German-born delegate proposed that instruction in languages other than English be permitted in school districts with many foreign-born residents. His proposal was defeated, but one historian contends that it lost "perhaps because it seemed unnecessary to grant express permission for something that was already common practice in such areas." The following year a new statute permitted Wisconsin school districts to authorize teaching in foreign languages "in connection with the English language," but in 1854 a flat requirement was made that the basic subjects were to be taught in English. Bilingual instruction was permitted in Milwaukee, but one of the city's German wards received no German instruction in its public school until 1857, and their inability to force the issue rankled among many Germans.

School district records indicate, however, that German continued to be used extensively in Wisconsin's public schools, sometimes for two days a week or an hour or so a day, occasionally during a separate term each school year. The inability to locate bilingual teachers forced many districts to maintain separate terms for German and English instruction, but school board minutes that record purchases of "kintling woot" demonstrate that immigrants were moving toward an accommodation with the English.

The language issue spilled over into the desire of many immigrants for schools run by their own churches or organizations. This was an outgrowth of European traditions, for in much of Germany and Scandinavia the Lutheran church was in partnership with the government in running the school system. The same held true for the Catholic church in Catholic-controlled regions of Germany. Even in British-controlled Ireland the Catholic church ran the schooling that reached the masses of Catholics. From these systems it followed that ideals, objectives, and methods were shaped principally by the dominant church in Europe, while funding and attendance requirements were (outside of Ireland) the province of the supporting governments.

In the changed environment of America the direct links between government and church in running public education were absent, but churches were drawn into school issues over their desires to control what their children were learning. Also, concern over loss of native language skills was so great that Milwaukee's German rationalists opened their own elementary school in 1851. Taught by a free-thinking former Lutheran teacher, it featured German as well as several other subjects not offered, or dealt with inadequately, in the city's public schools. It opened with 40 pupils, grew rapidly to 250, and soon had its own building as well as emulators around the city.

The most fervent devotion to private schools was shown by groups deeply concerned over maintaining their special brand of orthodoxy amid an environment filled with deluded or evil outsiders. Besides Catholics, who eventually built an extensive school system, this was true most notably of Old School Presbyterians, who established some sixteen schools of their own in Illinois after 1846, and the *Alt Lutheraner* from Germany, who entered the Mississippi Valley from 1839 on and established the Missouri Synod of the Lutheran church. The basic attitude of most of these churches was enunciated in 1845 by a group of German separatists in Milwaukee and Buffalo, who stated that "no Christian could with a good conscience send his child to a public school before its confirmation." The Norwegian Synod of the Lutheran church, operating principally in Wisconsin, voted that its children should be taught in their church school in Norwegian until age thirteen, because the common schools' discipline and spirit were "disturbing factors in the proper Christian nurture of the child."

The Missouri Synod group began immediately to control its children's education, forming a school within days of the first Saxon group's arrival in St. Louis in 1839 and dispatching agents to each *Alt Lutheraner* cluster to help launch a church and school. They eventually raised a string of parochial schools: 52 across the Old Northwest by 1851, at which time Missouri had 10, Iowa 9, Illinois 7, and Wisconsin 1; the total grew to 129 schools in 158 congregations by 1859. Related groups such as the German Lutheran Synod of Minnesota and the First German Evangelical Lutheran Synod of Wisconsin also moved rapidly to create their own schools separate from the public schools. One Missouri Synod historian wrote that these schools made the denomination "a body ever uniformly confessional in its doctrinal position, consecrated in its policies and practices, militant in its program, and thorough-going in its actions." A related English-language group, the Evangelical Lutheran Synod of Illinois, showed no interest in establishing its own schools; in this case a separate language and culture were not entwined with church doctrines.

Parochial schools were considered even more crucial to German and Irish Catholics. This was because they faced an opposition more vigorous about conversion, more determined to overpower the newcomers and their hated church of Rome. Initially the shortage of priests meant that much of the Catholic population was beyond the reach of the church, and while adults could hark back to earlier

"German Lutheran Trinity Church, Springfield."

An *Alt Lutheraner* congregation, organized in 1851, erected this building in 1860. The congregation launched its German-English Parochial School in 1855, the year it affiliated with the Missouri Synod Lutherans.

Courtesy of the Illinois State Historical Library.

training, their children could not. An Irish immigrant to Minnesota wrote home unhappily that "children brought young from Ireland to this country, also native-born of Irish parents, are brought up in a very careless way, so far as Catholicity is concerned, and most certainly the second generation are perverted, or else lose the faith to all practical intents and purposes." His concern was widespread among Catholic immigrants.

By the time the common school movement began its major campaigns across the Upper Mississippi in the 1840s, the East had already been scarred from Catholic-Protestant struggles over public schools, spurring latent Protestant fears of a foreign plot to control or subvert American institutions. Catholic leaders argued that their educational organization was nothing of the kind; Catholic children needed Catholic schools for proper upbringing, but the public schools were overwhelmingly Protestant, filled with Protestant publications, songs, and doctrines. In its Baltimore council of 1829 the church hierarchy called for establishment of parochial schools, and this call was reiterated in the provincial council of Baltimore in 1840. Catholic parents were urged to defend their rights against Protestant infringement in the public schools.

That was when the church in New York made its first concerted effort to gain public school funds for Catholic schools. Rebuffed by the city government and the legislature, Bishop John Hughes then began a massive campaign to build parochial schools so that Catholic children would not be forced to attend public schools. "In this age and country," he stressed, "the school is before the church." Philadelphia had a similar controversy, stemming from Catholic opposition to a state law requiring reading from the Protestant Bible in public schools. In 1842 a priest in New York burned a pile of King James versions of the Bible to protest such school laws. These incidents collided head-on with the long-festering anti-Catholic tradition in America, under which Catholicism was depicted as non-Christian, dominated by superstition and directed by European despots struggling to overthrow the United States.

At the heart of the school controversy was the issue of reading the King James version of the Bible in the classroom. The King James was a Protestant version not sanctioned by Roman Catholics, who had their own approved version. In the common schools of New England, Bible readings had traditionally been used as an integral part of the day's lessons, and the American Bible Society pledged continuous labor until the Scriptures were read in every schoolroom in the country. Chicago had a Bible requirement for schools by 1838, apparently enforced. An early meeting of Minnesota teachers resolved that "Christian morality being the basis of all true progress, its exponent, the Bible, should be read daily in the schools." Similarly, the *Common School Advocate* sought to imbue the Illinois public school movement with belief in the New Testament as a textbook. "Our teacher makes the Bible an important part of the instruction," a Protestant missionary reported proudly from Augusta, Illinois, in 1838. A year later a letter from another Illinois grade school stated that "by means of the daily devotional and scriptural exercises, the laws of Christ are brought to act upon the heart and conscience, and become the principal controlling influence in school."

This overriding Protestant system could not go unchallenged as immigration made the Irish and German Catholics more than local oddities. The mayor of Galena, capital of the lead region with its heterogeneous mining population, observed in 1852 that there was "a great deal of dissatisfaction" shown by "a large class of the community" over school instruction, and many parents held back from sending their children to school. He asked, "Would it not...be more consistent" with the principle of individual interpretation "to discard the use of 'Bible Commentaries' and 'Scriptural Explanations' in the public schools?" A Protestant missionary in Joliet in 1852 saw his efforts to run a school frustrated due to "some opposition in the community because prayer and the Bible are in the school." Similarly, at Fort Howard, Wisconsin, a missionary reported in 1855 that Catholics had resorted to "open and bold attacks" on such "venerable and customary usages" in the schools as Bible reading; even his own guest lecture to the pupils on self-government had become the subject of a newspaper tirade against sectarianism.

In Chicago the Bible controversy became a critical one. The *Chicago Tribune* emerged during the decade of the fifties as the city's most vociferous defender of Protestantism, urging Bible reading in the public schools because with it "we are

Saint Patrick's Church, Chicago (1870).

The Irish immigrants' first parish in Chicago was the frame structure at right in this 1870 photo. The frame building, erected in 1846, became Saint Patrick School for Boys (later Saint Patrick Commercial Academy, razed in 1874) after the dedication in 1857 of the building at left, still standing at Saint Patrick's, Chicago's landmark Irish parish.

Courtesy of the *Chicago Catholic.*

saved from all attacks of Romanism, and can bid defiance to the snares of papacy and the delusions of priestcraft." The *Western Citizen,* the city's leading reform journal early in the decade, charged that Catholics believed "all our free schools are anti-Catholic...and that the Bible itself is a sectarian book."

Resolutions passed in county and state teachers' meetings during most of the decade of the 1850s came down strongly on the issue, as at the Whiteside County, Illinois, teachers' meeting of 1855: "*Resolved,* That the Bible should be, and is hereby recommended, as a text book in all the schools in the county, and we earnestly recommend the practice of reading a lesson from the scriptures by the entire school at the opening each morning." The St. Louis teachers' conference in 1856 heard Horace Mann speak on a teacher's motivation, then listened to a local minister stress "the absolute necessity of the principles of the Bible being inculcated in our common schools." The topic was a persistent one at teachers' gatherings during the 1850s.

Those discussions prepared the ground for a heated debate that pitted the foreign-born against the native-born in many Upper Mississippi communities. Both Chicago's first Roman Catholic bishop, William Quarter, and the first bishop of Dubuque, Mathias Loras, became known for their zeal in establishing Catholic schools. Even without the organizational talents of the church hierarchy, Catholic schools frequently sprang up on the heels of the first Catholic arrivals in a community. Galena had seen a Catholic school started in 1832, and the La Salle mission opened one in 1838. Zealous priests soon launched a string of others across the region: in 1840 in Fort Madison and Burlington, Iowa; 1842 in Milwaukee; 1844 in Chicago; 1846 in Iowa City. These were followed by dozens in other communities. Minnesota's first Catholic school opened in 1851 in St. Paul, and by 1853 Chicago boasted twelve Catholic schools plus a Catholic university. The fact that some Protestant children were enrolled in these schools added desperation to the opposition's attacks.

If the forties were the decade of laying the foundations for a Catholic response to the common school movement in the region, the fifties were the time when Catholics opened a counterattack on their Protestant critics. Bishop James Van de Velde gave a series of lectures in Chicago in 1850 and again in early 1852 to refute

Protestant charges, and the Irish Catholic newspaper *Western Tablet* was launched at the same time. That newspaper became the impassioned spokesman for beleaguered Catholicism, denouncing the public schools as "nurseries of heathenism, vice and crime" and labeling them unjust and oppressive to Catholics. The *Western Tablet* frequently did battle with the *Tribune,* reminding Protestants that Catholics had also fought and died in the Revolution and arguing that Catholics were being forced by compulsory taxation to pay for others' schooling. "If Protestants choose to have their youth demoralized, and their salvation rendered next to impossible, that is no direct concern of ours," the Catholic newspaper editorialized, "but we are bound to see that the same calamity does not overtake the Catholic youth of the country."

Protestants lashed back. The *North-Western Christian Advocate,* a Chicago Methodist publication, said that Catholics were "not contented as citizens, and a sect of religionists, to be left on the same common footing with all others" regarding the school fund, but with "unparalleled insolence and audacity, they are asking and urging exclusive legislation in their behalf." To the similarly minded *Western Citizen,* the new Catholic offensive represented an open avowal of papal designs against American institutions. Critics saw no injustice. Catholics would lose out anyway if school funds were distributed on the basis of tax payments, for nearly three-fourths of the paupers of Chicago were Catholics.

The rise of Catholic opposition seemed contradicted by the reformers' increasing success with the Illinois legislature, where a new, more effective public school law was passed in 1855. That measure, put through by northern politicians over widespread southern Illinois opposition (except among the Germans of St. Clair County), provided for school taxation by linking population and territory. It also created the machinery for school boards to qualify for school funds. Private schools could receive tax funds only if they lost their private identity and submitted to the orders of district school directors. As a result, two-thirds of the state's private elementary schools either closed or became public schools within two years.

Wisconsin skirted some of these issues through a system of school fund loans, often distributed as political favors. Not surprisingly, the politically savvy Irish received 13.5 percent of the school loans made from 1848 through 1853, although the Irish accounted for but 7 percent of the state population. Germans made up 12.5 percent of the total population, but their schools received only 2.3 percent of the loans.

Despite these gains in providing funding for the common schools, the reformers were generally losing their campaign to have the King James Bible read in those schools. Wisconsin's state superintendent of education ruled in 1850 that district school boards could decide the issue, but a new superintendent in 1854 discouraged prayers and Bible reading during school time, noting that the Bible's "common English version is wholly repudiated by a very large class of our population." Such activities belonged in the family and church, he argued.

In Illinois the Bible was losing its proclaimed school role also. By 1858 the *Illinois Teacher* said there were counties in the state "in which an actual visitation reveals the fact that not in one-half the schools is the Bible read at all." Although Bible resolutions continued to win endorsement in teachers' meetings, by 1859 a different sentiment on the subject was appearing with more frequency. It was especially noticeable during the convention that year of the Illinois State Teachers Association, when "a large majority" of delegates supported a committee report rejecting use of the Bible or any religious tracts in public schools if opposed by anyone "who is compelled to contribute" toward the school's support. Any other view, the committee held, would permit Mormons or Catholics to force pupils to read their holy works if such groups had local majorities.

Another change was evident at that 1859 convention. La Salle's public school had as its delegate a Catholic teacher, his presence an indication of the changes that had come over the Upper Mississippi country since the time when New England Protestants almost single-handedly carried the torch for the common school movement. Delegate O'Connor of La Salle told the meeting that the practice of Bible reading "throws a firebrand among the schools. The dominant party controls it. If we [the Catholics] get the upper hand, we may choose to introduce our training."

Ultimately, the delegates in 1859 supported a statement that Illinois association members "recommend the reading of the Bible, without note or comment, in all our schools.'' That statement was still beyond what Catholics desired, but it might have provided some basis for compromise if divisions over the issue had not already hardened. Firmly rebuffed in their repeated bids for school funds, Catholics responded by throwing themselves even more vigorously into promotion of their own school system.

Clearly, in regard to the issue of common schools, the ''era of universal reform'' left a mixed legacy for the Upper Mississippi country. Earnest, righteous reformers were largely successful in building the foundations of a public school system across the region in the 1840s and 1850s, but their achievements fell far short of their goals. A major reason for this was that other groups in the population fought to keep portions of the past—doctrine, tradition, the mother tongue. And much less success was achieved by reformers in their Sabbatarian campaigns. Without question the Sabbath was more desecrated across the region in 1860 than in 1840 in the view of the reformers.

Through it all, those seeking to reform this new region were becoming increasingly angry at one group in the population—the immigrants. The feeling was reciprocal. Immigrants felt resentment toward those Americans who tried to change their customs, who labeled their traditions sinful. This was especially true in the debate over the use of alcoholic beverages.

7. Whiskey and Lager Bier

Opening a day of great expectations, the Sons of Temperance marched in communities across Illinois on June 4, 1855. Galvanized by Sabbath sermons of the previous day, the temperance forces formed ranks for what many believed would be the final victorious assault on Demon Rum—a statewide vote on prohibiting the manufacture and sale of alcoholic beverages.

At tiny Plainview in Macoupin County, Illinois, the Sons of Temperance met at their Temperance Hall at an early hour that Monday morning, then led the local citizenry to the Presbyterian church for a final series of speeches before the balloting. The program lasted three hours, with songs as well as lectures stressing the importance of the day. The crowd—"a large concourse of ladies and gentlemen from the country around"—spilled over outside the building, and afterward all lined up in another procession to march to the election hall. The ladies formed parallel lines for the men to pass through, urging them on with the "Prohibitory Song":

> Hurrah for Prohibition
> Hurrah for Prohibition
> Hurrah for Prohibition
> Give us the laws of Maine.

Inside the hall, the town's voters balloted 77 to 2 in favor of statewide prohibition. Plainview had spoken.

But Plainview was not Illinois nor did it reflect the growing heterogeneity of the Upper Mississippi country. Across the state on that June day, and in other states of the region during the mid-1850s, the wishes of the New England reformers and their allies collided with the desires of other newcomers from the upper South, from Europe, from lands outside the reformers' sphere of influence. In Illinois the voting showed that European immigrants and the residents of southern Illinois combined to defeat the reformers, as they had frustrated the Sabbatarian campaigns and many of the common school projects. The prohibition movement's failure, in turn, had a major impact on the antislavery movement and the development of the just-born Republican party.

Until that fateful vote, rising anger across much of the North over alcohol and its sway seemed to bode ill for the future of intoxicating beverages. This marked a change, for the past in both Europe and America had been a drinking past, with alcohol seldom far from the center stage of daily life. Prior to the opening of the nineteenth century, clergymen in Ireland, the German states, New England, and the rest of the United States generally took their rum, beer, whiskey, or wine openly, without shame. Drunkenness was often criticized by religious leaders, but drinking per se was seldom opposed. Ministers' salaries, in fact, were sometimes paid in part in alcoholic beverages.

The southerners who came into Illinois's Egypt, Iowa's river towns, and the Wisconsin lead region early in the nineteenth century carried their frontier drinking habits with them, occasionally shocking other newcomers who felt that the Bible commanded total abstinence from alcohol. Repelled by the sight of church members drinking and mingling with intoxicated persons at a southern Illinois barn raising, a missionary complained that "both lay members and preachers drink to intoxication whenever a convenient opportunity occurs, even on the Sabbath." The accuracy of this view was apparent when a Cairo newspaper stated that "the use of intoxicating drinks seems more natural than the use of water."

Then came the Europeans. Their cultural baggage included a host of traditions involving alcohol—social, religious, economic. Germans lost little time in establishing vineyards and building breweries, while the Irish became irrefutably linked with whiskey in the popular mind. Canal and railroad officials sought to bar liquor from their projects by firing contractors who brought it to the men, but such efforts had only temporary success.

The immigrants' holy men were part of these traditions. Ministers and priests drank, sometimes to excess. Bishop Loras of Dubuque complained in a letter to Dublin that many Irish clergymen "are not free of that mean vice which does more harm to religion in America than all the rest of the vices together." He accordingly urged Dublin to send him priests whose main virtue was temperance. A Muscatine priest's complaint to Bishop Loras indicated how real—and dangerous—the drinking problem was. A touring priest "caused several Catholics to go with him into groceries several times a day even on Sunday," the Muscatine clergyman wrote, and these actions did "more harm in a few days, than the most pious and devoted clergyman can repair for months." (Liquor was sold in groceries.)

All of this was observed by others coming into the Upper Mississippi country, some of whom were in a position to keep statistics. Of Chicago's 668 saloons, groceries, and other locales where alcoholic beverages were made or sold in 1855, a temperance lecturer noted, "six hundred are kept by foreigners—311 of them being Germans and the remainder nearly all Irish."

The fact that use of alcohol often led to violence was a major argument in the temperance arsenal. And conditions in 1853 and 1854 seemed to bring ever more violence. Immigration was increasing, a financial panic raised food prices sharply, and drinking seemed more widespread than ever.

To the reformer, both drinking and violence were to be attacked because they revealed a lack of self-control, an inability to dominate one's own body. Newspapers of the time were filled with reports of murders, beatings, rapes, suicides, and similar incidents stemming from immigrant drunkenness. Bodies of slain Irish women were periodically discovered, bruised and discolored, their intoxicated husbands slumped nearby. Chicago's frequent election-day riots always were linked with the activities of politicians who "pandered to the basest passions of man, by first inflaming them with whiskey." And efforts to block Sabbath liquor sales provoked Germans and Irish to reclaim their favorite beverages through savage fighting. The following news item was typical: "On Sunday last, six Irishmen came to [Dixon, Illinois] from Paolo station on a hand car, purchased a keg of whiskey, and soon became very drunk. Nearly all day they were running the

Drinking habits migrated with the Irish and Germans, creating monuments readily visible—and obnoxious—to temperance reformers. This ambrotype, circa 1855, shows some of the ambiance of Klinkel's Lager Beer Saloon, located in Chicago on the east side of North Wells Street, north of North Avenue.

Courtesy of the Chicago Historical Society.

car back and forth over the road, and finally left for Paolo a few minutes before the down train from Freeport was due. About three miles from Dixon they met the train in a curve of the road—the locomotive being nearly upon them before it was discovered. Three of the men were sober enough to spring from the car and save themselves, the others were not.''

The immigrant thus began to acquire a collective image: he drank, he was violent. These two aspects meshed to make him an unwelcome intruder in the eyes of those struggling to save the West. Everywhere they saw the drunken immigrants causing destruction, mayhem, and spoilation. One historian wrote that ''probably in no decade in American political history was there as much rioting as in the 1850s,'' usually involving the Irish and/or Germans on one side and Americans on the other. In the East, the decade was marked by Protestant-Catholic riots and by attacks on Catholic churches and touring church officials. These ranged from the Irish attack on a parade of the American Protestant Association in Newark, to a Cincinnati riot against the visiting papal nuncio, to Louisville's ''Bloody Monday'' in August of 1855, in which Germans were beaten by Americans.

Although Americans were the clear instigators of many of these outbreaks, the impression grew in the early fifties that immigrants were basically to blame for most of the violence and new troubles besetting the nation. They were behind the region's first labor disturbances, and immigrants organized most of the early trade unions, regarded as an unwelcome foreign growth by many Americans. As early as 1837 Irish canal workers in Illinois struck for higher wages, and canal laborers staged the first reported Chicago area strike ten years later, demanding a more agreeable foreman as well as a wage increase. (They lost.) A strike by railroad workers near Galena in late 1852 was followed quickly by arson against Illinois Central property in the area. Other strikes were launched from the 1850s onward as Chicago became the center for immigrant labor union activity.

Election days were increasingly riot days in the new urban centers, a development that worried as many natives as it angered. Liquor flowed freely around the polls, and politicians learned early that these newcomers' votes could be bought. Such incidents stirred the reformers to point out the un-American, as well as the un-Christian, aspects of this vast immigration. Democracy depended on intelligent voters who made their choices unswayed by outside pressures. But the immigrant hordes were being swayed by liquor and unscrupulous politicians as well as by their priests. Worse yet, they often voted for the wrong side. "Either the Irish population of the country are right in attempts to rule us—to control our elections—to vote illegally—to prevent American citizens from voting at all—or they are wrong," the Chicago reform journal *Free West* sermonized. "Either the American and fully naturalized citizens of this country and of this city are to control it, or they are to permit the foreign rabble to control it for them."

Milwaukee's spring election in 1854 provided the type of eruption that was becoming commonplace: an Irishman challenged a German's right to vote, and soon stones and brickbats were flying. The sheriff was powerless to stop the riot, for to call the military would have only added fuel to the fire—militia units were largely all-German or all-Irish. And one of the rioters was himself a city constable.

Five months later St. Louis exploded with an election riot after Irish voting irregularities were trumpeted and a disenfranchised Irishman stabbed a boy in a scuffle. "This," the newspapers reported, "was a signal for a general riot." The mob destroyed much of the waterfront in its attacks on Irish saloons, and Catholic churches and St. Louis University narrowly escaped destruction. Surveying such carnage, the *Chicago Tribune* asked, "Why do our police reports always average two representatives from 'Erin, the soft, green isle of the ocean,' to one from almost any other inhabitable land of the earth?...Why are the instigators and ringleaders of our riots and tumults, in nine cases out of ten, Irishmen?"

The immigrants' side of these incidents was usually unpublicized. Occasionally some inkling of a possible alternate cause leaked through, as when newspapers noted that a Milwaukee riot by three to four hundred laborers in July of 1853 erupted after their railroad subcontractor had not paid them their wages when due. In fact, wages—unpaid, overdue, or arbitrarily reduced—figured as the principal cause in several cases of violence by immigrants, including one of the region's most infamous incidents, the La Salle riot of 1853.

La Salle and its twin city of Peru had known immigrant-native tensions from earliest days, as easterners were drawn to the economic possibilities of the site on the Illinois River in north-central Illinois and Irish and Germans arrived for canal and railroad work. In 1838 Methodists organized and Catholic priests visited. Presbyterians had a church there the following year. A touring Irish priest found a "Catholic atmosphere" in the community in the early 1850s and a Protestant visitor agreed: "Catholics have a strong hold here—or, more properly speaking, 'Satan has his seat' here."

Reformers complained of the "grog shop" atmosphere and the large volume of liquor consumed. The Irish and German canal and railroad workers refused to take criticism silently and struck back in various ways, including a German assault on a temperance rally in Peru in 1854. (A witness asked, "Can the Germans hope to become worthy citizens...while they permit themselves to be used, as they now are, as pliant tools" of the saloon owners?)

The Reverend William H. Collins, who came to the First Congregational church of La Salle in May 1852, never got over the initial shock of what he found in that "modern Sodom." With forty-five dramshops serving a population of two thousand, plus two billiard saloons, a bowling alley, "and several houses which for infamy, deserve no mentionable name," he found La Salle to be the setting for "more wickedness in the shape of profanity, Sabbath-breaking, card-playing, fighting, debauchery, and intemperence" than he had ever before encountered. It was a community with women lying drunk on the sidewalk, justice corrupted by "foreign magistrates," and everywhere men with a "feverish thirst for gain." The Reverend Collins hoped for moral improvement after railroad crews moved on and new settlers moved in. However, the continued moral regression finally drove him from the community in 1858; he said that "the character of a large portion of the inhabitants of the place was not congenial."

The Irish and Germans of La Salle and Peru had to contend with more than the likes of the Reverend Collins. Their troubles were often of more immediate concern than whether liquor could be sold or the Sabbath would be kept holy. The issues they confronted often turned, rather, on questions of economic survival.

Immigrants learned early in the canal era that one of their principal barriers to an adequate existence was the uncertainty of wage payments. This problem would occur over and over for workmen as industrialism moved into the American frontier, where cash was in short supply and employers were often hundreds or thousands of miles away. The problem first hit the La Salle area during the 1830s, when canal laborers were repeatedly left unpaid for months while contractors scurried about the landscape rounding up cash. As the fifties dawned, the same phenomenon plagued railroad workmen, and their situation was worsened by the fact that thousands of them had been lured to the Upper Mississippi by the promise of high wages.

"WANTED! THREE THOUSAND LABORERS" the Illinois Central advertisements proclaimed in New York. One Irish carpenter reported in 1852 that after reading such handbills he had gone to the company's New York office, where agent Phelps had "positively asserted that I would have $2 per day, and that boarding could be had from $1.25 to $1.50." When this Irishman arrived in Illinois, however, he found that "no carpenters were wanted" by the line. Other Irishmen told of large numbers of their countrymen hired with similar inducements, $1 a day promised, spending $5 apiece for passage to Chicago, and then beginning to work only to discover that wages were being cut without notice. When this occurred at Dixon, Illinois, and a group of railroad laborers demanded to be paid, they were told to come back in another month. Desperate for his wages and unable to wait a month, one of the Irishmen pressed forward, complaining vociferously, but he was suddenly confronted by the contractor's revolver aimed at his head. The worker was informed that "if he uttered another word" the contractor "would blow his brains out."

With top-level decisions and lower-level practices all geared to producing an abundant supply of labor, immigrants continued to be victimized by false promises. The Illinois Central's construction chief received a frantic note in late September of 1852 that some six hundred destitute Irishmen had arrived at Chicago to begin work: "What shall be done? They say Phelps promised employment on arriving in Chicago."

Soon the *Western Tablet,* the Irish Catholic newspaper published in Chicago, was reporting numerous cases of "scoundralism" against Irish workmen. The incidents followed the same pattern, although sometimes recruitment had occurred in Chicago rather than New York. Two Irishmen wrote that they had responded to handbills seeking three hundred men to work on the Wisconsin and Chicago railroad line, some thirty miles north of Chicago, with wages of one dollar a day promised and "every necessary comfort would be provided for our accommodation at the work." Once employed, the pair found that the foreman's "brutality and tyranny would eclipse that of any Negro driver," while bed and board were "of the most filthy and abominable kind." The two described what happened next: "Having been employed for about two days and a half, the boss informed us that he considered he had already sufficient men in the two gangs—there were in all about forty-five, and yet he had advertised for three hundred—so he would dispense with our services. On going to the office for settlement, instead of allowing us for the full time employed, we were curtailed about half a day, and ordered to take our wages out in goods from the store."

There were many more of these incidents—workmen counting railroad ties walked away unpaid, immigrants wondering why they had left their homes across the sea for this. Resentment and cynicism followed. "The 'poor exiles of Erin' are gulled and fleeced enough by the vultures and harpies of New York," one infuriated Irishman wrote after learning of a company's false recruitment claims, "without being cozened by cheating advertisements of 'three thousand men wanted on the railroad.'" These developments formed a large part of the backdrop for the drama that unfolded in La Salle and Peru in December 1853.

The facts, as sifted from a variety of often contradictory records, appear to be as follows: the predominantly Irish crew of some 450 men, working on excavations and the embankment for the Illinois Central bridge over the Illinois River, were informed in early December that their $1.25 daily wage had been retroactively cut to $1. Those dissatisfied would be paid off and dropped December 15, announced contractor Albert Story. Many of the men then went on strike, seeking to block others from working, hoping to force the contractor to pay them the promised wage.

On the fifteenth, as wages were being given out, an error was found in payroll records, and payments were suddenly stopped. The angered employees rushed to the contractor's office the next day and demanded their pay; in the scuffle the contractor, Story, was struck. He drew his pistol, fired, and fatally wounded one of his attackers. Story then hurried home, unaware that a railroad superintendent had already rescued Mrs. Story and the children. When he found his family gone, Story ran to the stable to get his horse, but the mob caught him and pummeled him to death with picks, shovels, and stones. That evening the sheriff and a posse began arresting Irishmen in their shanties and on neighboring hills.

Coming at a time of increasing tensions between native-born Americans and immigrants and between industrial workers and employers, the La Salle killings provoked a storm of indignation. The reform journal *Free West* stated that Story was killed while "defending his property" and claimed that the mob also tried to kill his wife and children; the journal conceded, however, that the workmen attacked "in consequence of a reduction in wages." From the German community of Belleville, the *Belleviller Zeitung* reported simply that it was a riot of Irish workers, with no mention of the wage cut. Reporting the militia's roundup of Irishmen, the *Chicago Tribune* proclaimed: "Had the whole thirty-two prisoners that were taken been marched out and shot on the spot,...the public judgment would have sanctioned it at once." The *North-Western Christian Advocate* provided its analysis: "Probable cause—rum."

Closer examination reveals a more complex situation. One major point was that the contractor had advertised widely for workmen at the $1.25-per-day wage and hundreds had arrived by November as winter began. Then came Story's blunt announcement of the wage reduction. To Irish workmen in America in 1853, a notice of wage reduction and a delay in payment were simply repetitions of an old theme; all events conformed to the pattern. Because the Irish felt themselves surrounded by a hostile community that regarded them as intruders and derelicts, their vigorous reaction is perhaps more understandable. (As Albert Story ran to his stable he yelled back that he was "man enough for a hundred Irishmen.") In contrast to the implications of the newspaper reports, the *Western Tablet* described the slain Irishman, Ryan, as a father of two children, who "had the name of being an honest and peaceable man."

The Illinois Central quickly decided to "clear the bluff of any vestige" of the former crew and began the bridge project anew with different contractors as well as new employees, guarded by soldiers. Although it was reported in the aftermath of the riot that "the ringleaders have all fled," twelve men were indicted and four were convicted of murder, but Governor Joel A. Matteson pardoned them after a circuit judge noted that none of the four was ever shown to have been a leader or participant in the murder. The governor, perhaps with an eye to the enormous immigrant vote, but certainly aware as well of La Salle's social and political environment, justified mercy toward the four Irishmen by noting that Story "shot one of their countrymen at a time when the Irish felt they had not been very well used, and when a good deal of excitement had prevailed upon the work....A large number were present, and on the shooting of the man by Story there seemed to be created a general panic among the men and great excitement prevailed."

Reports in the Irish *Western Tablet* also went beyond the bare events, contending that "so long as railroad companies and contractors persist in holding out false promises to laborers, in order to allure them to leave comfortable employment and good homes, to live in rotten shanties and dismal swamps, we have no hope that this will be the last outrage of this kind."

The La Salle murders had a strong impact on the immediate area. Governor Matteson was hung in effigy when he visited La Salle, and the local native-born element grew bitter over the lack of a crackdown against the Irish. The following summer twenty-six community leaders informed the editor of a La Salle newspaper that they were withdrawing their patronage because, since Story's murder, he had "both truckled and bowed to Irish arrogance and outrage," and he had supported the governor's pardons for those convicted.

Across the broad valley of the Upper Mississippi, gory incidents such as the La Salle strife and the multiplying tales of immigrant drunkenness spurred the temperance movement to new levels of activity. It was a diverse movement, both in types of participants and in their motives. Modern students of temperance contend that status defense played a large role in such campaigns. The higher-status group, according to this argument, tried to avoid being identified with the lower-status group. The best way to do this was to abstain from practices shared with the lower-status group. In the antebellum era the use of alcohol was such a shared custom; by choosing total abstinence, native-born Americans could separate themselves and distinguish themselves from foreign-born immigrants.

Historians note also that most of the temperance crusades arose during periods of tumultuous change, when Americans felt threatened by drastic shifts in accustomed patterns. This was the case between the 1830s and the Civil War, as migration and immigration confronted thousands with unfamiliar surroundings. Sentimental reverence for the supposed virtues of olden times and the tradition-bound extended family increased the popularity of such songs as "Home Sweet Home," "The Old Oaken Bucket," and "Old Folks at Home." In this transformed world, former easterners spoke longingly of their childhood, when the village church symbolized a united people. (The fact that intoxicating beverages had been common in those olden times, in New England as elsewhere, was overlooked.)

The temperance movement grew rapidly in such an environment, spreading through voluntary organizations in the tradition of American reform. First came the American Temperance Society (1826), followed by the American Temperance Union (1833), the Washington Temperance Society (1840), the secretive Sons of Temperance (1842), and a host of local societies and clubs, most with strong connections to Christian evangelism. By late 1843, Chicago had 1,989 persons (out of a total population of 7,580) enrolled in four temperance groups.

Just as other reform movements were swerving away from moral suasion and gradualism toward the goal of immediate perfection, so the temperance reformers began demanding total abstinence from alcohol rather than just its temperate use. One prominent reformer told his formula for determining drunkenness: "He is drunk, if you can smell his breath." Others would sign "T = Total" after their names to indicate their support of total abstinence. This usage survives in the modern term, *teetotaler*.

The Presbyterian general assembly began shifting against drink by 1816, paralleling developments in the Congregational church. Methodist and Baptist clergymen were drawn to total abstinence sporadically down to the 1850s. The movement grew especially fast among Americans in those frontier districts receiving heavy European immigration. Iowa had a Sons of Temperance organization

WASHINGTONIAN ASSOCIATION OF DANBY.

PLEDGE.

We, whose names are annexed, desirous of forming a Society for our mutual benefit, and to guard against a pernicious practice which is injurious to our health, standing, and families:—Do pledge ourselves as gentlemen, that we will not drink any spirituous or malt liquor, wine or cider.

Danby, Ill., _____ 185__

This is to Certify, *That _____*

having subscribed _____ name to the foregoing Pledge, is by virtue thereof, a Member of the **WASHINGTONIAN**

ASSOCIATION OF DANBY, *Du Page County, Ill., and by appointment, a Member of the Vigilance Committee.*

Secretary. _____ **President.**

**Pledge certificate, Washingtonian
Association of Danby, Illinois.**

The Washington Temperance Society, launched in Baltimore in 1840, quickly spread into the Upper Mississippi Valley. It separated the temperance cause from church leadership, appealed to the actual drinker rather than the potential imbiber, and broke tradition with its use of theater (such as "Ten Nights in a Bar-Room"), music, and personal testimonies.

Courtesy of the Chicago Historical Society.

soon after achieving statehood in 1846, and it multiplied so rapidly that there were 80 local groups in the state by 1850; by that time the organization also claimed some 3,000 members in Wisconsin. In Illinois the Sons of Temperance was launched in 1847 and listed over 330 local divisions and more than 10,000 members by 1852. The Good Templars organization, a national temperance group, reported in 1858 that Illinois was its national leader with 145 lodges, followed closely by other states of the region; New York had only 15. Protestant churches often doubled as centers for local temperance agitation, and when the first convention of the "friends of prohibition" was held in Illinois, some 200 of the 240 delegates were clergymen.

Catholics became active in the cause as well, belying the popular view of Irish and Germans as inevitable drinkers. That Protestant America used the Irishman's drunkenness to censure him and his church was widely known in Ireland, and this fact was used to advertise the temperance cause throughout the island. The *Cork Abstainer* in 1841 reported there were signs in New York proclaiming "No Irishman Need Apply," and commented: "For what reason was this?—because the Irishman got the credit of being a drunkard; he came from Ireland, and, according to the closeness of Yankee logic, coming from such a country, he must necessarily be addicted to the national vice of drunkenness."

The Italian priest Samuel Mazzuchelli made a similar observation after serving in the states of the Upper Mississippi Valley from 1830 to 1843. "The greater number of the emigrants from Ireland" became "slaves to the sin of intemperance," he wrote, and zealous Protestants, "chiefly the Presbyterians," used this as an excuse to attack the Catholic church. While Irish Catholics joined the temperance movement to improve their way of life, Father Mazzuchelli said, they also sought "to remove that occasion of scandal which made fruitless so many discussions in defense of the truths contradicted by Protestants."

The major Catholic exponent of changing these habits and that reputation was Father Theobald Mathew of County Tipperary, who devoted most of his adult life to the cause of total abstinence. By 1841 he claimed to have convinced half of the Irish population to sign the pledge. Father Mathew visited the United States from 1849 to 1851, dined at the White House, was given a parade in Boston, was feted in Chicago, and signed half a million Roman Catholics to the pledge. Some of the

Catholic hierarchy were angered, however, by his joint appearances with Protes-tant temperance leaders known for their attacks on Catholicism.

In Chicago, Catholic temperance groups claimed two thousand members by 1847, and they often demonstrated on the Fourth of July. The Catholic Sons of Temperance, "attired in the beautiful regalia of their order," marched in the Joliet parade in 1852, and the following summer Springfield's Independence Day festivities were marked by the appearance of the Roman Catholic Total Abstinence Society. "The entire procession (with one or two exceptions) was com-posed of Irishmen."

Despite—or perhaps because of—the troubles at La Salle, Father John O'Reilly, the community's priest in the early fifties, was "thoroughly a temperance man," and a Protestant activist noted with approval that the priest announced a local temperance meeting from the pulpit. Many other Catholic priests and high-ranking church officials were identified with the temperance campaigns. Bishop Van de Velde of Chicago, who invited Father Mathew to speak in the Chicago diocese, occasionally preached temperance sermons. At one such occasion in the Chicago cathedral in 1851 eight hundred persons took the pledge. Bishop Loras of Dubuque invited Catholics there to vote for a statewide Iowa prohibition law, and Minnesota's first Catholic bishop, Joseph Cretin of St. Paul, was known for his support of temperance.

From these varied origins grew the wide-ranging temperance movement of the early fifties. But with new levels of activity and determination came greater frustration. It was increasingly clear that reform by example, by moral suasion, was not winning many converts among the hordes of foreign-born. A new ap-proach, a new direction, was called for. That new direction led into coercive reform through law. But laws are created through politics, and politics had tradi-tionally been spurned by religious leaders as corrupt and sordid, something to avoid because it involved compromise. And there could be no compromise with sin.

The dilemma over political action bothered many. It was succinctly stated by the grand worthy patriarch of the Illinois Sons of Temperance in 1850. Neither he nor his organization thought their movement could be a political party, he said, "striving with others for the loaves and fishes of office." But he now realized that temperance was "of great political importance," and the Sons of Temperance could not shirk from requiring lawmakers to deal with the subject. Other organizations went through a similar soul-searching before carrying their fight into the political arena.

And the legislators began to bend, sometimes only slightly, often just enough to calm the temperance advocates. As this happened, the issue moved out of the exclusive realm of religion into the open field of political combat. In 1849 Wisconsin's legislators passed a short-lived law requiring liquor dispensers to post a bond and pay for damages caused later, beyond the saloon or grocery, by their drinking customers. In 1851 both the Iowa and Illinois legislatures banned the sale of intoxicants (except beer in Illinois) in amounts of less than a quart. Illinois also prohibited the sale of liquor for drinking on the premises and barred sales to persons under eighteen. These laws, aimed mainly at the immigrant groggeries, were allowed to pass by saloon lobbyists who "were shrewd enough to see the impossibility of enforcement." A Belleville clergyman hailed the new Illinois law and wrote, "I shall rejoice exceedingly if it can be enforced, especially in this town." There was little cause to rejoice, for the Belleville minister or for his fellow laborers elsewhere in the temperance movement. But then a momentous event took place in the East and rallied the reformers to try again.

The event was a breakthrough in New England; passage in Maine of a state prohibition on the manufacture and sale of alcoholic beverages, with numerous provisions for ferreting out violators. Its author was Neal Dow, mayor of Portland, and he was rapidly elevated to hero status in the new frenzy of political activity by temperance groups around the United States. The Maine victory transformed the 1853 Sons of Temperance convention in Chicago into a massive endorsement, really a sanctification, of the Maine law. It also encouraged renewed political efforts. When the Illinois Maine Law Alliance was formed later that year its cardinal tenet was that members pledged never to vote for a candidate "not unequivocally pledged to the Maine law." As legislators met in 1853 and later, they encountered piles of petitions from similar groups demanding passage of a prohibitory law.

The movement in Iowa, Wisconsin, and Illinois still lacked the ingredients of victory in 1853. Wisconsin voters narrowly endorsed adopting the Maine law, but the two houses of the state legislature disagreed and so blocked passage. The Illinois legislature also failed to come up with a bill, stirring the *North-Western Christian Advocate* to chide the state's citizens: "How many, on the morning of the last election day, around the family altar, prayed, 'let Thy kingdom come,'... then went and voted for some of these men, or others like them. If the Legislature closes its present session without passing the Maine Liquor Law, how many murders will be committed....Think of this, Christian politician, and remember, that if you helped to elect these men, you helped make those speeches....Remember that you are accessory to the crimes, and accountable to God."

The frustration that drove many reformers to politics drove others to rush the groggeries and beer gardens. Women led "liquor riots" against saloons in a string of Illinois communities—Milford, Farmington, Canton, Plano, Tonica, Towanda, Liberty, La Salle, and Winnebago—and grog-selling groceries in Bloomington owned by Thomas Malony, John O'Brien, and Patrick O'Brien were smashed by mobs following a "mass temperance meeting." After a Methodist preacher in Baraboo, Wisconsin, openly wished during a church service that "the thunderbolts of heaven would shiver the brick tavern," a group of church women promptly invaded the brick tavern and laid waste to its bottled goods. In Mount Pleasant, Iowa, citizens took up a collection and purchased all the liquor in the community and turned it over to local physicians, who were instructed to control its use for medicinal purposes.

Politics was the new order for most temperance reformers. Sunday closing laws were passed in cities ranging in size from Quincy to St. Louis, while liquor was banned outright in several more, including Carbondale, which used its first city ordinance to prohibit liquor within its limits. Temperance candidates carried every ward of Janesville, Wisconsin, during the spring election of 1855, "and on that night, hundreds of torches and a multitude of bonfires illuminated our streets." The temperance, or more accurately, the prohibition movement was on the attack by mid-decade across the Upper Mississippi country.

Southerners and immigrants rose to meet it. In southern Illinois there were few Maine law alliances. Isolated New Englanders working in Egypt wrote of their shock in discovering that local Baptist and Methodist clergy openly criticized temperance and the Maine law. But the perils of raising the issue in Egypt were most dramtically revealed to the Reverend W.H. Bird, an agent of the American Home Missionary Society at DuQuoin. When he began actively speaking up for temperance, the wrath of the local "rum party" was stirred: "I soon became a term of reproach among them and all manner of insult has been given. Men have frequently come out of their dirty den, (drinking place) which was not far from us, and tottered along opposite our house, and turned about in the presence of my wife or daughters pulled down their clothes and exhibited themselves in the most shameful manner possible. Frequently in my absence, on Saturdays, my wife and daughters have been compelled to shut themselves up closely in the house.... Hardly a week has passed without some mischief being done, at night about my dwelling, such as taking off my gate—turning hogs into my yard, stoning or egging my house—fastening up our doors, and firing crackers under the windows while we were at our family devotions." The opponents even wrote obscenities on the church pulpit, and following a public debate on the Maine law they "marched around my house in rank and file, barking like dogs, howling like wolves, squalling like cats, and cursing like devils."

These responses of native-born Americans in southern Illinois had their counterparts in the region's cities, where Germans and Irish also were incensed by the clamor for temperance legislation. Milwaukee Germans were angered by an 1849 law requiring saloon keepers to post a $1,000 bond and remain liable for "all damages to the community" caused by their inebriated customers, up to a day after the drinking took place. To protest this, a mostly German mob stormed the home of a protemperance politician, and a rally was held to voice opposition to "wooden nutmeg legislators" (New Englanders) and the "ukases of the temperance aristocracy." Milwaukee Germans also attempted to block a protemperance demonstration eleven days later, and they almost succeeded. In Quincy, Illinois, part of the membership of a German Lutheran church split off when the minister raised the subject of temperance; he was accused of "blowing into the same horn as Presbyterians and Methodists do." When immigrants successfully urged a loophole in an Illinois prohibition proposal to permit beer sales by the barrel, the *Aurora Guardian* struck back: "Thus has FOREIGN INFLUENCE overpowered the expressed will of the majority of the native population."

Reformers foresaw a total change for the better if drinking would end. This 1842 temperance poster depicts "Eden" and "Sodom," the main difference being the presence of alcohol. "Eden" is compared to New England, the model for most reformers.

THE CONTRAST

A correspondent of the Peoria (Illinois) Register, thus describes two towns, both situated on the Illinois river, of about three years' growth, containing a population of three hundred each; yet in the character and conduct of the inhabitants, they form a perfect contrast to each other:

Look on this Picture!

One has no grog shop in it; no spirits or intoxicating drinks are sold at any of their stores; none are to be obtained by the glass within six miles. Wine is not to be found within twenty miles. No citizen of the neighborhood has been seen intoxicated there for more than a year. During the past year they have enjoyed the labors of a devoted Presbyterian minister; a church was organized by him ten months since, of thirty-three members; it now contains more than one hundred. There is also a flourishing Methodist church. The Sabbath has the delightful stillness and solemnity of that sweet day of rest in New England. A young man came last winter to establish a grog shop among that happy people; they called a public meeting on the occasion, and unanimously begged he would not afflict them with such an *intolerable nuisance*. He complied with their request.

And then on this!!

In the other town every store has a full supply of what they call *choice spirits*. The taverns and the groceries very cheerfully deal out the treacherous dram, artfully prepared to suit the taste of every patron. As the traveller entered that town from the north, he saw a spectacle which would move the hearts even of those citizens but for its being so common, *a man dead drunk* by the side of the road. In going out of the town at the south end on the same day, he saw another in the same beastly condition. There the Sabbath is distinguished from the other days of the week by the greater number that are seen strolling with their fishing rods and their guns, the greater amount of idleness and profanity.

There is no organized church of any name, and the few who once professed piety, are generally ashamed to have it known.

Who are the most guilty, they that license to sell, they that sell, or they that drink the poison that turns an Eden into a Sodom?

Conscientious father and mother, in which of these two towns would you train your children? You are helping to make your own town like one or the other.

Some of this new influence came from the immigrant press. When a proposal was advanced calling for Sunday-closing of all saloons within two miles of a church, the *Anzeiger des Westens* of St. Louis facetiously suggested a better way—Sunday could be changed to Monday. In Iowa, prominent German editor Thomas Guelich attacked the Maine law as "a despotic curtailment of the natural rights of man." Immigrants from Holland were vociferous in attacking the Maine law in Sheboygan County, Wisconsin, and in the Pella, Iowa area, using their newspapers as well as the pulpit.

In Illinois the two major German-language newspapers, the *Illinois Staats-Zeitung* of Chicago and the *Belleviller Zeitung,* lashed out at the Maine law. The *Staats-Zeitung* feared "the ghost of the old European police state" would develop as police searched houses, used paid informers, and destroyed property in ferreting out illegal beverages. "Instead of getting the best of European culture and humanity to the United States," the editor complained, "the incomparable silliness of the police state is being taken across the sea."

The Belleville German newspaper agreed, arguing that the Maine law principle contradicted both the Illinois constitution and the Declaration of Independence. It was "fanaticism," and it would "give the first deadly blow to the present blooming of our material conditions" under democracy. "We ourselves think sometimes that in our dear old town, Belleville, there are too many saloons," the editor said, but he argued that the license law and the proposed Maine law tended to increase the popularity of these businesses.

The Upper Mississippi Valley's heaviest concentration of Irish and Germans was in Chicago, which had four times as many Irish as the rest of Illinois by decade's end. In that city occurred the region's and the era's major explosion against prohibition. It came in the spring of 1855, as Illinois, Iowa, Wisconsin, and states to the east were reeling under the divisiveness of Maine law campaigns. Everywhere the temperance cause was becoming entwined with nativist politics, as the Know-Nothing party made its move into open candidacies. The nativists' bellicose speech was matched by that of its opponents, however. In 1852 appeared the *Western Tablet*, the quick-to-anger spokesman of Chicago's Irish Catholics, which repeatedly denounced nativists and the *Chicago Tribune* ("the organ of the Second Presbyterian church"). The Germans' *Illinois Staats-Zeitung* joined the *Western Tablet* in many of the Chicago battles against nativists.

The nativists had a growing army of sympathizers too, for many Americans were becoming disgruntled over both the actions and the power of immigrants. This was a period when an organization of "Old Settlers" of Chicago was formed, which limited membership to those who had arrived before 1837 and thereby shut out the bulk of the immigrants. Protestant religious publications sprouted in Chicago in the late forties and early fifties, frequently adding to the journalistic criticism of the foreign-born. From Chicago's religious soil came the *Congregational Herald,* the *Christian Times* (Baptist), the *North-Western Christian Advocate* (Methodist), and the *Chicago Evangelist* (New School Presbyterian).

The tone in these church publications was often circumspect and mild regarding the foreign-born, flaring only occasionally. The temperance issue spurred the *North-Western Christian Advocate* to describe the audience at an anti-Maine law rally as "almost wholly composed of foreigners.... Red noses, carbuncled cheeks, watery eyes, scarred lips, bloated forms, and uncombed heads, with loathsome breaths, expired in the utterance of horrible profanity, pronounced with a trans-Atlantic accent."

These denominational newspapers frequently reprinted *Chicago Tribune* articles approvingly and joined the journalistic affrays involving that anti-immigrant journal. (Opponents of the *Tribune* scored a minor victory, however, when a judge castigated one of its reporters but decided to allow him in the court-room, "because anything he says in his paper will do no harm.... If any man who has lived in Chicago two years believes anything he reads in the *Tribune,* unless it is consistent and self-evidently true on the face of it, it would be regarded as evidence of insanity or of a depraved mind.")

The temperance movement in Chicago needed the newspapers' support, for it had achieved few victories by the mid-1850s. In 1834 a city Sunday-closing ordinance was passed, and twelve years later a move to prohibit the sale of all intoxicants in Chicago failed only by a 7 to 5 vote in the city council. Temperance groups, including Catholic total abstinence societies, were prominent in city parades, and by the latter 1840s the city could boast of three temperance hotels. Switching to political action in 1854, temperance forces united behind Amos Gaylord Throop in the Chicago mayoral election. But Throop lost to Isaac L. Milliken, who favored giving Catholics a share of the school fund and who disagreed with the temperance cause. A Methodist newspaper blamed Throop's defeat on the opposition of Catholic priests, rum sellers, Irish whiskey drinkers, and German beer drinkers.

In early 1855 the campaign began for the March 6 Chicago city election. Religious, ethnic, and political spokesmen argued for weeks over a variety of issues that were woven into what rapidly became a nativist campaign—such topics as the school fund controversy, foreigners on night police duty, saloon brawls, the Democratic party's splintering over the 1854 Kansas-Nebraska Act. The major issue, however, remained the legislature's decision to submit to the voters in June the question of whether Illinois should prohibit the manufacture and sale of alcoholic beverages.

This was to be the Illinois Maine law. If passed it would be the ultimate achievement of the temperance reformers in their quest to create a utopia in the Upper Mississippi Valley. Agitation over the coming Maine law election in June quickly became intermixed with the campaign for the city election scheduled in March, some three months earlier. And this drew the immigrant question further into political strife.

Dr. Levi Boone, temperance candidate for mayor, challenged and finally defeated incumbent Isaac Milliken in the 1855 Chicago race. Boone was reputed to be a Know-Nothing; he was clearly a nativist. At the victory celebration the day after his 3,186 to 2,841 triumph, his supporters stressed the American aspects of his candidacy. The new city attorney rejoiced "that there was to be no more Jesuitical rule in this city." The *Tribune*'s spokesman at the rally described the Boone administration as one which came from "the American people of the city, possessing nine-tenths of the means, and nineteen-twentieths of the brains of the community." He called the victory a setback for "men who had pandered to the foreign population for ten years to his certain knowledge."

Boone performed as his supporters expected. In his opening speech to the new council he called for an end to Sunday liquor sales and said new liquor licenses should not be authorized, obviously expecting the prohibitory bill to be approved in June by the electorate. (The council raised the fee for licenses to $300 but continued to issue them.) Boone appointed eighty native-born Americans as policemen and leveled charges at "the existence in our midst of a powerful politico-religious organization" whose members held allegiance to "a foreign despot, boldly avowing the purpose of universal dominion over this land" by bloody means if necessary. The Methodist newspaper enthusiastically described what happened under a "no-two-ways-about-him" Maine law mayor: "Sabbath last, our six hundred grog and lager-bier shops were closed, and in the language of one, 'it was the only Sunday, that looked like Sunday, ever witnessed in Chicago.' Its effects were magical. The Monday morning police court, always crowded, was found with room enough and to spare. Mayor Boone's inaugural...breathed persistent prohibition in every line—a sound and healthy document—a paper for the times, abounding in temperance, righteousness, and municipal judgment to come."

But the seeds of conflict had been planted. Early in Boone's administration seventeen saloonkeepers were arrested for Sunday opening, and in response to this, mass meetings were held where "a determined resistance" to the law was mapped by liquor sellers and their allies. Most of the speakers were Germans, convinced of the justice of their cause. Since Boone's adherents were also convinced of the justice of their cause, only a spark was needed to ignite a major native-born versus foreign-born conflagration.

That spark appeared April 21 at a trial of several saloonkeepers charged with operating without a city liquor license. Their supporters had vowed to throng the courtroom, and so on that Saturday morning a crowd—almost all Germans—collected at Müller's beer hall on Randolph Street and marched by drumbeat across the street to the courthouse. Shoving began as police sought to clear the corridors. The melee was quickly carried outdoors, where "a terrible fight ensued between the police and the rioters in the middle of the street."

The group's drummer then beat an alarm tattoo, and over the next several hours Germans and other supporters of the saloonkeepers rushed to gather at different points around the city. Rumors spread rapidly. Witnesses claimed to have seen Germans with "muskets or guns or clubs," and warnings came that "the Dutch are crossing the bridge!" One man later testified he had seen "about thirty" Germans going by "with bludgeons." The Germans who pushed into the courthouse square in the afternoon demanded the release of those arrested during the morning fracas. When Mayor Boone saw this armed crowd approaching the courthouse, he called out troops he had previously alerted—the Light Guards, the National Guard, and the Chicago Light Artillery. These eventually brought quiet to the city the following day. Two police and two Germans died in the rioting; fifty-three Germans were arrested. Only two of those charged were ultimately convicted, however, receiving one-year prison terms.

These events of April 21–22 set off a storm of condemnation against the Germans. The *Daily Democratic Press,* usually the immigrants' friend, called it "the first instance that we are apprised of, in which, as a class, [the Germans] have openly and illegally arrayed themselves against the constituted authorities." The newspaper urged law-abiding Germans to influence the others to "bring no deeper stain upon themselves" and on Chicago.

The *North-Western Christian Advocate* held that, "as with ninety-nine hundredths of all the mobs, murders, and misery that infernalize our large cities, this riot originated in rum." The Methodist newspaper went on to tie the entire event to the irritation over the license changes felt by "the restive, infidel, beer-soaked, muddy-headed Germans, of whom the mobocratic party was wholly composed."

The *Belleviller Zeitung,* on the contrary, attempted to report the riot by printing the differing accounts of two witnesses, saying, "We are not like the English press, confident of the police officers." One of the witnesses said the police had suddenly, without announcement, charged too energetically into a crowd gathered at a beer saloon and ordered the customers to disperse. The lawmen then forced their way through nearby restaurants, threatening customers. However, the other witness quoted by the Belleville newspaper said that "even several German people protested" against the German group's initial plan to rally, and the police were belligerent because just one day previous they had been forced to break up a near-riot. "Be that as it may," the *Belleviller Zeitung* added, "everybody seems to be of the opinion that in the morning there had been wounded people only on the German side—and weapons used only by the police."

The spotlight now turned to the coming June 4 vote in Illinois on the Maine law. "Prohibition alone can eradicate the seeds of such outbreaks," the Methodist journal warned. "Let every voter remember the Chicago mob in June next, not forgetting that its chief instigators were infidel foreigners…uniting in imprecations upon 'American tyranny,' and adopting for their watch word, 'Great is whiskey and lager bier.'"

Temperance picnics, massive rallies and parades (three thousand children marched in a "Temperance Turn-Out" in Chicago), and the vociferous debates between newspapers helped rivet the attention of Illinois voters on the Maine law in the weeks following the Chicago riot. In the meantime, other states of the region were also facing decisions on the issue.

The Wisconsin controversy was complex; in 1853 voters had endorsed passage of a law modeled after Maine's by a vote of 27,519 to 24,109, with Milwaukee opposing it 4,381 to 1,243 and the Yankee counties heavily in favor of it (Rock County cast 2,494 ballots for the law, 432 against). The voter-approved measure then went to the legislature, which failed to enact it before the session ended. In 1855 a new legislature passed the measure, but Governor William Barstow then vetoed it. Germans were jubilant; they held mammoth torchlight parades, and Milwaukeeans gave the governor a hundred-gun salute. Iowa voters narrowly approved a Maine law in 1855, balloting 25,555 to 22,445 in its favor.

Some prominent Illinois politicians came out against the prohibition proposal, including Senator Stephen A. Douglas, senatorial aspirant Abraham Lincoln, and German-born Lieutenant Governor Gustave Koerner. Lincoln had fought against the prohibition concept years earlier in the legislature, charging that it struck "at the very principle upon which our government was founded." He supported individual, voluntary avoidance of intoxicants, and when asked in 1855 where he stood on the question facing the voters, he replied, "I am not a temperance man, but I am temperate to this extent—I don't drink." Koerner refuted the zealots' claims that victims of drink filled the jails and insane asylums, and he labeled the Maine law "a ruthless attempt on personal liberty."

Election day came June 4, 1855, and the Sons of Temperance marched expectantly in communities around the state. Thousands of Germans and Irish were out as well, helping assure the largest voter turnout ever recorded in Illinois to that time. As expected, southern Illinois and the immigrant centers went heavily against the plan. Counties in Egypt rolled up antiprohibition margins such as Franklin's 925 to 168, Union's 1,065 to 296, and Williamson's 1,132 to 278. St. Clair County, which includes Belleville, went 4,408 to 919 against the Maine law; Adams (Quincy), another German county, recorded a 2,885 negative to a 1,907 positive vote, while Effingham voted 775 to 190 against it. In Chicago the plan lost by 3,964 to 2,785, and the heavily immigrant seventh ward voted 759 no, 84 yes—333 more ballots than had been cast in the highly emotional March mayoral election. Cook County balloted against the measure 5,182 to 3,807.

Areas of Illinois largely settled by New Englanders supported the 1855 prohibition referendum. Bureau County (Princeton) voted in favor by 1,550 to 680, Knox County (Galesburg) went for it 1,623 to 1,087. The banner county was Winnebago (Rockford), which produced a margin for the Maine law of 2,153 to 363. The statewide total was 79,010 for the Maine law, 93,102 against.

The philosophies behind the Illinois rejection of the temperance crusade were enunciated later in the month, when four thousand persons held an anti-temperance rally in Chicago. Resolutions passed at the culminating program in Dearborn Park included:

1. That we condemn the Prohibitory Act and rejoice at its defeat, not because it was aimed at intemperance, an evil which all good citizens and good men deprecate, but because it was founded on a mistaken view of the powers and duties of government, and would have resulted in evils incalculably greater than those sought to be prevented.
2. That it is not within the legitimate province of government to take away rational liberty in order to prevent a crime or a vice which may result from its abuse....
3. That intemperance in legislation is an evil more dangerous and deadly by far than intemperance in eating or drinking....

The Maine law defeat severely deflated and disheartened the temperance leaders. One reason for its reversal was plain to see, however. The movement had the undesired effect of uniting immigrants in opposition. By 1856, eight states around the nation had enacted prohibition in some form, but the newfound strength of the foreign-born was the main force responsible for halting the movement in the Upper Mississippi Valley. One of Wisconsin's temperance advocates sadly watched the movement collapse and charged that both Republicans and Democrats now feared to frighten "our German friends." Even in Iowa, where the Maine law had scraped through in 1855, the reaction against it by immigrants was so vehement that modifications began to come almost immediately. By 1857 "homemade" cider and wine could be sold, and a year later wine and beer were legally defined as nonintoxicants. Breweries and saloons were also given legal sanction. The counterrevolution was victorious.

All this was evidence of a new political and social environment developing across the Upper Mississippi. Now immigrants were finding their own articulate spokesmen in politics and the press, they were developing a network of their own voluntary organizations, and they were proving that they could join *as immigrants* to aggressively work for common goals. The riots in La Salle and Chicago were not forgotten by Americans, but they were diminished in importance as other characteristics came more readily to be associated with the foreign-born.

Those who sought other reforms, changes not clashing with immigrant traditions, might have read lessons from 1855 events as they searched for support amid the decade's political breakup.

8. The Politicians

The handbills pressed eagerly into the hands of passersby on that spring evening demanded attention:

KIDNAPPERS!!

Citizen arrested under the Fugitive Slave Law!
All Citizens who feel interested in the Liberties of one of their number, are invited to meet at the United States Court Room, Saloon Buildings, corner of Lake and Clarke Streets, to-morrow morning, at 10 o'clock. Citizens! VIGILANCE IS THE PRICE OF LIBERTY.

These notices were effective in Chicago of 1851. The courtroom was packed the next morning, and the story quickly unfolded. Moses Johnson, a Negro, had been seized on the streets of Chicago by a U.S. marshall and several of his agents, acting under the 1850 Fugitive Slave Law. They charged that he was an escaped slave whose Missouri owner was offering a $200 reward for his return.

The case stirred enormous interest. The *Democrat* and the *Western Citizen* seized upon the incident and condemned Johnson's arrest and the city's call for militia to ward off expected violence. The judge discharged Johnson for lack of sufficient proof that he was a slave, and in seconds the freed man was passed exuberantly over the heads of the crowd to his Negro friends outside and whisked away to safety.

The determined crowd that pushed into the Chicago courtroom—"nine-tenths of them were the friends of the slave"—was said to include many Scotch, English, and Germans. This immigrant presence in the courtroom was a portent, for during the crucial decade then beginning, the foreign-born would play important roles as the nation and region grappled with issues that led to civil war. Ten years after Moses Johnson's joyful exit from the Chicago courtroom, there were anger, tears, and blood mingling in the struggle between Union and Confederate forces. And between the two dates—1851 and 1861—the Mississippi Valley was torn as the slave controversy was imposed upon the stresses accompanying the influx of immigrants and the native-born.

Just as other reforms had worked into the political system, so the slavery issue in this decade became irrevocably a political question, carried now beyond moral suasion and religious discussion into the realm of legal coercion. This meant that politicians confronted several moral controversies and were struggling to build voter majorities in a heterogeneous, shifting population burgeoning with massive immigration.

One of the crucial aspects of the 1850s was the breakup of the national party system. The Whigs, the Democrats' major opposition since the early 1830s, stumbled on the growing North-South division while suffering from a reputation as opponents of the "common people" during an era that gloried in that class. Although able to win occasional election races and to elect two presidents (1840 and 1848), the Whigs had few victories in the Upper Mississippi Valley.

A critical problem for the Whigs in the region was their lack of support among immigrants. Democrats had more success in courting specific groups, such as Mormons and immigrants, through special legislation or political appointments. The awarding of postmasterships, assistance in expediting township organization for religious colonies, and especially Senator Stephen A. Douglas's success in blocking an 1839 court ruling that would have barred all Illinois voting by noncitizens were prominent items in the list of Democratic accomplishments. The work among Mormons pointed toward the party's efforts among immigrants, for Democrats aided in protective legislation for the Nauvoo experiment and in turn received the group's ballots: "We give our voats to Democrats and by hour great numbers we can gain the voat for we all give our voats one way," an English Mormon wrote home from Nauvoo in 1845. This special attention by politicians of-

8

fended many non-Mormons, of course, just as attention to immigrants by candidates would stimulate anger among the native-born. New immigrants participated in politics, often soon after their arrival, and this justified special appeals to them by politicians.

The Northwest Ordinance had defined a voter as a white male citizen over twenty-one, resident two years in the district, and owner of fifty acres. The latter provision was inoperative on the frontier due to the large numbers of squatters who settled ahead of land surveys, and Illinois in 1812 won congressional approval for granting suffrage to all free white males of one year's residence in the territory. By 1829 Irishmen in Illinois were voting without a year's residence. Citizenship with a six-month state residence was added to the franchise requirements when a new state constitution was approved in 1848, but previous voters were allowed to continue voting even without citizenship. Chicago permitted voting in city elections to males over twenty-one if they had been in Illinois when the 1848 constitution went into effect.

Wisconsin that year permitted noncitizen males to vote if they had a year's residence in the state, registered their intent to become a citizen, and took an oath of allegiance. When Minnesota came into the Union in 1858, it beat back efforts by Congress to change its liberal suffrage rules. White foreign-born residents could vote if they had lived in the state four months and in the United States one year and had declared their intent to become citizens.

There is some evidence that even these slight prerequisites for voting were waived in some districts. The openness of the system surprised a Swedish visitor to the region in 1849 and she noted that Europeans were casting ballots with only a single year's residence. Democratic governor Joel Matteson sought without success in 1853 to lower Illinois's suffrage requirements to only a flat one-year residence, without citizenship.

Political participation was a two-way street. Immigrants expected to gain from it, perhaps police protection or the appointment of a local postal clerk who could read German. Milwaukee's Germans organized politically as part of an 1844 campaign to assure that voting on the Wisconsin statehood question would be open to all free white males who were twenty-one or over and had at least three months' residence. They teamed with the city's Irish to win that struggle and in the process formed the German Democratic Association to continue their political activity.

Amid such conditions, it was suicidal for the Whigs to line up against immigrants. But oppose them they did, coming out against the Wisconsin 1844 voting plan, urging a ban on alcohol in Iowa, trying to block preemption rights for foreign-born landseekers, and repeatedly lashing out in frustration at the Democrats' courting of immigrant voters. One estimate in 1840 put the support for Democratic candidates in Illinois at 90 percent of the 10,000 votes cast by the foreign-born. Failing in another desperate attempt to attract the rising immigrant tide to their banner, the Whigs were crushed in the 1852 presidential race. A Whig journal in Chicago said this loss came because the party's candidate had the image of native Americanism and "there is no ism, perhaps, that would be as fatal to the success of a candidate in the northwestern states."

The Whigs' disintegration was well under way when the Kansas issue erupted in 1854. Eager to create new states on the Great Plains, part of his grand plan for a railroad to the Pacific, Illinois Senator Douglas helped push through Congress a plan to create Kansas and Nebraska territories out of remaining sections of the Louisiana Purchase, and to permit settlers there to decide for themselves whether to permit slavery within their borders. This "popular sovereignty" held the possibility of establishing slavery north of the westward extension of Missouri's southern border—the famous 36°30′ boundary decreed by the 1820 Missouri Compromise as the dividing line between slavery and nonslavery in the West.

There was an added difficulty with the Kansas-Nebraska Act as Douglas shepherded it through Congress. Southerners had inserted an amendment barring noncitizens from both voting and office holding, a sharp contrast with tradition, under which all of a territory's free, adult male residents were eligible to vote almost immediately after its official organization. It became evident that the South had special reasons for keeping the immigrants out of the decision-making process in Kansas's early days, and this was noted by an editor in Belleville. Traditionally, he wrote, new state constitutions allowed all (free, adult, male) residents to vote. Why was this not being followed in the Kansas-Nebraska Act? "The answer is easy and simple," he said, "the Germans are against slavery." Although the Clayton amendment was dropped from the bill before it became law on May 30, 1854, it had already served to stimulate massive opposition from immigrants, especially Germans, in the Upper Mississippi country. (Later that year these sensitivities were rankled again when a Mississippi Democrat introduced a bill into Congress to require a twenty-one-year residence before citizenship.)

All across the region in the spring and summer of 1854 lights burned late in schoolhouses and churches as citizens and future citizens denounced the Kansas-Nebraska Act and Senator Douglas, who was charged with being lax in opposing the South. New groups appeared, such as the Free-Soil Democrats, the Free Democrats, and the Anti-Nebraska Democrats. Antislavery groups moved quickly into the fray, their Chicago newspaper urging formation of a new political party that would seek repeal of both the Kansas-Nebraska Act and the 1850 Fugitive Slave Law and restrict slavery to the South by banning it from the western territories.

Immigrants and reformers figured prominently in all these activities. In March, when the Kansas-Nebraska debate was still raging in Congress, Chicago's Germans held an impassioned rally. Resolutions were passed denouncing Douglas as "an ambitious and dangerous demagogue" and the proposed legislation as an "attempt to import southern aristocracy and southern contempt of free labor, into the North." Douglas was burned in effigy. A similar protest was held on the Fourth of July in Chicago in 1854, when German Turners marched with the Hibernian Society and the Scandinavian Union, symbolizing the rising immigrant political consciousness. Twenty-six Chicago clergymen wrote a joint letter to Douglas attacking him for his inequity in repealing the Missouri Compromise. The senator in turn attacked them for using the pulpit for political purposes.

Defections from the Democratic cause were frequent during those months as editors wrangled and Kansas-bound emigrants from New England addressed multitudes in Chicago and other cities. One of the most famous politicians to break with Douglas was Lieutenant Governor Gustave Koerner, German immigrant and long-time Democrat, who had stood "shoulder to shoulder" with the

Gustave Koerner (1809-1896).

Gustave Koerner came to America in 1833 at age twenty-two, having fled the unsuccessful 1830 revolt in the German states. He settled in Belleville, Illinois, studied law, and soon became a law partner of Irish native, James Shields. Koerner was elected to the state legislature in 1842 and became a Democratic state leader, rising to justice of the Illinois Supreme Court, 1845-1848, and lieutenant governor in 1852. He broke with his party over the Kansas-Nebraska Act and led the exodus of many Germans over to the new Republican party.

Courtesy of the Illinois State Historical Library.

GUSTAVUS P. KOERNER

senator during the previous campaign. The list of defectors also included such influential German editors as George Schneider of the *Illinois Staats-Zeitung* in Chicago and Theodore Guelich of the Davenport newspaper, *Der Demokrat.*

The first test of this political regrouping came in the fall of 1854. Douglas met hostility as he campaigned across northern Illinois and was shouted down at a massive September meeting in Chicago. He nevertheless predicted that the Democrats would win "all along the canal line," still a heavily Irish district, as well as elsewhere. The difficulties Douglas faced may be suggested by the fact that five of the state's nine representatives in Congress had voted against passage of his Kansas-Nebraska Act, and a sixth had opposed it but had been too ill to vote. An additional fact gave the 1854 campaign extra importance; the next legislature would elect a U.S. senator for the seat held by Irish-born Democrat James Shields.

The results were not as devastating as many Democrats had feared, but several details must have given pause to the party. The Democrats still managed to elect four of the nine congressmen from Illinois, but the largely German area around Belleville chose Lyman Trumbull, an anti-Nebraska Democrat, to go to Congress, and in rapidly growing Chicago the anti-Nebraska candidates won all offices they contested. (Trumbull was promptly selected for the U.S. Senate by the new legislature.) An examination of voting precincts would have revealed important German areas going 75 percent or better against supporters of Douglas, and this among a group previously known for its near-unanimity with the Democrats.

In Iowa, however, the Whigs made one of their last successful stands across the region, managing to win the governorship by soft-pedaling the temperance issue and attacking the Kansas-Nebraska Act. The Whig platform was a cornucopia of planks appealing to various groups, some of them, such as Germans and temperance reformers, mutually antagonistic. In this the Whig campaign foreshadowed the Republican efforts across the region in ensuing years.

Republicans formed a political organization in Wisconsin in 1854 and scored a near-sweep in their initial election run that year: two of three congressional races, control of the state assembly, a new U.S. senator, and many local officials. The future looked bright for the party, although it was clear that many Germans had sat out the balloting.

These 1854 debates and campaigns stemming from disagreement over the Kansas-Nebraska Act proved to be the beginning of an increasingly acrimonious, polarizing controversy that would only end with war in 1861. Douglas's legislation may be seen as the lid of a Pandora's box, which when opened produced more extensive questioning of the institution of slavery. Juxtaposed with this debate were continued arrivals of escaped slaves. Chicago, for example, counted only 323 blacks in the 1850 census, but during 1854, 482 escaped slaves crossed through the city in a seven-month period, many of them receiving newspaper publicity and appearing at rallies. Wisconsin erupted in 1854 over the events surrounding the capture of Joshua Glover, an escaped slave from Missouri, who was rescued by a mob from a Milwaukee jail and whisked to Canada. From that year until the Civil War, similar cases contended for newspaper space with lurid tales of the Kansas warfare between free-state and slave-state forces.

The growing network of antislavery organizations clutched at the opportunity presented by these 1854 events. Like other reform activists, opponents of slavery had turned to politics to espouse their cause, holding an Illinois antislavery political convention in 1841. Eight hundred persons signed a petition to the Illinois legislature in its 1844–45 session urging repeal of all laws making a distinction between white and colored persons. The Reverend Owen Lovejoy, brother of Elijah Lovejoy, who had been slain by a proslavery mob at Alton in 1837, ran an unsuccessful congressional race as an abolitionist in 1846, receiving 3,531 votes (he would win the seat in 1856). By 1850 antislavery groups were active throughout the Upper Mississippi country.

These organizations rested securely on the foundations of the general reform campaigns already sprouting across the region. They were transported west by New Englanders, spread through perfectionist arguments, and were operating in most cases through evangelical Protestant denominations. A typical leader of the abolitionist reformers was a "York stater" named Sherman M. Booth, who arrived in Milwaukee in 1848 after having helped organize the Connecticut Liberty party. Booth became editor of the *American Freeman,* the voice of political antislavery in Wisconsin, and soon enmeshed himself in temperance and related causes and in the formation of the new Republican party in 1854. Booth gained

Zebina Eastman (1815-1883).

Abolitionist editor and champion of many reform causes, Zebina Eastman typified the New England reformer in the Upper Mississippi country. A native of North Amherst, Massachusetts, he came to Chicago in 1842 and soon was editor of the antislavery *Western Citizen*. Eastman and his wife led organization of the Plymouth Congregational church in 1852 because of dissatisfaction over the weaker stand against slavery shown by the First Presbyterian church of Chicago.

Courtesy of the Chicago Historical Society.

Zebina Eastman.

Sherman M. Booth (1812-1904).

A "York Stater," Sherman Booth arrived in
Wisconsin in 1848 after helping organize a
Liberty party among antislavery enthusiasts in
Connecticut. He became editor of the aboli-
tionist *American Freeman* and later of the
Free Democrat, a Republican organ. Booth
became a leading Wisconsin reformer, helping
free a slave and defying the federal Fugitive
Slave Act.

Courtesy of the State Historical Society of Wisconsin.

fame for aiding the rescue of Joshua Glover from a Milwaukee jail that year, leading to the Wisconsin Supreme Court's controversial ruling that the 1850 federal Fugitive Slave Law was unconstitutional.

Some Protestant churches were split by the slavery controversy, often feuding not over whether the institution was good or bad but over the relative importance of antislavery compared with other reforms. An AHMS missionary in Vanceboro, Illinois, complained in 1853 that "my feelings have been much tried of late by ultra abolitionists" who oppose those "who do not sacrifice every other cause for their favorite one and always harp on it." Many others felt this way about abolitionism, and the electorate showed definite opposition to blacks on several occasions: when Illinois voters supported an 1847 constitutional provision to permit legislation barring entry of free blacks (the vote was 50,261 to 21,297); when Iowa's few hundred blacks were prohibited by a 49,387 to 8,489 statewide vote in 1857 from holding legislative seats and voting; and when Wisconsin's voters defeated a Negro-suffrage proposal 41,345 to 28,235, also in 1857. (Earlier, however, a Negro-suffrage plan had received 5,265 yes votes and 4,075 no votes in Wisconsin. This was insufficient for passage, since less than a third of the voters in the 1849 election cast ballots on the suffrage question.)

Some churches moved only gradually into open opposition to slavery. Baptist John Mason Peck was a leader in the successful 1820s fight against legalizing slavery in Illinois, and his denomination's publications regularly lambasted slavery and its northern supporters by the 1850s. But many in southern Illinois resisted this. Methodists, like the Baptists, suffered from internal arguments over the issue, but local conferences in Iowa, Wisconsin, and Illinois were attacking slavery vigorously as the fifties proceeded. The Rock River conference in 1855 requested that the Methodist national conference change the church's constitution to achieve "the utter extirpation of slavery" from the denomination.

Germans and Irish, the Upper Mississippi's two major groups of foreign-born, began to develop contrasting views on the issue. Although German Catholics, like most other Catholic groups, took no official stand on slavery, and Missouri Synod Lutherans found Biblical justification for owning slaves, other German church groups and even the national *Turnverein* condemned the slave system. By the mid-1850s, antislavery meetings often featured German-language speakers, and a contemporary survey found that eighty of the country's eighty-eight major German-language newspapers opposed the Kansas-Nebraska Act. The leading national antislavery organization made special note of this "great unanimity" against slavery among German newspapers and German immigrants in general. Many German leaders, especially the Forty-Eighters, became prominent opponents of slavery. This included Gustave Koerner, whose feelings on the issue led him in 1857 to pay the fine of a Negro caught under the Illinois ban on entry of free blacks into the state. By 1860 the support of this group for antislavery was so widespread and well known that a missionary describing an immigrant church in the river town of Canton, Missouri, added, "They are all right on the peculiar institution, of course, being Germans."

Perhaps the Germans' antagonism to the South and slavery and the Irish people's immunity from such feeling can be partly explained by their contrasting European backgrounds. Blocked in attempts to obtain land in the German states, the German immigrants saw their dreams coming true in America until the specter of a slave-owning West was suddenly spread before them in 1854. The Irish came from a different environment, one that included bouts with Protestant proselytizers and British officials, many of whom were critics of slavery as well as of Catholicism. It was what they often found in America: "In some cases the agitator for abolition was also an agitator against the Catholic foreigner." Since Britain was constantly presented as the world's antislavery leader, it was asking much of the anti-British Irish to adopt the philosophy of their traditional enemy.

There were antislavery Irish people, but contemporary observers agreed that the bulk of the Irish population in the 1850s was not moved by the abolitionists' arguments. A fervent plea on the subject came from across the ocean, when a Dublin journal urged Irish emigrants to cease their support of slavery. The editor was especially pained by cases where the Irish had been prominent in "aiding to slip the slave's collar on and snap the lock." Seizing upon this Dubliner's call, the anti-Catholic *Chicago Tribune* presented an economic and status explanation: the Irish feared that free blacks would displace them in the work force and in society. Without slavery, the *Tribune* charged, there would be no race beneath the Irish,

"KEPT beneath them by chains and stripes, and not by any intellectual or moral inferiority."

The *Tribune*'s attempt to link the Irish to slavery betrayed the developing quandary of nativists in the aftermath of the Kansas-Nebraska controversy. When such reforms as temperance and Sabbatarianism were high in popularity, immigrants in general could be easily identified as the enemy, and the nativist, secretive Know-Nothings led a popular crusade. When slavery emerged as the critical issue, it was difficult to continue labeling immigrants as the enemy, especially when large numbers of immigrants were joining the antislavery campaigns.

This turn of events was surprising to many because there had been indications that the Know-Nothings were developing as a major party in the region as the Whigs broke apart. The nativist party thrived on the broadly based anti-Catholicism of the era, as seen in the controversies over public funds for Catholic schools, and it benefited from the anti-immigrant feelings generated by the temperance and Sabbatarian movements.

An AHMS clergyman in Rock Island, Illinois, complained in the late summer of 1854 that grogshops and crime were increasing, but he concluded, "We hear of the footsteps of a wonderful order of Know Nothings moving upon our populations and they are literally Do Somethings." His hopes were echoed in the cheers that many other reformers, frustrated over immigrant sinfulness, gave to the new order. Chicago's nativist mayor in 1855 was praised by a Methodist gathering for "his efforts to suppress the liquor traffic, and the open desecration of the Sabbath by the sale of liquor." Similarly, the Chicago Methodist newspaper expressed the hope that "the 'Know-Nothings' as well as those who know something will watch with sleepless vigilance the anti-American tendencies of German infidelity in this country."

With this sort of linkage to reformers, the Know-Nothing movement spread rapidly across the region in 1854, although its size must remain conjectural because no membership records have been located. "There was scarcely a day but fist fights and rows between Know-Nothing rowdies and German and Irish born citizens took place," a German editor from Iowa recalled. This was particularly true in Davis and Van Buren counties, which had taken in many proslavery southerners. Houses of the foreign-born were "chalked with an X and thus marked for espionage and persecution." Know-Nothing lodges and newspapers were reported in Muscatine, Keokuk, Des Moines, Dubuque, and Oskaloosa, and the order saw one of its Iowa members elected to Congress. Illinois Know-Nothing lodges were in operation by 1854 in Joliet, Ottawa, Grayville, Canton, Vermont, Alton, Chicago, and Quincy. In the Quincy area, according to one of Senator Douglas's friends, there were at least seventeen Know-Nothing lodges, "and the smallest number of Democrats in any of them is twenty, which makes the changes enough to upset our majority and lose the district." Usually running as the "American Party," Know-Nothings carried several city council elections including La Salle's, where memories were still strong of the murder of a railroad contractor by Irish workmen. In Wisconsin the party supported the Republicans and apparently received its payoff in the subsequent abolishment of the state's immigration agency.

The Know-Nothings required members to be Protestant born, reared, and wed, and to swear to vote only for native-born American citizens, excluding all foreigners and aliens "and Roman Catholics in particular." Their journals were filled with tales of loathsome conduct by Catholics and foreigners, as in Stevens Point, Wisconsin: "The week before election a Catholic priest came here and spent three days, and with his own hands distributed the tickets for catholics to vote.... 'The Church' exercised a complete surveillance over all votes cast. A majority of the town board belonged to the party of the fag-ends, and foreigners were asked no questions when offering their votes. If they were challenged the oath was read to them, they answering 'Yaw,' although more than half of them could not understand one word of the oath."

By 1855, however, Levi Boone's victory in the Chicago mayoral race stood as virtually the only bright star in the Know-Nothing sky, and the organization's basic belief that immigrants should be excluded from American life was being challenged by the political requirements of other causes, especially the rising antislavery sentiment. Opponents won back city council control in La Salle, Alton, and most other communities where it had been lost during the Know-Nothing surge.

The American party's much-heralded candidate for judge of central Illinois, Stephen T. Logan, was defeated by 1,100 votes despite the fact that a year earlier he had finished first by 800 votes in a legislative race.

The demise was general, and it came about because of several factors. The Know-Nothings were a rising group only so long as there was widespread enthusiasm for reforms that focused opposition on the immigrants. Antislavery, rapidly ascending at mid-decade, was not such a movement. Their doom was sealed when Know-Nothings themselves began debating the issue, as they did in 1855 and 1856 when they split into "Sam" (proslavery) and "Jonathan" (antislavery) factions.

The Know-Nothings were also discovering that politics meant compromise. In addition to seeking support from antislavery enthusiasts, some leaders of the movement began softening their flat opposition to immigrants, warning in their Milwaukee mouthpiece that soon the Democratic party would be entirely composed of "priest-led foreigners" while the American party would stand against it, "upheld in a great measure, by the protestant foreign population." The newspaper added that there should be "no political distinction" between native-born and foreign-born, completely reversing the traditional position of the party.

But these efforts were to no avail. The organization collapsed after 1855. Attacks on immigrants were no longer enough to guarantee success, as the Know-Nothing candidate learned in the Chicago mayoral race in 1856. He vowed "to hold the noses of the Dutch and Irish to the grindstone," and he was defeated. When the order held a Chicago rally in August it drew five hundred persons; at a similar event in October the attendance fell to seventeen. The day after the party's election defeat that year in Illinois, its newspaper discontinued publication for good.

Among the results of nativist agitation was one that was perhaps unexpected and certainly unwanted: political consciousness developed rapidly among the immigrants at the same time that they were developing their own organizations for recreation, religion, music, and mutual aid, groups capable of acting in self-defense when threatened. Several groups were formed specifically in response to nativist attacks, including the *Bund freier Männer,* created in 1853 to coordinate

German political activity and sponsor of conventions that year in Wisconsin, Illinois, and Ohio. A year later antichurch Germans formed the Central Union of Free Germans, vowing to oppose slavery, despotism, and the Bible. In 1855 the *Deutsche Römisch-Katholische Central-Verein von Nord-Amerika* was organized, partly for mutual aid but also to help German Catholics beat back Know-Nothing attacks. Such groups as the Ancient Order of Hibernians and the local Irish military companies could be stimulated to defend Irish honor. Immigrant newspapers proliferated. The cultural renaissance among immigrant groups that was underway by the early fifties was thus channeled into political muscle-flexing as a result of nativist attacks.

The immigrants built these responses on a foundation of pride, for by the 1850s these groups had already supplied large numbers of soldiers for the Mexican War of 1847, including volunteer companies "mostly of gallant young Germans" who had rushed to the colors from St. Clair and Monroe Counties. The Irish had their own Illinois hero from the Mexican War: Irish-born U.S. Senator James Shields, elected in 1849, then reelected by the Illinois legislature months later to meet the constitutional requirement of nine years' citizenship. The controversy over seating Shields in 1849 and his defeat for reelection in 1855 kept Irish political feelings high. By the latter date Daniel O'Hara had launched the *Western Tablet* as the Irish Catholic newspaper in Chicago, filling its columns with defense of Irish actions and praise for Irish greatness. Milwaukee's German Catholics had their *Seebote*. Catholicism itself had become more aggressive by the fifties, when its leadership had been taken over by Irish clergymen who displaced the small Anglo-American group that had led the tiny, meek church of earlier days.

These shifting conditions formed the backdrop as opponents of the Kansas-Nebraska Act and a conglomeration of supporters of other causes came together in various communities across the northern states to create a new opposition group in 1854, 1855, and 1856. In each state of the Upper Mississippi the new Republican party had varying success in freeing itself from the stigma of nativism. A group of Illinois abolitionists and nativists called an 1854 meeting in Springfield to create a "Republican party," and succeeded mainly in frightening away

James Shields (1810-1879).

The immigrants' rapid adaptation to American politics had no better example than James Shields. Born in Dungannon, County Tyrone, Ireland, Shields came to the United States in 1826. He began practicing law in Kaskaskia, Illinois, in 1832 and launched his political career with election to the state legislature in 1836. Shields became a hero of the Mexican War when he was wounded twice. His political record in the Democratic party included appointment as governor of the Oregon Territory and service as U.S. senator from three states—Illinois (1849-1855), Minnesota (1858-1859), and Missouri (1879). This photo was taken at the height of his political career, circa 1855.

Courtesy of the Chicago Historical Society.

Lincoln and other politicians afraid of being linked to extremists. The new party was not successfully launched in Illinois until 1856. Wisconsin's anti-Democrat activists progressed rapidly, giving birth to the Republican party at a convention in Madison on July 13, 1854, with only three Germans present. When the Iowa Republican party was organized in 1856, three German editors withheld their expected support because the convention refused to attack Know-Nothings.

Events in all three states illustrated how fragile the new party's coalition was and how important the immigrant vote had become. The three Germans attending the Madison sessions were promptly named to various top committee positions, while Sherman Booth and other Whig and Free-Soil veterans carefully limited the delegates' activities to the slavery question. The Wisconsin convention resolved "that we accept this issue [freedom or slavery], forced upon us by the slave power, and in the defense of freedom will cooperate and be known as Republicans."

Temperance and the Sabbath issue were to be avoided and nativism ignored in these organizing sessions, but the participation of Whigs, reformers, and Know-Nothings made this difficult. This was especially true in Iowa, where new Republican Senator James Harlan was known as a nativist, where opponents barely defeated a Republican attempt in the legislature to force naturalized citizens to exhibit their papers when challenged at the polls, and where the American party merely "confirmed" the 1856 Republican state nominees as their own. Similarly, in Wisconsin the Know-Nothing newspaper endorsed the state Republican ticket in 1855.

Irishmen generally stayed away from this new party because of such incidents. Many Germans went along only halfheartedly or stressed that antislavery was the overriding issue of concern in national politics, but temperance could be an important state or local issue. Karl Roeser, a German Forty-Eighter and *Manitowoc Democrat* editor, exulted that there had been "not a word about temperance in the platform" after he left the 1854 Madison convention. As other reform elements became more visible in the Wisconsin Republican campaign in later months, he counseled Germans to avoid voting for a temperance candidate for governor, while still retaining party loyalty.

Democrats labored to make such selectivity difficult. The Milwaukee German Catholic *Seebote* argued that the Republican party was made up of "temperance men, abolitionists, haters of foreigners, sacreligious despoilers of churches, Catholic killers." Other Democrats pointed to the incongruous Republican alliances and warned the immigrants away.

Germans therefore sent up warnings as Republicans prepared to organize in Illinois in 1856. At a Decatur editors' meeting in February, George Schneider of the *Illinois Staats-Zeitung* cautioned that Germans needed assurances the party had no connections with Know-Nothings. The editors drew up a platform that attacked the Kansas-Nebraska Act, called for maintenance of the Missouri Compromise 36°30′ line to limit slavery's growth, and stated that slavery would not be touched where it already existed. Then they were asked by Schneider to add another resolution: to come out for religious tolerance and the continuance of existing naturalization laws. Meeting vociferous opposition, Schneider asked for the opinion of the only politician present, Abraham Lincoln. According to Schneider's later recollection, Lincoln responded that the resolution was not new but was already contained in the Declaration of Independence. You cannot, Lincoln added, "form a new party on proscriptive principles." The Decatur meeting then endorsed Schneider's resolution, slapping the Know-Nothings publicly and establishing the immigrants as a crucial component of the new organization.

A similar development occurred at the Republican state convention three months later. That party leaders recognized the need to placate immigrants and disassociate themselves from the Know-Nothings was apparent in the preconvention maneuverings by several persons, especially *Chicago Tribune* editor C.H. Ray. Ray, who was helping his newspaper tear loose from its nativist moorings, wrote to Senator Lyman Trumbull in March: "It is of the utmost importance that, in the approaching state convention of the anti-Nebraska men of Illinois, there should be some distinct ground assumed on which the 20,000 anti-slavery German voters of this state can stand, or we shall lose them in [a] body.... We need no denunciation—nothing to excite angry feeling—only a plain and unequivocal declaration that the party do not contemplate any change of the naturalization laws....It will not do to leave the whole matter without any expression upon it, and confine the platform to an exposition of our views upon the greater question of slavery. If that is done, we shall be obliged to carry two or more K.Ns on the state ticket, and that the Republicans will not attempt to do.''

A further warning came from Lieutenant Governor Gustave Koerner, a German Democrat who was preparing to leave his party if, as expected, its 1856 national convention pledged support for Douglas's Kansas-Nebraska Act. In a widely published letter to the Republican State Central Committee, Koerner stated that if he joined the new party it would have to support the philosophy that ''all American citizens without distinction of birth and religion should be entitled 'to rule America''' and naturalization laws ''should not be modified in an illiberal spirit.''

The Republican convention, with delegates drawn from the northern two-thirds of Illinois, followed the wishes of Ray, Lincoln, Koerner, and the German editors and approved a resolution vowing to ''proscribe no one, by legislation or otherwise, on account of religious opinions, or in consequence of place of birth.'' It also nominated a German, Francis A. Hoffman of Chicago, as its candidate for lieutenant governor.

Know-Nothings may have lost out in the resolutions debates, but their widely noted presence within the new Republican organizations placed the immigrant question at the center of the 1856 political campaign across the Upper Mississippi country—less important than the slavery controversy, but ranking high on the list among other critical issues. Just before the campaign opened that year, the Illinois State Democratic Committee blasted ''the malcontents, the intolerants, and the religious bigots'' who were merging to form a new party: ''One day they profess to be charmed by 'that rich Irish brogue and that sweet German accent,' and the next day they shoot down, burn and murder men, women and children for not being born in the same country as themselves.'' The 1856 Illinois Democratic convention endorsed Douglas's Kansas-Nebraska Act, thereby driving out men like Koerner, but the platform also stressed religious freedom and opposition to the proscription of foreign-born citizens. The party launched a German-language newspaper to carry the Democratic banner in Chicago. At a typical Democratic

The American party, the political organization
the nativistic Know-Nothings, grew rapidly
1855 and 1856 and appeared to be en route
replacing the Whigs as the region's second
rty. However, by the time of this rally in
eenville, Illinois, on October 18, 1856, the
rty's fortunes were ebbing. In 1856 the
vement collapsed, losing to the broader-
sed Republicans, who accepted Know-
thing support but thereby had to deal with
e anger of immigrant voters who bitterly op-
sed the Know-Nothings.

eenville (Ill.) American Courier, Oct. 16, 1856.
urtesy of the Illinois State Historical Library.

rally in Springfield, speeches in German were presented, and the Irish were given an important location in the parade.

Common Democratic themes in 1856 hit at the unpopularity of the reformers among the foreign-born. Gustave Koerner recalled hearing a visiting Democrat orator tell a German Catholic crowd that the "black Republicans" were made up mainly of Yankees who "would not allow a man to cook meals on the Sabbath, or kiss his wife, or take a walk for pleasure." These Republicans, the orator charged, included in their ranks temperance agitators who "hated the Germans because they would drink beer even on Sundays and would sing and dance on the Lord's day," while the rest were abolitionists and Know-Nothings.

Republicans were painfully aware that they needed many of the same groups already attracted to the nativists. Months before the 1856 campaign opened, Lincoln wrote to reformer Owen Lovejoy that until their new party could "get the elements" of the Know-Nothings "there is not sufficient materials to successfully combat the Nebraska democracy with." Lincoln said that many leading Know-Nothings were his "old and personal friends," but he hoped the group "would die out without the painful necessity of my taking an open stand against them."

This proved to be a difficult balancing act for the Republicans, particularly when Douglas stepped up his attacks on the nativist presence within the new party. (Anti-Nebraska legislators blocked Senator Shields's reelection, Douglas charged, because "he had been guilty of the crime of being born in Ireland.") As part of their efforts to erase or obscure the nativist connection, Republicans assured immigrants of their importance within the party while lashing out at Democratic abuses of the foreign-born. Frederick Hecker, a well-known German Forty-Eighter, was hired to campaign for the Republicans, and when Hecker's house was burned the party trumpeted the incident as a Know-Nothing attack. The *Belleviller Zeitung,* which had moved firmly into the Republican camp, acknowledged that there were Know-Nothings within the party's tent, but the editor stressed that he supported the new organization because it "has made its aim to fight more and more against the growing power of the slaveholder." Know-Nothings were not so dangerous, the editor added, "that we would separate ourselves from the Republican party, which generally follows very good aims."

The Belleville newspaper went to considerable lengths, in fact, to link local Democrats to the Know-Nothings. And it noted that all efforts in Congress to change citizenship laws had come from the Democratic South, source as well of the restrictive Clayton amendment to the Kansas-Nebraska Act.

As the 1856 campaign wore on, there were hints that changes were taking place within the electorate. Trumbull received a letter from a Belleville Republican in July informing him that "the Germans are warming up finely.... The Protestant Germans I think are pretty much all with us and some of the Catholic Germans." Although Germans had generally sided with Democrats in the Chicago mayoral election earlier in the year, by the time of the fall campaign it was said that anti-slavery feeling ran so high there that "no German in the city" was "willing to advocate publicly the doctrines of slavery extension." This was held to be largely attributable to the leadership of George Schneider of the *Staats-Zeitung*.

Election day 1856 bore out the effectiveness of the Republican strategy. Bissell, a Catholic, carried the Illinois governorship for the new party, and the state Senate now stood at thirteen Democrats, eleven Republicans, and one American (Know-Nothing); in the House there were thirty-seven Democrats, thirty-one Republicans, and six Americans plus a contested seat. Democrat Buchanan won the presidential race in the state as in the nation, but in Illinois the combined Republican and American party votes exceeded those given to the Buchanan.

Southern Illinois remained solid Douglas country. The Republican presidential candidate, John Frémont, received only five votes in Jackson County and two in an adjoining county, recalled Gustave Koerner, "and one of these voters, a schoolmaster, was driven out of the county after the election." The northern counties and Chicago had gone for Frémont, and they were the fastest-growing areas of the state.

There was an ominous note in the returns; many German areas had gone Republican. This included the city of Belleville, formerly a Democratic stronghold but a Frémont district on election day: 658 for the Republican presidential candidate, 464 for Buchanan, and 224 for the American party's Fillmore.

One study of the 1856 balloting estimates that 55 or 60 percent of Illinois German voters sided with the Republicans, and over 85 percent of those in recently settled German areas supported the new party. German Catholic communities remained up to 80 percent Democratic, however, perhaps revealing the depth of concern over the Know-Nothing presence in the Republican tent.

But the Illinois pattern was not followed elsewhere in the Upper Mississippi. The Republicans won the Wisconsin governorship and control of the legislature, and the party carried every Iowa state office by 7,500 votes or better. Within the 1856 precinct returns in the two states was abundant evidence that the victors had not fared well among the immigrants. In both states the Republicans were linked closely to temperance, and the Iowa Republican platform had been silent on the subject of nativism, a key test for many immigrants. The party's success rested instead on the fact that northern groups now predominated in the American population of the two states. These voters were being drawn to strong antislavery positions because of the depredations in Kansas and the continued appearances in their streets and churches of Negroes fleeing from southern plantations.

It was a new electorate, doubting, wondering, changing. This complexity increased the importance of voters who as a group could be appealed to with a chance of success. The foreign-born constituted such a group, but courting them meant that reforms considered obnoxious to immigrants would have to be jettisoned. This action had been urged by some observers months earlier. "The result of the late elections," the *Aurora Guardian* concluded in 1855, "must have taught Republicans everywhere a valuable lesson; that to succeed in the great battle of 1856 THERE MUST BE BUT ONE ISSUE," opposition to the extension of slavery.

This realization came gradually to many reformers from 1854 on, causing them to switch their emphasis from temperance, Sabbatarianism, the common schools, and other causes to antislavery. The *Chicago Tribune* finally quieted its anti-immigrant barrage and began to concentrate instead on attacking "the slave power." Given the intensity of the earlier reform crusades, the change to antislavery was difficult for many, and a Methodist committee reported in 1857 that "the great subject of temperance...has been sadly neglected." The church's Illinois annual conference was informed that "leading temperance men have been almost silent" in previous months, few temperance leaders made the circuit any more, and "the men of the pulpit have lost their wonted zeal in this great cause."

Enthusiasm was flagging on other causes because reformers now rushed to join the antislavery crusade. Following the lead of groups in New England, reform elements in the Upper Mississippi region began to aid the settlement of Kansas by free-state emigrants. Men and women reformers who formerly had been aloof from politics were now drawn into the developing fray. One was Julian Sturtevant, a Connecticut native who was president of Illinois College at Jacksonville. He enlisted in the Republican campaign in 1856, rejoicing that he could help "advance the righteous principles embodied in the platform." This was more than a political movement, he wrote, "it was a great moral upheaval." By 1858 the *Chicago Daily Democrat* noted one of the results of the reformers' transfer of allegiance from isolated causes to a common effort: "There is scarcely a Protestant church member in Chicago, or a temperance man, who is not an ardent Republican."

These developments came as the nation began to stagger under the burdens of sectional discord. Debts, injuries, and insults began to accumulate as North and South drifted further apart, and the polarization only increased the need of each side for allies. Immigrants were now being scrutinized more carefully as potential voters.

The search for their support involved more than simply attacking nativism, for the immigrants' earlier attachment to the Democrats rested on a variety of issues and philosophies, including the party's stand as spokesman for the common people. A German editor in Alton pointed to the importance of issues in this competition when he asserted to Republican Senator Lyman Trumbull in 1857, "If our party will take the right steps in regard to the banking-system, to Kansas and if the same would make the 'Homestead Bill' as one of their 'Creed,' I belief our success would be unconquerable." Another Republican in southern Illinois assured Trumbull that the Homestead Bill "is our best chance to convert the wavering foreigner" in that district. It was a reality that politicians kept in their minds as their search for a majority proceeded.

Another issue—slavery—was gaining prominence rapidly. Kansas would not quiet. The proslavery group there forced through its Lecompton constitution in

1857, and Senator Douglas broke with the Buchanan administration to attack it because the lack of majority support was obvious. (The proslavery constitution required that a governor have twenty years of U.S. citizenship before taking office.) This split within the Democratic party drew several prominent foes of the national administration, including some Germans, to Douglas's side as he met the challenger, Lincoln, in the battle for the U.S. Senate seat. Since the coming legislature would choose the next senator, the Lincoln-Douglas contest of 1858 was conducted with legislative races in mind.

The decision by the Republican press to link slavery and Catholicism as "the two despotisms" pointed to the direction the campaign was moving. Nativism was not completely removed. A severe Irish versus German division in the 1857 Chicago municipal campaign, during which a German was killed in a fight and an Irish Democrat candidate defeated a German Republican amid charges of vote fraud, helped to create further disunity among the foreign-born. Milwaukee's Germans became increasingly divided over political issues as the rift widened between liberal Forty-Eighters and German Catholics. Having been invited to join with the Irish to battle nativism, the future leader of Milwaukee's German Republicans instead lashed out at the Irish, "who stand nearer barbarism and brutality than civilization and humanity." They were the "natural enemies" of Germans, he added, "not because they are Irishmen, but because they are the truest guards of popery." Such sentiments, in turn, worked against a large-scale Irish desertion from the Democrats.

Beset by attacks from the northern-oriented Republicans and a southern-dominated administration in Washington, Stephen A. Douglas struggled to maintain his party as a national organization, which meant retaining its northern immigrant support—Irish and German. Democrats confronted "the allied forces of Abolitionism, Know-Nothingism, and every other 'ism'," he proclaimed late in the 1858 campaign, arguing that while those two major "isms" were first cousins generally, "in Illinois they were at least brothers, and SIAMESE TWINS AT THAT." The southern slant of the Democrats discouraged the allegiance of Germans. Douglas was warned during the campaign that the Dred Scott decision was "the great bugbear of the German Republican leaders and must be answered on the stump," and with this suggestion and under Lincoln's prodding he developed his "unfriendly legislation" doctrine. Under it, Douglas held that despite Supreme Court rulings, a territory could effectively bar slavery by withholding police protection.

As in 1856, the balloting of 1858 brought victory and defeat to both sides. The Democrats' legislative majority after the election in Illinois was 54 to 46, enough to reelect Douglas to his Senate seat but not representative of the state's population, due to population changes since the previous drawing of district lines. Republicans won the races for state treasurer and state superintendent of public instruction, thus gaining total control of the state administration.

In Iowa the revulsion against the bloody Kansas incidents was widespread, helping ensure election of the entire Republican state ticket in 1858, including a solid Republican congressional delegation. Know-Nothings had seen their Iowa vote totals fall steadily since 1856, and now the Republican margins seemed so large that immigrant ballots were not needed as a balance of power. Wisconsin's Republican party again carried two out of three congressional races and had majorities in both houses of the state legislature.

All this was watched closely by one candidate who lost in 1858 but who was working to join disparate elements under the Republican banner for the 1860 campaign. Abraham Lincoln had made the decision to reject nativism earlier than had some of his Whig kinsmen. It was he who helped guide the editors at Decatur to a resolution desired by Germans, who supported this concept in state and national Republican conclaves, who briefly owned a German newspaper, and who took the extreme step of trying to master German grammar. During the 1858 campaign Lincoln once turned to the foreign-born in his audience and assured them that their European forebears were spiritually "blood of the blood, and flesh of the flesh" of the American founding fathers. Such assurances came often from him in the campaign.

But the distasteful fact of nearly solid Irish opposition kept intruding on this Republican defense of the foreign-born. Lincoln met this issue on his 1858 campaign tour when he encountered, for example, "about fifteen Celtic gentlemen, with black carpet-sacks in their hands," whom he believed were representatives of the "floating Hibernian" population imported to swing the election to the Democrats. His law partner, William Herndon, assured a friend that the rumor of imported Irishmen was "no humbug cry," and he asked, "What shall we do? Shall we tamely submit to the Irish, or shall we arise and cut their throats?" The Reverend Owen Lovejoy urged that "a lot of regulators" be organized "and have every Irishman by the neck that you find in the county!" However, the Republican State Central Committee sent around circulars detailing how to prevent illegal voting, and this tactic rather than violence was the response to the rumored threat of imported "Celtic gentlemen."

While slavery extension had become the predominant issue dividing the two parties (Wisconsin's Democratic leaders charged that "republicanism and niggerism" had become one), much of the political maneuvering for 1860 still centered on the parties' real or alleged relations with the Know-Nothings. This development revealed the growing importance of the immigrant vote. At a county Democratic convention in Iowa, each delegate was required to stand and pledge that he was a Democrat and had no sympathy with Know-Nothings. Senator Douglas thrived on the nativism stories, pointing eagerly to the presence of Know-Nothings in the Republican party and warning also that the "white basis" of American government would suffer if Negro equality were forced on the nation.

Republicans fought back, content that prominent Know-Nothings generally remained quiet within the party. One way to weaken the charges of Know-Nothing links was to demonstrate support for—and by—Catholics and immigrants. Accordingly, the Republicans put forward German candidates for many local races and for lieutenant governor posts in Wisconsin in 1857, Iowa in 1857, and Illinois in 1860. William Bissell, a Catholic, had been chosen by the Republicans to run for governor of Illinois in 1856, and he won.

But the Republicans' efforts ran into a sudden embarrassment, a near-derailment, in March 1859. Like a firebell in the night, the Republican-controlled Massachusetts legislature voted to amend the state constitution to require a naturalized citizen to live two years in Massachusetts before he could vote. This was two years more than required for any native-born male.

From frantic Republicans across the Upper Mississippi country came an eruption of denunciation. Iowa's Republican State Central Committee branded the act "an unjust and offensive discrimination between citizens on account of their births" and called upon the people of Massachusetts to reject the proposed amendment. The German-language newspaper in Muscatine, Iowa, switched to the Democrats over the *Zwei-jahrs* issue, and several German leaders threatened to likewise bolt the Iowa Republican ticket if the Massachusetts proposal were not condemned. Several German political leaders sent a questionnaire to the state's senatorial delegation, demanding to know whether the congressmen opposed lengthening the naturalization process and specifically how they stood on the Massachusetts plan. The Iowa senators promptly responded that they opposed the Massachusetts measure.

Wisconsin's Germans were vituperative in attacking the Massachusetts amendments. One group demanded that the state Republican party run Carl Schurz for governor, so that the party could "disprove the charges of Knownothingism made against it." When Schurz's bid for nomination failed, many German Republicans stayed away from the polls, and the German Republican Club of Manitowoc denounced the party's eventual gubernatorial candidate as a Know-Nothing.

In Illinois the German Republicans sought action also. Some radical editors called for Germans to return to the Democratic fold and urged Gustave Koerner to draw up a manifesto for a German convention on the Massachusetts question. Koerner refused, but he and other prominent Germans spoke out angrily on the issue. The editor of the *Illinois Staats-Anzeiger* asked Lincoln how he stood on the Massachusetts plan, and the angular Republican replied that he opposed "its adoption in Illinois or in any other place where I have a right to oppose it." Lincoln noted his own support for Negro rights and said it would be inconsistent if he favored "any project for curtailing the existing rights of white men, even though born in different lands, and speaking different languages from myself." The letter was widely reprinted.

These efforts betrayed Republican panic. Despite denials and denunciations by Upper Mississippi Republicans, the Massachusetts plan made the German vote suddenly less certain than it had seemed. And with eastern Republicans possessing great power within the party, the possibility remained that the Republican national convention in 1860 might take some similar step that would frighten away what remained of immigrant support.

In an effort to head off such a development, a group of German Republicans called a preconvention gathering in 1860 at the Deutsches Haus in Chicago. The structure itself had become a symbol of immigrant resistance since its construction in 1856 to provide a German meeting place during the Know-Nothing agitation. With its ranks including leading Forty-Eighters and a heavy sprinkling of German editors, the Deutsches Haus gathering drew up resolutions endorsing a free Kansas and a homestead act and repudiating the Massachusetts amendment. The repudiation asserted bluntly: "The Republican party is opposed to any change in our naturalization laws, or any state legislation, by which the rights of citizenship heretofore accorded to immigrants from foreign lands will be abridged or impaired, and is in favor of giving a full and sufficient protection to all classes of citizens, whether native or naturalized, both at home and abroad." The Germans presented this as a "must" resolution to the Republican convention, with Schurz warning that 300,000 German votes hung in the balance. The convention adopted the "Dutch plank" unanimously, despite efforts by a prominent Massachusetts Republican to block it.

German delegates to the convention generally favored the presidential candidacy of New York's William Seward, who had an impressive antinativist record and enjoyed widespread support among the German press. The major contribution by German delegates in the nominating process, however, lay in blocking the advance of Missouri's Edward Bates, a conservative Free-Soiler who had supported American party candidates. Lincoln, though not the Germans' first choice, was acceptable because of his past stand on issues considered important to the Germans, especially his opposition to nativism and his support for a homestead bill.

With Douglas nominated by one wing of the badly splintered Democrats and Lincoln named by the Republicans, the 1860 national presidential race was in many ways a replay of the 1858 Illinois Senate contest. Slavery extension was the all-prevailing issue, but in the Upper Mississippi country both parties rushed to af-

Rebelling against the nativism of the mid-1850s, Chicago Germans built *Das Deutsche Haus* in 1856 to provide themselves with a place to hold meetings. One writer states that this became "a sort of German townhall and theater and assembly room for bunds, clubs, lodges, societies and *vereins* of various kinds." It was here that the German Republican leaders met before the 1860 Republican National Convention opened to prepare a list of demands on the party. The structure was at the southeast corner of Indiana and Wells streets in Chicago.

Courtesy of the Illinois State Historical Library.

firm their opposition to nativism. Democrats and Republicans in Iowa, for example, both called for equal protection for native-born and foreign-born citizens, regardless of residence (a reference to the growing fear that immigrants visiting Europe might be drafted into armies in the native lands). Iowa Democrats also condemned the Maine law, but by then it had been so emasculated under German pressure that it was virtually dead as a campaign issue. In Scott County the Republican organization carefully selected its delegates to the national party convention: five Germans, five Americans, and three Irish. But the Dane County Democrats in Wisconsin went beyond this, nominating in local races an Irishman, a Pole, a German, a Scot, a Dane, and three native-born Americans; these were pitted against a Republican slate featuring one Norwegian and seven Americans.

Were Germans the crucial element in Lincoln's 1860 presidential victory? Students of that campaign disagree. Despite extensive campaigning by Carl Schurz ("The Germans are coming over in masses," he reported jubilantly), most recent examinations of voting precincts indicate that Germans in Wisconsin and Iowa generally voted Democratic, retaining their former allegiance. Lincoln's loss in Missouri included defeat in some German areas. Joseph Schafer's early Wisconsin study has not been seriously challenged by more recent findings. He estimated that perhaps five-sixths of the votes of Wisconsin Germans went to Douglas but that Lincoln had adequate support at the polls without them. Milwaukee's vote went 58 percent to Douglas, although the citywide Democratic majority was down considerably from 1856. Both Catholic German newspapers and anti-Catholic German newspapers remained Democratic.

A similar electoral situation apparently prevailed in Iowa, where Germans and Hollanders ignored their leaders and editors and returned to the Democratic fold, perhaps influenced by the Massachusetts question or the Republicans' identification with temperance. It was said that the Dutch in the area around Pella, Iowa, "were suspicious of the abolitionist elements in the new party." A study of Minnesota townships having more than half their population made up of Germans found that twelve went Republican and two went Democratic in 1860. Germans were important but not crucial in Lincoln's victory in that new state.

Lincoln's victory in Illinois included two major German centers—Chicago, where he received 58 percent of the total vote, and St. Clair County, which gave him 54.8 percent. One examination of the German balloting reported that "in precinct after precinct" in St. Clair County "a preponderance of Germans is always associated with a Lincoln majority." Basically agreeing, James M. Bergquist, the major student of the Illinois 1860 immigrant vote, found that "a fair estimate might place the Republican portion of the German vote at from 60 to 65 percent." This matched or slightly exceeded the 1858 percentages, indicating that "the political transformation of the German community begun in 1854 was now complete." There were variations, but generally these were predictable. Republicans did better among German Lutherans than among German Catholics.

German votes were not crucial in Lincoln's Illinois win, Bergquist argues, but he stresses the Germans' importance in forcing Republicans to take stands that appealed to the foreign-born. Efforts to win immigrant support joined with the immigrants' own increasing activism within the political system to create a vastly different political environment as the decade of the fifties came to a close.

This was evident when an Irishman wrote home from Chicago in 1860 that there was "the greatest kind of excitement" between Democrats and Republicans, "just what there would be prodestant and Catholick." And he described a rather simple political division: "All Catholics here is Democrats or for slavery and all Republicans is prodestants or not for slavery but it is not known yet which will beat."

Which will beat? That was known the day after the balloting. But the campaign itself and the efforts by politicians to lure the immigrant vote emerge from the historical record as evidence that the immigrant influx of the 1840s and 1850s had finally been drawn into the American political system. They were mere onlookers no longer. And they entered the system, not as submerged, cowed exiles and wanderers, but as free men, proud of their Turnverein and their Saint Patrick's Day, their lager beer and their whiskey, and their continental Sundays.

Epilogue

Both a new region and a new nation were forming in the decades leading up to America's Civil War. The United States was sweeping its boundaries westward, taking in Texas, the Southwest, and the Oregon country as it conquered the Mexicans and prevailed over the British in the Pacific Northwest. While this expansion was proceeding, the Mississippi Valley became an emerging power center, arbiter between North and South, en route to dominance in economic and political affairs.

This new America was marked by a sharp transformation in internal composition, and nowhere was this more evident than in the Upper Mississippi country. No longer a nation of the native-born with a smattering of aliens, guided by the Founding Fathers and marked by distinct regional identities, the United States was fast becoming a heterogeneous conglomeration, a hodge-podge of peoples. The upsurge of mobility and immigration after 1830 was shattering the former stability in many spheres.

Drastic changes were occurring in the positions of various groups. Catholics had formerly survived as a tiny breath of a church led by meek French priests; now they had a massive, aggressive organization with considerable influence in many districts. Within Protestantism, Methodists and Baptists had developed the theology and the church-planting methods needed to thrive in the Great Valley. Even political stability was disrupted during this era, as one major party disintegrated and another was born.

This was no land immobilized in the vise of tradition. And yet, traditions were extremely important in the course of events from 1830 to 1860 across this Upper Mississippi region, for all peoples arriving there had been prepared by their

233

respective pasts for the drama that was unfolding. Southerners were leery of New Englanders long before the two groups traded epithets in the Shawnee Hills, the lead diggings, and the river towns. New Englanders headed west with the confidence that comes from participating in a divine mission, a confidence bred into them by generations of dedicated Puritan forebears. If their spirit helped them survive severe tests to create churches and schools across the region, that spirit often was accompanied by intolerance of those clinging to different beliefs.

This new America had foundations in the Old World across the Atlantic as well. Driven from their homes by famine or landlords, pressured by economic disaster or revolutionary agitation, Germans and Irish and other European groups carried bundles of experiences and expectations with them across the water. Irishmen had already been taunted at home by Anglicans and Presbyterians about their drinking and Sabbath displays; their quick, blunt rejection of such complaints from American proselytizers was quite predictable. Similarly, Germans who had witnessed a strong government merging churches in Prussia or who had been threatened by rationalists in local disputes did not forget these conflicts after they crossed to America. Those leaving lands of "Young Ireland" and "Young Germany" were no strangers to abuse.

This mingling of peoples during the decades straddling midcentury changed the midcontinent frontier and the nation drastically. The suddenness of the influx was overwhelming; Wisconsin's foreign-born, who constituted 37 percent of its population in 1860, helped the state rise from twenty-ninth in total population rank in 1840 to fifteenth by the outbreak of the Civil War. The new state of Minnesota—launched in 1858—already recorded 34 percent foreign-born by 1860. That last prewar census also reported that Iowa's 106,081 immigrants made up 16 percent of the state's population, but four-fifths of those aliens had arrived since 1850. Missouri stood eighth in U.S. population in 1860, its 160,541 foreign-born representing 14 percent of the state's people.

The Illinois census statistics were especially dramatic by 1860; the southern-dominated frontier state that had ranked twentieth in United States population in 1830 now stood fourth, with 1.7 million. The foreign-born constituted 19 percent of that 1860 total, and two-thirds of them had entered Illinois since the last census had been taken a decade earlier.

These bare statistics held within them many stories. One of the most important was the rapid movement of vastly different groups into a region unprepared for them. The change was drastic in many localities. St. Louis by 1860 bore no resemblance to a sleepy French river town; Milwaukee had lost its early Yankee air, and the opportunity had passed for many smaller towns like La Salle to be anything other than immigrant communities. The cold facts of the census reports and the drama of the politicians' convoluted appeals to different groups both revealed a region in 1860 far closer to modern America than to the America of just two or three decades earlier. By the outbreak of the Civil War a wide diversity of national origins and beliefs had been implanted into the American domain.

This transformation did not come without turmoil, and the people who rushed to win the Upper Mississippi were conscious above all that something new was being created. But this sudden juxtaposition of people and ideas, this clash of tradition and hope, stirred apprehension in many. Some feared that this Great Valley so pregnant with future greatness would be lost to the ungodly. Missionaries from distant centers struggled to gain a foothold, feeling increasingly uneasy as settlers poured in.

But others found a different meaning in it all: more people to settle the prairies, build the canals and railroads, help new enterprises thrive. And for some, especially politicians, this diverse population also brought new opportunities to recruit allies. Their actions were constrained by the demands of the American electoral system to create voting majorities rather than construct alliances between parties. This need, paired with the immigrants' speedy acquisition of the ballot, meant that the scowl of the local missionary was eclipsed—overwhelmed—by the welcoming handshake of the candidate for office. Abraham Lincoln's effort to master German grammar was a clue to the larger search underway for immigrant votes. If "native Americanism" became unacceptable during the 1850s, this change was mainly due to the fact that immigrants had established themselves resolutely within the political system. In politics they found a warm reception.

This rapid politicization pointed to another factor: the penchant of immigrants no less than native-born Americans to organize for protection whenever necessary. If the region's heavily immigrant cities served as "decompression chambers" (to use Kathleen Neils Conzen's sobriquet for Milwaukee) where

Belleville became an early German center of Illinois and the Upper Mississippi, especially through the presence of many veterans of Germany's 1830 and 1848 revolutions. With singing societies, a *Turnverein*, and their own newspaper, Belleville Germans like these enjoying watermelon, circa 1860, shaped their new community as well as being shaped by it.

newcomers could adjust to American life among familiar faces and customs, it was also true that the new residents pushed beyond narrow concerns rapidly. Milwaukee had an Irish mayor by 1852, Chicago, a German mayor by 1860, while numerous foreign-born candidates entered the state legislative arena. And it was not unusual for candidates of the same foreign nationality to be pitted against each other. But such political organization was scarcely original. The immigrants were following the course they had already taken in America in religion, music, education, and other endeavors. And each Know-Nothing eruption, each attack on groggeries, Sabbath festivities, or parochial schools only stirred the foreign-born to further defensive action.

As they fought these battles, the immigrants relied more and more on arguments based on rights—rights that both Americans and immigrants now shared. When the Irish canal workmen were angered by harsh treatment, they went on strike for a better foreman "so as not to have white citizens drove even worse than common slave Negroes." Similarly, the German editor of the *Belleviller Zeitung* attacked the proposed prohibition law because it "destroys all the freedom of the citizen and of business," contradicts "the principles of our state constitution and those of the Declaration of Independence," and would carry the public to a narrowness so extreme "that the European police-state would be bearable in comparison with this." Such were the thoughts of those who had grown to political maturity elsewhere before encountering men who wanted to reform them in the Great Valley. They knew their rights.

The outbreak of war in 1861 marked the end of this time of "planting," the close of the "seedtime" for both reformers and other participants in the Upper Mississippi's pioneer era. As the fighting began between North and South, the presence of diverse peoples within national life became dramatically visible across the valley. It was seen in the rush of support for the Union, in the creation of the Irish Brigade and the Schwarze Jaeger, the "preachers' regiment" and the Rock River Rifles, and in such incidents as the capture of a prosecession Missouri militia unit by a Union troop composed almost entirely of Germans. ("Damn the Dutch!" the prisoners yelled as the Germans led them away from the captured St. Louis camp.) Events of those anxious months make it plain that most immigrants as well as most of the native-born in the Upper Mississippi had come to share a common belief—that Kansas no more than the prairies and oak openings could be transformed into slave territory and still remain the object of these settlers' dreams. They were now a people with something to hold, something to preserve. And part of that something lay in their expectations that America meant a chance to move on, to start over again, to build anew.

But part of what they held lay in the past, too, for all had been pioneers. "We are the founders of this beautiful queen of the West," the German Old Settlers of Milwaukee declared as they met in 1858 to recall events of former years. No late-comers here; immigrants as well as the native-born were involved from the start with shirt-sleeves rolled up. The canals, the railroad lines, the churches and schools and whole communities—the labor pains of this birth, and much of the glory and pride, were their own.

This Great Valley would cast its shadow across the nation in ensuing years. As war began, the new territories to the west as well as the national government now headed by an Illinois settler would show the imprint of the struggles and the accommodation that took place in the Upper Mississippi country in those antebellum decades. Once it had been New England, New France, and New Spain that the searching Europeans launched in the Americas. Now the line of settlement had reached midcontinent and embraced New Erin and New Baden, New Virginia and Yankee Settlement. An old process, a new land.

Sources

Much of the source material for this book has come from letters sent from residents of the Upper Mississippi Valley to family members, church leaders, politicians, and others, in most cases in Ireland, Germany, New England, New York, or other coastal areas. Letters of American Home Missionary Society agents were extremely useful for all sections of this book; originals are located at Dillard University, New Orleans. The letters from Illinois are on microfilm at the Chicago Theological Seminary. Many letters were printed in the AHMS publication, the *Home Missionary.*

Other major sources of letters included the All Hallows College Missionary Correspondence, 1843–1877, at All Hallows College, Drumcondra, Dublin, Ireland; the massive collections of Irish immigrant letters gathered by Professor Kerby Miller of the University of Missouri at Columbia and by Professor Arnold Schrier of the University of Cincinnati; the Dr. E. R. R. Green collection and the James Finton Lalor letters in the National Library of Ireland, Dublin; the America Letters in the Cork Archives Council, Cork, Ireland, and in the Public Records Office, Belfast, Northern Ireland; and "Letters of Emigrants to America, 1745–1911" in the British Library of Political and Economic Science, London School of Economics.

Religious history studies proved extremely useful. Two general works provided much of the background: Sydney E. Ahlstrom, *A Religious History of the American People* (New Haven: Yale Univ. Press, 1972), and Clifton E. Olmstead, *History of Religion in the United States* (Englewood Cliffs, N.J.: Prentice-Hall, 1960). Two books on German church groups were also of help: Carl E. Schneider, *The German Church on the American Frontier: A Study in the Rise of Religion among the Germans of the West* (St. Louis: Eden Pub. House, 1939), and the Reverend Emmet H. Rothan, *The German Catholic Immigrant in the United States (1830–1860)* (Washington, D.C.: Catholic Univ. Press, 1946).

Two general works on the Irish provided basic information: Carl Wittke, *The Irish in America* (Baton Rouge: Louisiana State Univ. Press, 1956), and Arnold Schrier, *Ireland and the American Emigration, 1850–1900* (Minneapolis: Univ. of Minnesota Press, 1958). The problems besetting the Irish and other immigrant groups are given careful study in the standard work on nativism: Ray Allen Billington, *The Protestant Crusade, 1800–1860* (New York: Macmillan, 1938).

Three works on historical figures proved useful for many portions of this book. They include two on Stephen A. Douglas written or edited by Robert W. Johannsen: *Stephen A. Douglas* (New York: Oxford Univ. Press, 1973) and *The Letters of Stephen A. Douglas* (Urbana: Univ. of Illinois Press, 1961). Also, the *Memoirs of Gustave Koerner, 1809–1896*, edited by Thomas J. McCormack (Cedar Rapids, Iowa: Torch Press, 1909), vols. 1 and 2, provided insights into the reactions of a thoughtful immigrant to the changing scene throughout the antebellum period.

Major sources of information on Illinois included Arthur C. Cole's vast accumulation of excerpts from Illinois newspapers at the Illinois Historical Survey, University of Illinois; and these Chicago newspapers: *Western Citizen, Free West, Western Tablet,* and *Daily Democratic Press.* General studies used extensively included Arthur Charles Cole, *The Era of the Civil War—1848–1870* (Springfield: Illinois Centennial Commission, 1919); Robert P. Howard, *Illinois—A History of the Prairie State* (Grand Rapids, Mich.: Eerdmans, 1972), and Bessie Louise Pierce, *A History of Chicago,* vols. 1 and 2 (New York: Knopf, 1937 and 1940). Document collections used most frequently included Pierce's *As Others See Chicago: Impressions of Visitors, 1673–1933* (Chicago: Univ. of Chicago Press, 1933), and *The Prairie State—A Documentary History of Illinois,* vol. 1, edited by Robert P. Sutton (Grand Rapids, Mich.: Eerdmans, 1976).

Major sources of information on Iowa were Morton M. Rosenberg, *Iowa on the Eve of the Civil War: A Decade of Frontier Politics* (Norman: Univ. of Oklahoma Press, 1972); Leland L. Sage, *A History of Iowa* (Ames: Iowa State Univ. Press, 1974); and *Patterns and Perspectives in Iowa History,* edited by Dorothy Schweider (Ames: Iowa State Univ. Press, 1973).

The outstanding book on immigrant participation in the growth of a specific city is Kathleen Neils Conzen's *Immigrant Milwaukee 1836–1860—Accommodation and Community in a Frontier City* (Cambridge: Harvard Univ. Press, 1976). Other works useful in describing Wisconsin's experiences under the influx of immigration included Richard N. Current, *The History of Wisconsin,* vol. 2, *The*

Civil War Era, 1848–1873 (Madison: State Historical Society of Wisconsin, 1976); M. Justille McDonald, *History of the Irish in Wisconsin in the Nineteenth Century* (Washington, D.C.: Catholic Univ. of America, 1954); Bayrd Still, *Milwaukee—The History of a City* (Madison: State Historical Society of Wisconsin, 1948); and Robert C. Nesbit, *Wisconsin: A History* (Madison: Univ. of Wisconsin Press, 1973).

In addition to the above, special sources of information were used as noted for specific chapters:

Chapter 1

Travelers' comments were found in *Prairie State—Impressions of Illinois, 1673–1967, by Travelers and Other Observers,* edited by Paul M. Angle (Chicago: Univ. of Chicago Press, 1968), as well as the Pierce and Sutton document collections noted above. Useful for settlement patterns were William V. Pooley, *The Settlement of Illinois from 1830 to 1850,* Univ. of Wisconsin History Series (Madison: Univ. of Wisconsin Press, 1908); Truman O. Douglass, *The Pilgrims of Iowa* (Chicago: Pilgrim Press, 1911); Douglas K. Meyer, "Southern Illinois Migration Fields: The Shawnee Hills in 1850," *The Professional Geographer,* May 1976, pp. 151–60; Douglas K. Meyer, "Native-Born Immigrant Clusters on the Illinois Frontier," *Proceedings of the Association of American Geographers 8* (1976): 41–44; and William J. Petersen, "Population Advance to the Upper Mississippi Valley 1830–1860," *Iowa Journal of History and Politics 32,* 4 (Oct. 1934): 312–53.

Chapter 2

Ireland's travail during the period of the exodus to America is recounted in *The Course of Irish History,* edited by T.W. Moody and F.X. Martin (Cork: Mercier Press, 1967); Joseph Lee, *The Modernisation of Irish Society, 1848–1918* (Dublin: Gill and Macmillan, 1973); and Cecil Woodham-Smith, *The Great Hunger—Ireland 1845–1849* (New York: Harper and Row, 1962). This background is also vividly described in the journals of Sir John Benn-Walsh, published in *The Journal of the Cork Historical and Archaeological Society 80,* 230 (July–Dec. 1974): 86–123, and *81,* 231 (Jan.–June 1975): 15–42.

These Irish newspapers proved helpful in examining Irish life of the 1840s and 1850s: the *Constitution; or, Cork Advertiser* (Cork); the *Cork Southern Reporter and Cork Commercial Courier* (Cork); the *Galway Vindicator and Connaught*

Advertiser (Galway); the *Kerry Evening Post* (Tralee); the *Kilkenny Journal and Leinster Commercial and Literary Advertiser* (Kilkenny), and the *Waterford Mail* (Waterford). All were used in the British Library Newspaper Library, Colindale, England.

The invaluable records of the Crown Estate of Kingwilliamstown, County Cork, regarding famine conditions and the emigration of tenants were used at the Dublin Public Record Office. British official reports were also used: House of Lords, *Fifth and Sixth Reports. Operation of the Irish Poor Law,* no. 507 (1849); House of Commons, *Fourteenth Report from the Select Committee on Poor Laws (Ireland),* no. 572 (1849); Parliamentary Papers, *Emigration (North American and Australian Colonies),* no. 593, part 2 (1849), and Parliamentary Accounts and Papers, vol. 40: *Emigration,* (1851).

In addition, the following articles in recent Irish historical journals contained helpful information: Eilish Ellis, "State-Aided Emigration Schemes from Crown Estates in Ireland, c. 1850," *Analecta Hibernica,* 22 (1960): 329–94; Timothy P. O'Neill, "The Catholic Church and Relief of the Poor 1815–45," *Archivium Hibernicum* 31 (1973): 132–45; James Coleman, "Voyage of the 'Jamestown,'" *Journal of the Cork Historical and Archaeological Society* 10, 2d series (1904): 23–31; and two articles in the *Journal of the Kerry Archaeological and Historical Society*: Sean O'Luing, "Some Travellers in Kerry," 1 (1968): 56–72; and Padraig O'Riain, "Two Welsh Visitors to Kerry in 1852," 4 (1971): 98–105.

In addition to earlier cited works, Irish activities in the Upper Mississippi Valley are described in the 1853 diaries of Dr. James Donnelley, a touring Irish priest (copy in the Public Records Office, Belfast), and in David Dominic Costigan, "Irish Immigration and Settlement in Illinois, 1845–1880" (master's thesis, Illinois State Univ., 1959).

Chapter 3

Major studies of the background of German emigration are Mack Walker, *Germany and the Emigration—1816–1885* (Cambridge: Harvard Univ. Press, 1964); Marcus Lee Hansen, *The Atlantic Migration—1607–1860* (Cambridge: Harvard Univ. Press, 1940); Marcus Lee Hansen, "The Revolutions of 1848 and German Emigration," *Journal of Economic and Business History 2,* 4 (Aug. 1930): 630–58; and Oscar J. Hammen, "Economic and Social Factors in the Prussian Rhineland in 1848," *American Historical Review 54,* 4 (July 1949): 825–40.

Two contemporary German journals that trumpeted the emigrants' cause and provided them with information on America were the following, used at the Commerz-Bibliothek in Hamburg, West Germany: *Allgemeine Auswanderungszeitung* (Rudolfstadt), and *Der Deutsche Auswanderer* (Frankfort a. M.).

Useful in tracing the settlement of Germans in an often hostile American environment were Carl Wittke, *Refugees of Revolution—The German Forty-Eighters in America* (Philadelphia: University of Pennsylvania Press, 1952); *The Forty-Eighters—Political Refugees of the German Revolution of 1848,* edited by A.E. Zucker (New York: Columbia Univ. Press, 1950); Sister M. Hedwigis Overmoehle, "The Anti-Clerical Activities of the Forty-Eighters in Wisconsin 1848-60—A Study in American Liberalism" (Ph.D. dissertation, Saint Louis Univ., 1941); Albert Bernhardt Faust, *The German Element in the United States* (Boston: Houghton Mifflin, 1909), vol. 1; and Theodore Schreiber, "Early German Pioneers of Scott County, Iowa," *The American-German Review 8,* 2 (Dec. 1941): 20–23. Catholic colonization attempts by Germans and Irish are traced in Sister Mary Gilbert Kelly, *Catholic Immigrant Colonization Projects in the United States, 1815–1860* (New York: U.S. Catholic Historical Society, 1939).

Reminiscences and diaries by German immigrants abound in such publications as the *American-German Review.* Two from that journal used here were Johann Konrad Dähler, "The Kind of Stuff That Made America What It Is Today," *10,* 6 (Aug. 1944): 28–29, and *11,* 1 (Oct. 1944): 26–29; and "The Hour-Glass of Migration," edited by H.W. Elkinton, *11,* 5 (June, 1945) 18–20; *11,* 6 (Aug. 1945): 13–16, *12,* 1 (Dec. 1945): 30–33. The John Konrad Meidenbauer letters and diaries in the State Historical Society of Wisconsin were also useful.

Chapter 4

General works on railroads and canals include John F. Stover, *History of the Illinois Central Railroad* (New York: Macmillan, 1975); Paul Wallace Gates, *The Illinois Central and Its Colonization Work* (Cambridge: Harvard Univ. Press, 1934); Howard Gray Brownson, *History of the Illinois Central Railroad to 1870,* Univ. of Illinois Studies in the Social Sciences (Urbana: Univ. of Illinois Press, 1909); James William Putnam, *The Illinois and Michigan Canal—A Study in Economic History* (Chicago: Univ. of Chicago Press, 1918); and David L. Lightner, "Construction Labor on the Illinois Central Railroad," *Journal of the Illinois State Historical Society 66,* 3 (Autumn 1973): 285–301.

Papers, letters, and other records of canal and railroad companies were used extensively. The Illinois State Archives provided the Illinois and Michigan Canal papers, including Letter Books of Jno. A. McClernand, treasurer; Robert Stuart, secretary; and records of payments and supplies. The papers of William Henry Swift, president of the canal trustees, were found at the Chicago Historical Society. The canal commissioners' 1900 report (published in 1901) includes a history of the canal's beginnings and early operations. The Newberry Library holds the papers, reports, and records of the Illinois Central Railroad and other regional railroad companies. Especially useful for the I.C. were the B.F. Johnson and D.A. Neal letter-books and the New York office in-letters.

Letters of persons active in political maneuverings and early operations of the canal and railroads provided much insight into the laborers' activities. These included the letters of Mason Brayman in both the Illinois State Historical Society and the Chicago Historical Society; the Wm. H. Bailache papers in the Illinois State Historical Society; the letters of Augustus French in the Illinois State Historical Society; and the letters of Charles Floyd-Jones, a young railroad engineer, in the Floyd-Jones Family Papers at the Bancroft Library, University of California, Berkeley.

Chapter 5

Meeting records of local churches and the personal accounts of pioneer missionaries were used extensively in recounting the religious developments of the era in the Upper Mississippi Valley. Especially helpful were *The Memoirs of Father Samuel Mazzuchelli, O.P.* (Chicago: Priory Press, 1967, reprinted from a 1915 translation of the 1844 edition); and the *Autobiography of Peter Cartwright* (New York: Carlton and Porter, 1857). Letters from the AHMS and All Hallows missionaries, cited above, were extremely important in ascertaining the goals and trials of individual church leaders, while Catholic hierarchical aims and problems were drawn from the Leopoldine Society of Vienna correspondence and the Archdiocese of Cincinnati papers, both in the University of Notre Dame Archives. Minutes of the Iowa, Rock River, Central Illinois, and Illinois conferences of the Methodist Episcopal church; the Clear Creek Monthly Meeting of Hicksite Quakers; the Baptist General Association of Illinois; the Nine Mile and the Apple Creek Baptist associations; and the Mount Pleasant Baptist church and Whetstone Creek Freewill Baptist church were also used. These are in the Illinois

Historical Survey, the Illinois State Historical Library, and the archives of the United Methodist church Central Illinois Conference.

The church history studies by Olmstead, Ahlstrom, Schneider, and Rothan, cited for chapter 1, provided much of the background on the movement of denominations into the American frontier. Special mention should be made of the volumes on *Religion on the American Frontier,* edited by William Warren Sweet, especially those on the Baptists (New York: Henry Holt, 1931), Presbyterians (New York: Harper and Bros., 1936), Congregationalists (Chicago: Univ. of Chicago Press, 1939), and Methodists (Chicago: Univ. of Chicago Press, 1946). *The Indomitable Baptists—A Narrative of Their Role in Shaping American History* (Garden City, N.Y.: Doubleday, 1967), by O.K. and Marjorie M. Armstrong, was helpful also.

Several scholars have written on phases of the Catholic church's entry into the American frontier. The most useful for this study were the following: Thomas T. McAvoy, *A History of the Catholic Church in the United States* (Notre Dame, Ind.: Univ. of Notre Dame Press, 1969); Rev. Theodore Roemer, *The Ludwig-Missionsverein and the Church in the United States (1838-1918)* (Washington, D.C.: Catholic Univ. of America, 1933); Edward John Hickey, *The Society for the Propagation of the Faith—Its Foundation, Organization and Success (1822-1922)* (Washington, D.C.: Catholic Univ. of America, 1922); James J. McGovern, *The Catholic Church in Chicago* (Chicago: Archdiocese of Chicago, 1891); Gilbert J. Garraghan, S.J., *The Catholic Church in Chicago, 1673-1871* (Chicago: Loyola Univ. Press, 1921); Rt. Rev. Msgr. Peter Leo Johnson, *Crosier on the Frontier: A Life of John Martin Henni, Archbishop of Milwaukee* (Madison: State Historical Society of Wisconsin, 1959); Rev. John Rothensteiner, *History of the Archdiocese of St. Louis—In Its Various Stages of Development from A.D. 1673 to A.D. 1928,* vol. 1 (St. Louis: Blackwell Wielandy, 1928); Sister Mary Petrina Peters, "The Pioneer German Catholics of Iowa, 1833-1860," (unpublished dissertation, Catholic Univ. of America, 1941); and Alice O'Rourke, O.P., *The Good Work Begun—Centennial History of Peoria Diocese* (Chicago: Lakeside Press, 1970).

Works on Protestant activities in the Upper Mississippi include: Rev. A. D. Field, *Memorials of Methodism in the Bounds of the Rock River Conference* (Cincinnati: Cranston and Stowe, 1886); Lois Kimball Mathews Rosenberry, *The Expansion of New England—The Spread of New England Settlement and Institutions to the Mississippi River, 1620-1865* (New York: Russell and Russell, 1962, reprint of 1909 ed.); Charles C. Cole, Jr., *The Social Ideas of the Northern Evangelists, 1826–1860* (New York: Octagon Books, 1966, reprint of 1954 ed.); Colin Brummitt Goodykoontz, *Home Missions on the American Frontier: With Particular Reference to the American Home Missionary Society* (New York: Octagon Books, 1971, reprint of 1939 ed.); and Carrie Prudence Kofoid, "Puritan Influences in the Formative Years of Illinois History," *Transactions of the Illinois State Historical Society for the Year 1905,* pp. 261–338.

Chapter 6

Letters of church leaders—especially the AHMS collection—provided much material for examining the Sabbatarian and common school controversies, as did contemporary church journals and reform newspapers: *Western Citizen, Free West, North-Western Christian Advocate,* and the *Christian Times.* German reaction was noted mainly from the *Belleviller Zeitung,* which reprinted articles from other German publications. The Cole collection of newspaper excerpts was invaluable for reform topics.

Previously cited works that were extensively used here included the studies by Billington, Conzen, Garraghan, Overmoehle, Current, and Charles C. Cole, Jr. Philip Gleason's *The Conservative Reformers—German-American Catholics and the Social Order* (Notre Dame, Ind.: Univ. of Notre Dame Press, 1968) and Robert T. Handy, *A Christian America—Protestant Hopes and Historical Realities* (New York: Oxford Univ. Press, 1971) were also used.

Many studies have been published on the common school movement and resulting controversies with immigrants. The *Illinois Teacher* for 1855–1858 presented the reformers' goals and reports on debates. Secondary works relied upon included Walter H. Beck, *Lutheran Elementary Schools in the United States—A History of the Development of Parochial Schools and Synodical Educational Policies and Programs* (St. Louis: Concordia Pub. House, 1939); Daniel W. Kucera, *Church-State Relationships in Education in Illinois* (Washington, D.C.: Catholic Univ. Press, 1955); Rev. James A. Burns, *The Principles, Origin and Establishment of the Catholic School System in the United States* (New York: Arno Press, 1969, reprint of 1912 ed.); James W. Sanders, *The Education of an Urban Minority—Catholics in Chicago, 1833–1965* (New York: Oxford Univ. Press, 1977); Lloyd P. Jorgenson, *The Founding of Public Education in Wisconsin* (Madison: State Historical Society of Wisconsin, 1956); David Nasaw, *Schooled to Order: A Social*

History of Public Schooling in the United States (New York: Oxford Univ. Press, 1979); John Pulliam, "Changing Attitudes toward Free Public Schools in Illinois, 1825-1860," *History of Education Quarterly 7*, 2 (Summer, 1967): 191-208, and Jacob A. Swisher, "A Century of School Legislation in Iowa," *Iowa Journal of History and Political Science 44*, 2 (Apr. 1946): 174-204.

Chapter 7

Letters of missionaries, contemporary newspapers, and the Illinois Sons of Temperance *Journal of Proceedings* for 1847-1855 provided much of the source material for the examination of temperance and violence. In addition, excerpts from the *Milwaukee Sentinel* and *Milwaukee Daily American*, compiled by the State Historical Society of Wisconsin's History of Wisconsin Project, provided insight into the Know-Nothing controversy.

Still the major study of nativism in the region is Sister M. Evangeline Thomas's *Nativism in the Old Northwest, 1850-1860* (Washington, D.C.: Catholic Univ. Press, 1936), which was used in conjunction with the Billington book. The German divisions are examined in the Overmoehle study and in John A. Hawgood, *The Tragedy of German-America* (New York: Putnam's, 1940).

The temperance crusade has received much attention from historians. Three of the best general works are Joseph R. Gusfield, *Symbolic Crusade: Status Politics and the American Temperance Movement* (Urbana: Univ. of Illinois Press, 1963); Norman H. Clark, *Deliver Us from Evil: An Interpretation of American Prohibition* (New York: W. W. Norton, 1976); and John Kobler, *Ardent Spirits—The Rise and Fall of Prohibition* (New York: Putnam's, 1973).

These articles were also useful: Joseph Schafer, "Yankee and Teuton in Wisconsin," *Wisconsin Magazine of History 6*, (Dec. 1922): 125-45; (Mar. 1923): 261-79; and (June 1923): 386-402; Frank L. Byrne, "Maine Law versus Lager Beer: A Dilemma of Wisconsin's Young Republican Party," *Wisconsin Magazine of History, 42*, 2 (Winter 1958-59): 115-20; Herbert Wiltsee, "The Temperance Movement, 1848-1871," *Papers in Illinois History and Transactions for the Year 1937* (Springfield: Illinois State Historical Society, 1938): 82-92; Dan Elbert Clark, "The History of Liquor Legislation in Iowa 1846-1861," *The Iowa Journal of History and Politics 6*, 1 (Jan. 1908): 55-87; and Henry S. Lucas, "The Political Activities of the Dutch Immigrants from 1847 to the Civil War," *Iowa Journal of History and Politics 26*, 2 (Apr. 1928): 171-203.

Most of the La Salle riot information is drawn from newspaper reports, Illinois Central Rail Road correspondence, and these sources located in La Salle: Record Book of the First Congregational church of La Salle for 1852-1903; Stuart Duncan, et al., *La Salle Illinois—an Historical Sketch* (La Salle, 1952), and the centennial report for adjacent Peru, *Commemorating One Hundred Years of Peru's Existence* (1935).

The Koerner memoirs and the studies by Conzen, Pierce, Current, and A. C. Cole were also valuable sources of information on the controversies over temperance and violence.

Chapter 8

The political ferment of the 1850s has received extensive study, but the immigrants' roles in the decade's shifting alliances have traditionally been examined in connection with election results. The Lyman Trumbull papers in the Illinois Historical Survey; *The Collected Works of Abraham Lincoln*, vols. 2 and 3 (New Brunswick, N.J.: Rutgers Univ. Press, 1953); plus the previously noted Koerner memoirs and the study of Douglas by Johannsen were invaluable in tracing the politicians' efforts among immigrants. Newspapers and church records, already cited, were also important.

Studies of the immigrants' involvement in the changing political situation of the 1850s are collected in *Ethnic Voters and the Election of Lincoln*, edited by Frederick C. Luebke (Lincoln: Univ. of Nebraska Press, 1971). Other articles used for this chapter were Thomas M. Keefe, "Chicago's Flirtation with Political Nativism, 1854-1856," *Records of the American Catholic Historical Society of Philadelphia 82,* 3 (Sept. 1971): 131-58; H. P. Scholte, "The Coming of the Hollanders to Iowa," *Iowa Journal of History and Politics 9,* 4 (Oct. 1911): 528-74; William Vocke, "The Germans and the German Press," *Transactions of the McLean County Historical Society 3* (Bloomington, Ill., 1900): 52-53; Louis Pelzer, "The History and Principles of the Democratic Party of Iowa 1846-1857," *Iowa Journal of History and Politics 6,* 2 (Apr. 1908): 163-246; Louis Pelzer, "The History of Political Parties in Iowa from 1857 to 1860," *Iowa Journal of History and Politics 7,* 2 (Apr. 1909): 179-229; Erik McKinley Eriksson, "The Framers of the Constitution of 1857," *Iowa Journal of History and Politics 22,* 1 (Jan. 1924): 52-88; and Ernest Bruncken, "The Political Activity of Wisconsin Germans, 1854-1860," *Proceedings of the State Historical Society of Wisconsin* (Madison, 1902): 190-211.

Also valuable were four articles by F. I. Herriott: "Iowa and the First Nomination of Abraham Lincoln," *Annals of Iowa,* vol. 8 (Des Moines, Iowa, 1911); "Memories of the Chicago Convention of 1860," *Annals of Iowa 12,* 6 (Oct. 1920): 446–66; "The Premises and Significance of Abraham Lincoln's Letter to Theodore Canisius," *Deutsch-Amerikanische Geschichtsblätter, Jahrbuch der Deutsch-Amerikanischen Historischen Gesellschaft von Illinois—Jahrgang 1915,* vol. 15 (Chicago, 1915); and "The Conference of German-Republicans in the Deutsches Haus, Chicago, May 14–15, 1860," *Transactions of the Illinois State Historical Society for 1928* (Springfield, Ill., 1929).

Secondary studies that were especially helpful included Jay Monaghan, *The Man Who Elected Lincoln* (Indianapolis: Bobbs-Merrill, 1956); Willard L. King, *Lincoln's Manager: David Davis* (Cambridge: Harvard Univ. Press, 1960); Alexander Davidson and Bernard Stuvé, *A Complete History of Illinois from 1673 to 1873* (Springfield: Illinois Journal Co., 1874); Frederick Irving Kuhns, *The American Home Missionary Society in Relation to the Antislavery Controversy in the Old Northwest* (Billings, Mont., 1959); Don E. Fehrenbacher, *Prelude to Greatness: Lincoln in the 1850's* (Stanford, Calif.: Stanford Univ. Press, 1962), and the previously cited works by Pierce, Conzen, Rosenberry, Current, and Overmoehle. Information on the Know-Nothings was drawn from most of the above, for a general study is lacking, but special note should be made of the Thomas work, already cited; Robert P. Sutton, "Against the 'drunken Dutch and low Irish': Nativism and Know-Nothings in Illinois," in Sutton, *Prairie State,* vol. 1, pp. 326–41, and Ronald Deane Rietveld, "The Moral Issue of Slavery in American Politics, 1854–1860" (Ph.D. dissertation, Univ. of Illinois, 1967).

Index

priests in, 133–34; and slavery, 209; trusteeship disputes, 131–32. *See also* Churches; Germans; Irish

Sabbatarian movement, 149–55
Sac Prairie, Wis., 137
St. Clair County, Ill.: Baptists in, 120; election of
1860, 231; German settlers in, 63; in Mexican
War, 214; prohibition vote, 196. *See also*
Belleville, Ill.
Saint John's Abbey, Minn., 134
St. Louis, Mo.: *Alt Lutheraner* in, 53; Americans in,
9–10; Bible controversy, 167; Catholic losses
in, 134; cholera epidemic, 96; election riot,
176; French settlers in, 9; German language in
schools of, 160; German newspapers in, 68;
Germans in, 11, 63, 67; language dispute, 138;
liquor laws, 187; opposition to sabbatarianism
in, 152; rationalists, 70; stagecoach service, 6;
Ursuline nuns in, 134
St. Marie, Iowa, 67
St. Paul, Minn., 167
Scandinavian Evangelical Lutheran Augustana
Synod, 128
Scandinavians, 148–49. *See also* Norwegians;
Swedes
Schneider, George, 205, 217, 221
Schurz, Carl, 70, 227, 228, 230
Scots, 11
Scott County, Iowa, 230
Seebote (Milwaukee), 214, 217
Sheboygan County, Wis., 64, 190
Sheffield, Ill., 78
Shelbyville, Ill., 97
Shields, James, 214, 220
Slavery issue, 216, 217, 222. *See also* Kansas-
Nebraska Act; Negroes
Sons of Temperance, 171, 182–84, 185–86, 195.
See also Maine law; Prohibition; Temperance
movement
Southerners: in Illinois, 9–10, 17; in Iowa, 10, 17
Southern Illinois: drinking, 172; in 1856 election,
221; New England influence in, urged, 112;
opposition to sabbatarianism in, 151–52; pro-
hibition vote, 196; settlement of, 9–10; and
temperance movement, 187–88. *See also* Il-
linois
Springfield, Ill., 79; Democratic rally, 218–20;
Germans in, 64; railroad, 84, 86; Repub-

licans in, 214–16; temperance movement
in, 185
Stagecoach travel, 6
Statehood, 8
Steamboats, 5–6, 58–59, 75
Stearns County, Minn., 137
Strikes and wage disputes: by immigrants, 104,
175; by Irish canal workers, 83–84; by railroad
workers, 92–93, 176–81
Sturtevant, Julian, 223
Swedes, 11, 128

Temperance movement: fading by 1857, 222;
growth of, 182–84; and Republicans, 216–17.
See also Maine law; Prohibition; Sons of
Temperance
Terre Haute and Alton Railroad, 97
Teutopolis, Ill., 67, 138
Tonica, Ill., 187
Towanda, Ill., 187
Trumbull, Lyman, 217; elected, 205; hears of Ger-
man support, 221; letters to, 223

Union County, Ill., 160, 196
Union Grove, Ill., 99
Upper Alton, Ill., 112
Ursuline nuns, 134

Van Buren County, Iowa, 212
Vanceboro, Ill., 209
Vandalia, Ill., 76, 146
Van de Velde, Bp. James Oliver, 131, 132;
opposes Protestant charges, 167–68; and
temperance, 185
Vermont, Ill., 212
Voting: changes proposed, 216, 221; rules on, 201,
203. *See also* Politics

Wabash-Erie Canal, 80
Walcott, Iowa, 64
Walther, Rev. C.F.W., 53
Warsaw, Ill., 152
Washington County, Wis., 147
Watertown, Wis., 72
Watertown Railroad, 92–93
Waukesha County, Wis., 73, 87, 90–91
Weather, 93–94
Welsh, 11, 38
Weninger, Fr. Francis Xavier, 134–35, 138, 149